POVERTY
IN A RISING
AFRICA

POVERTY
IN A RISING
AFRICA

KATHLEEN BEEGLE
LUC CHRISTIAENSEN
ANDREW DABALEN
ISIS GADDIS

 **WORLD BANK GROUP**

ISBN: 978-1-4648-0723-7
eISBN: 978-1-4648-0724-4
DOI: 10.1596/978-1-4648-0723-7

Library of Congress Cataloging-in-Publication Data
Names: Beegle, Kathleen, 1969- author. | World Bank, issuing body.
Title: Poverty in a rising Africa / [Kathleen Beegle, Luc Christiaensen, Andrew Dabalen, Isis Gaddis].
Description: Washington DC : World Bank, [2016]
Identifiers: LCCN 2016009159 | ISBN 9781464807237
Subjects: LCSH: Poverty—Africa. | Economic development—Africa. | Africa—Economic conditions.
Classification: LCC HC800.Z9 P6187 2016 | DDC 339.4/6096—dc23
LC record available at http://lccn.loc.gov/2016009159

Cover design: Bill Pragluski, Critical Stages LLC.
Cover image: Africa Footprints, lithograph © Richard Long/World Bank Art Program. Further permission required for reuse.

Contents

Boxes

Figures

Maps

Tables

Foreword

After two decades of unprecedented economic growth, how much have the lives of African families improved? The latest estimates from the World Bank suggest that the share of the African population in extreme poverty did decline—from 57 percent in 1990 to 43 percent in 2012. At the same time, however, Africa's population continued to expand rapidly. As a result, the number of people living in extreme poverty still increased by more than 100 million. These are staggering numbers. Further, it is projected that the world's extreme poor will be increasingly concentrated in Africa.

With the adoption of the Sustainable Development Goals, including the eradication of extreme poverty by 2030, successful implementation of the post-2015 development agenda will require a solid understanding of poverty and inequality in the region, across countries and population groups, and in different dimensions.

Poverty in a Rising Africa is the first of two sequential reports aimed at better understanding progress in poverty reduction in Africa and articulating a policy agenda to accelerate it. This first report has a modest, but important, objective: to document the data challenges and systematically review the evidence on core measures of poverty and inequality, along both monetary and non-monetary dimensions. The findings are both encouraging and sobering.

Considerable progress has been made in terms of data for measuring the well-being of the population. The availability and quality of household survey data in Africa has improved. At the same time, not all countries have multiple and comparable surveys to track poverty trends. Reevaluating the trends in poverty, taking into account these data concerns, suggests that poverty in Africa may be lower than what current estimates suggest. In addition, Africa's population saw progress in nonmonetary dimensions of well-being, particularly in terms of health indicators and freedom from violence. While the available data do not suggest a systematic increase in inequality within countries in Africa, the number of extremely wealthy Africans is increasing. Overall, notwithstanding these broad trends, caution remains as data challenges multiply when attempting to measure inequality.

While these findings on progress are encouraging, major poverty challenges remain, especially in light of the region's rapid population growth. Consider this: even under the most optimistic scenario, there are still many more Africans living in poverty (more than 330 million in 2012) than in 1990 (about 280 million). Despite improvements in primary school enrollment rates, the poor quality of learning outcomes, as evidenced by the fact that two in five adults are illiterate, highlights the urgency of policies to improve educational outcomes, particularly for girls. Perpetuation of inequality, in the absence of intergenerational mobility in education, further highlights the long-run consequences of failure to do so. Not surprisingly, poverty reduction has been slowest in fragile states. This trend is compounded by the fact that violence against civilians is once again on the rise, after a decade of relative peace. There is also the paradoxical fact that citizens in resource-rich countries are experiencing systematically lower outcomes in all human welfare indicators controlling for their income level. Clearly, policies matter beyond resource availability.

To maintain and accelerate the momentum of progress of the past two decades, concerted and collective efforts are also needed to further improve the quality and timeliness of poverty statistics in the region. Domestic political support for statistics can be the most important factor in the quest for better data. Development partners and the international community also have an important role to play in terms of promoting regional cooperation, new financing models, open access policies, and clearer international standards. This volume is intended to contribute toward improving the scope, quality, and relevance of poverty statistics. Because, in the fight against poverty in Africa, (good) data will make a difference. *Better data will make for better decisions and better lives.*

Makhtar Diop
Vice President, Africa Region
World Bank

Acknowledgments

This volume is part of the African Regional Studies Program, an initiative of the Africa Region Vice Presidency at the World Bank. This series of studies aims to combine high levels of analytical rigor and policy relevance, and to apply them to various topics important for the social and economic development of Sub-Saharan Africa. Quality control and oversight are provided by the Office of the Chief Economist for the Africa Region.

This report was prepared by a core team led by Kathleen Beegle, Luc Christiaensen, Andrew Dabalen, and Isis Gaddis. It would not have been possible without the relentless efforts and inputs of Nga Thi Viet Nguyen and Shinya Takamatsu (chapters 1 and 2), Umberto Cattaneo and Agnes Said (chapter 3), and Camila Galindo-Pardo (chapters 3 and 4). Rose Mungai coordinated the massive effort to harmonize data files; Wei Guo, Yunsun Li, and Ayago Esmubancha Wambile provided valuable research assistance. Administrative support by Keneth Omondi and Joyce Rompas is most gratefully acknowledged.

Francisco H. G. Ferreira provided general direction and guidance to the team. Additional contributions were made by Isabel Almeida, Prospere Backiny-Yetna, Yele Batana, Abdoullahi Beidou, Paolo Brunori, Hai-Anh Dang, Johannes Hoogeveen, La-Bhus Jirasavetakul, Christoph Lakner, Jean-François Maystadt, Annamaria Milazzo, Flaviana Palmisano, Vito Peragine, Dominique van de Walle, Philip Verwimp, and Eleni Yitbarek.

The team benefited from the valuable advice and feedback of Carlos Batarda, Haroon Bhorat, Laurence Chandy, Pablo Fajnzylber, Jed Friedman, John Gibson, Jérémie Gignoux, Ruth Hill, José Antonio Mejía-Guerra, Berk Ozler, Martin Ravallion, Raul Santaeulalia-Llopis, and Frederick Solt. Valentina Stoevska and colleagues from the ILO provided valuable data.

Stephan Klasen, Peter Lanjouw, Jacques Morisset, and one anonymous reviewer provided detailed and careful peer review comments.

The World Bank's Publishing and Knowledge team coordinated the design, typesetting, printing, and dissemination of the report. Special thanks to Janice Tuten, Stephen McGroarty, Nancy Lammers, Abdia Mohamed, and Deborah Appel-Barker. Robert Zimmermann and Barbara Karni edited the report.

About the Authors and Contributors

Kathleen Beegle is a lead economist in the World Bank's Africa Region. Based in Accra, she coordinates country programs in Ghana, Liberia, and Sierra Leone in the areas of education, health, poverty, social protection, gender, and jobs. Her broader area of work includes poverty, labor, economic shocks, and methodological studies on household survey data collection. She was deputy director of the *World Development Report 2013: Jobs*. She holds a PhD in economics from Michigan State University.

Umberto Cattaneo is a research assistant at the World Bank and a doctoral fellow at the European Center for Advanced Research in Economics and Statistics at the Université Libre de Bruxelles. His research interests include development economics, civil war, poverty analysis, applied microeconometrics, and agricultural and environmental economics. He recently completed a study on the impact of civil war on subjective and objective poverty in rural Burundi. He holds a master's degree in development economics from the School of Oriental and African Studies of the University of London and a master's degree in economics and finance from the University of Genova.

Luc Christiaensen is a lead agriculture economist in the World Bank's Jobs Group and an honorary research fellow at the Maastricht School of Management. He has written extensively on poverty, secondary towns, and structural transformation in Africa and East Asia. He is also leading the "Agriculture in Africa: Telling Facts from Myths" project. He was a core member of the team that produced the *World Development Report 2008: Agriculture for Development*. He holds a PhD in agricultural economics from Cornell University.

Andrew Dabalen is a lead economist in the World Bank's Poverty and Equity Global Practice. His work focuses on policy analysis and research in development issues, such as poverty and social impact analysis, inequality of opportunity, program evaluation, risk and vulnerability, labor markets, conflict, and welfare outcomes. He has worked in the World Bank's Africa and Europe and Central Asia Regions on poverty analysis, social safety nets, labor markets, and education reforms. He has coauthored regional reports on equality of opportunity for children in Africa and vulnerability and resilience in the Sahel and led poverty assessments for several countries, including Albania, Burkina Faso, Côte d'Ivoire, Kosovo, Niger, Nigeria, and Serbia. He has published scholarly articles and working papers on poverty measurement, conflict and welfare outcomes, and wage inequality. He holds a PhD in agricultural and resource economics from the University of California-Berkeley.

Isis Gaddis is an economist in the World Bank's Gender Group. She previously served as a poverty economist for Tanzania based in Dar es Salaam. Her main research interest is empirical microeconomics, with a focus on the measurement and analysis of poverty and inequality, gender, labor economics, and public service delivery. She holds a PhD in economics from the University of Göttingen, where she was a member of the development economics research group from 2006 to 2012.

Camila Galindo-Pardo worked as a research analyst in the Chief Economist's Office of the Africa Region of the World Bank, where she studied the link between sectoral economic growth and poverty, income inequality and extreme wealth, gender based-violence, and the prevalence of net buyers of staple foods among African households. She is a PhD student in economics at the University of Maryland-College Park.

Rose Mungai is a senior economist/statistician with the Africa Region of the World Bank and the region's focal point on poverty data. She has more than 15 years of experience designing household surveys and measuring and analyzing poverty. For several years she led production of the Bank's annual *Africa Development Indicators* report. Before joining the World Bank, she worked as a senior economist/statistician at the Kenya National Bureau of Statistics, where her core role was measuring poverty. She holds a master's degree in development economics from the University of Manchester.

Nga Thi Viet Nguyen is an economist in the World Bank's Poverty and Equity Global Practice, where her work involves poverty measurement and analysis, policy evaluation, and the study of labor markets and human development. She was part of the team that produced the 2013 report *Opening Doors: Gender Equality and Development in the Middle East and North Africa*. In Africa she investigated the impact of Nigeria's import bans on poverty, the role of social safety net programs in rural poverty in Malawi, and the contribution of labor income to poverty reduction in five African countries and contributed to various poverty assessments. She holds a master's degree in public policy from Harvard University.

Agnes Said is a lawyer who has been working with the World Bank since 2009. Her work focuses on public sector governance and social protection. She is part of the management team of a multidonor trust fund for the Middle East and North Africa Region that is striving to strengthen governance and increase social and economic inclusion in the region. Her work on justice and fundamental rights has been published by the European Commission and the European Parliament. She holds a master of laws degree from the University of Gothenburg and a master's degree in international relations and international economics from the School of Advanced International Studies of the Johns Hopkins University.

Shinya Takamatsu is a consultant in the Poverty and Equity Global Practice of the Africa Region of the World Bank, where he is a core member of the region's statistical development team. He has published several working papers on poverty imputations and survey methodology and conducted research on the educational spillover effect of a conditional cash transfer program and the poverty impacts of food price crises. He holds a PhD in agricultural and resource economics, with a minor in statistics, from the University of Minnesota.

Abbreviations

AIDS	acquired immune deficiency syndrome
BMI	body mass index
CPI	consumer price index
DHS	Demographic and Health Survey
GDP	gross domestic product
GHS	General Household Survey
HIV	human immunodeficiency virus
ICP	International Comparison Program
IDP	internally displaced person
MDG	Millennium Development Goal
MICS	Multiple Indicator Cluster Survey
MLD	mean log deviation
PPP	purchasing power parity
S2S	survey-to-survey
SDG	Sustainable Development Goal
SWIID	Standardized World Income Inequality Database
WGI	Worldwide Governance Indicators

Key Messages

Measuring poverty in Africa remains a challenge.

- The coverage, comparability, and quality of household surveys to monitor living standards have improved. Still, by 2012, only 27 of the region's 48 countries had conducted at least two comparable surveys since 1990 to track poverty.
- Regular and good-quality GDP, price, and census data are also lacking.
- Technical approaches can fill in some gaps, but there is no good alternative to regular and good-quality data. A regionwide effort to strengthen Africa's statistics is called for.

Poverty in Africa may be lower than current estimates suggest, but more people are poor today than in 1990.

- The latest estimates from the World Bank show that the share of Africans who are poor fell from 57 percent in 1990 to 43 percent in 2012. Limiting estimates to comparable surveys, drawing on nonconsumption surveys, and applying alternative price deflators suggest that poverty may have declined by even more.
- Nonetheless, even given the most optimistic estimates, still many more people are poor because of population growth: more than 330 million in 2012, up from about 280 million in 1990.
- Poverty reduction has been slowest in fragile countries, and rural areas remain much poorer, although the urban-rural gap has narrowed. Chronic poverty is substantial.

Nonmonetary dimensions of poverty have been improving.

- Health, nutrition, education, and empowerment have improved; and violence has diminished.
- But the challenges remain enormous: more than two in five adults are still illiterate, and the quality of schooling is often low; after a decade of relative peace, conflict is on the rise.
- Nonmonetary welfare indicators are weaker in resource-rich countries, conditional on income, pointing to the unmet potential of natural resource wealth.

Inequality in Africa has many dimensions.

- The data do not reveal a systematic increase in inequality across countries in Africa. But these data do not capture extremely wealthy Africans, whose numbers and wealth are increasing.
- Spatial inequalities (differences between urban and rural areas and across regions) are large.
- Intergenerational mobility in areas such as education and occupation has improved, but mobility is still low and perpetuates inequality.

1

Overview

Perceptions of Africa changed dramatically over the past 20 years. Viewed as a continent of wars, famines, and entrenched poverty in the late 1990s, there is now a focus on "Africa rising" and an "African 21st century."[1] At 4.5 percent a year, average economic growth was remarkably robust, especially when contrasted with the continuous decline during the 1970s and 1980s.

Substantial improvements in well-being should have accompanied this expansion. Whether or not they did remains unclear given the poor quality of the data (Devarajan 2013; Jerven 2013), the nature of the growth process (especially the role of natural resources) (de la Briere and others 2015), the emergence of extreme wealth (Oxfam 2015), the heterogeneity of the region, and persistent population growth of 2.7 percent a year (Canning, Raja, and Yazbeck 2015).

Expectations are also rising. All developing regions except Africa have reached the Millennium Development Goal (MDG) of halving poverty between 1990 and 2015 (UN 2015). Attention will now shift to the set of new global development goals (the Sustainable Development Goals [SDGs]), which include the ambitious target of eradicating poverty worldwide by 2030. The potential for a slowdown in economic growth

and projections that the world's poor will be increasingly concentrated in Africa even if the average 1995–2014 growth rates are maintained suggest the need to focus the global poverty agenda on Africa.

This report is the first of a two-part volume on poverty in Africa. This study documents the data challenges and revisits the core broad facts about poverty in Africa; the second report will explore ways to accelerate its reduction.

The report takes a broad, multidimensional view of poverty, assessing progress over the past two decades along both monetary and nonmonetary dimensions. The dearth of comparable, good-quality household consumption surveys makes assessing monetary poverty especially challenging. The report scrutinizes the data used to assess monetary poverty in the region and explores how adjustments for data issues affect poverty trends.[2]

At the same time, the remarkable expansion of standardized household surveys on nonmonetary dimensions of well-being, including opinions and perceptions, opens up new opportunities. The report examines progress in education and health, the extent to which people are free from violence and able to shape their lives, and the joint occurrence of various types of deprivation. It also reviews the distributional aspects of poverty, by studying various dimensions of inequality.

To shed light on Africa's diversity, the report examines differences in performance across countries, by location, and by gender. Countries are characterized along four dimensions that have been shown to affect growth and poverty: resource richness, fragility, landlockedness (to capture geographic openness and potential for trade), and income status (low, lower-middle, upper-middle, and high income).

Assessing the Data Landscape

According to World Bank estimates from household surveys, the share of people living on less than $1.90 a day (in 2011 international purchasing power parity [PPP]) fell from 57 percent in 1990 to 43 percent in 2012, while the number of poor still increased by more than 100 million (from 288 to 389 million).

These estimates are based on consumption surveys in a subsample of countries covering between one-half and two-thirds of the region's population. Poverty rates for the rest of the countries are imputed from surveys that are often several years old using gross domestic product (GDP) trends, raising questions about the accuracy of the estimates. On average only 3.8 consumption surveys per country were conducted in Africa between 1990 and 2012, or one every 6.1 years. In the rest of the world, one consumption survey was conducted every 2.8 years. The average also masks quite uneven coverage across countries. For five countries that together represent 5 percent of the African population, no data to measure poverty are available (either because no household surveys were conducted or because the data that were collected are not accessible, or, as in the case of one survey for Zimbabwe, were collected during a period of hyperinflation and unsuitable for poverty measurement). As of 2012, only 27 of 48 countries had conducted at least two comparable surveys since 1990 to track poverty.

To be sure, the number of household surveys in Africa has been rising. Africa now ranks second to South Asia in terms of the number of national household surveys per country, according to the International Household Survey Network catalog. The region has an average of 24 surveys per country conducted between 1990 and 2012—more than the developing world average of about 22. This expansion was confined almost entirely to surveys that do not collect consumption data, however.

The increase in household consumption surveys, which are the building blocks for measuring poverty and inequality, was sluggish, though coverage increased. Since 2009 only 2 countries did not conduct a single consumption survey over the past decade (down from 10 in 1990–99). The number of countries that either did not conduct a consumption survey or do not allow access to the microdata declined from 18 in 1990–99 to 4 in 2003–12; and the number of countries with at least two consumption surveys increased, from 13 in 1990–99 to 25 in 2003–12. Many fragile states—namely, Chad, the Democratic Republic of Congo, Sierra Leone, and Togo—were part of this new wave of surveys. Nonetheless, fragile states still tend to be the most data deprived.

The lack of consumption surveys and accessibility to the underlying data are obvious impediments to monitoring poverty. But the problems do not end there. Even when available, surveys are often not comparable with other surveys within the country or are of poor quality (including as a result of misreporting and deficiencies in data processing). Consequently, countries that appear to be data rich (or have multiple surveys) can still be unable to track poverty over time (examples include Guinea and Mali, with four surveys each that are not comparable).

At a country level, lack of comparability between survey rounds and questions about quality issues often prompt intense technical debates about methodological choices and, national poverty estimates within countries (see World Bank 2012 for Niger; World Bank 2013 for Burkina Faso; World Bank 2015b for Tanzania). But much regional work in

MAP O.1 **Lack of comparable surveys in Africa makes it difficult to measure poverty trends**

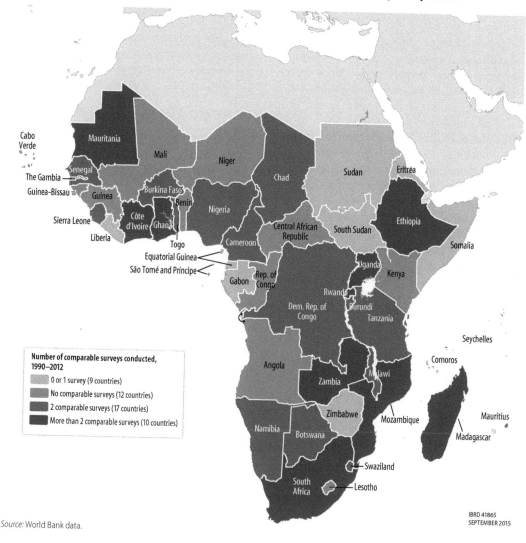

Number of comparable surveys conducted,
1990–2012

- 0 or 1 survey (9 countries)
- No comparable surveys (12 countries)
- 2 comparable surveys (17 countries)
- More than 2 comparable surveys (10 countries)

IBRD 41865
SEPTEMBER 2015

Source: World Bank data.

Africa and elsewhere disregards these important differences, relying on databases such as the World Bank's PovcalNet that has not consistently vetted surveys on the basis of comparability or quality.

If surveys that are not nationally representative (covering only urban or rural areas, for example), that were not conducted at similar times of the year (in order to control for seasonality in consumption patterns), and that collected consumption data using different instruments or reporting periods are dropped, the typical African country conducted only 1.6 comparable surveys in the 23 years between 1990 and 2012.

The challenge of maintaining comparability across surveys is not unique to Africa or to tracking poverty (see, for example, UNESCO 2015 for data challenges in tracking adult literacy). However, in Africa lack of comparability exacerbates the constraints imposed by the already limited availability of consumption surveys. It becomes especially problematic when the challenges concern populous countries, such as Nigeria. Only 27 countries (out of 48) conducted two or more comparable surveys during 1990–2012 (map O.1). On the upside, they represent more than three-quarters of Africa's population.

The estimation of poverty also requires data on price changes. For cross-country comparisons of poverty in a base year, 2011 in this case, nominal consumption must be converted to 2011 price levels. The main method used to make this adjustment is the consumer price index (CPI), which relies on both the collection of country-specific price data and basket weights of consumer items to measure inflation. The CPI suffers from three specific problems in Africa, in addition to the more general technical difficulties. First, in many countries prices are collected only from urban markets. Second, the basket weights rely on dated household surveys and sometimes only on market purchases (excluding home-produced foods). Third, computational errors sometimes bias the data, as in Tanzania (World Bank 2007) and Ghana (IMF 2003, 2007).[3]

Across the globe, when surveys are not available in a given year, researchers use GDP to compute annual poverty estimates. Missing data are interpolated (between surveys) and extrapolated (to years before and after the previous and latest surveys) using GDP growth rates (see World Bank 2015a). Not all of these GDP data are reliable, however. Ghana, for example, leapt from low-income to low-middle-income country classification after rebasing its GDP in 2010; following rebasing, Nigeria surpassed South Africa overnight as the biggest economy in Africa. These examples suggest that GDP growth rates—and by extension the extrapolated poverty reductions—may be underestimated.

Another issue is that imputation based on GDP growth rates assumes that GDP growth translates one-to-one into household consumption and that all people see their consumption expand at the same pace. But GDP includes much more than household consumption: on average across a large sample of African countries, household consumption surveys captured just 61 percent of GDP per capita. The assumption that growth is evenly distributed can also be tenuous when growth

is driven by capital-intensive sectors such as mining and oil production (Loayza and Raddatz 2010) and may lead to poverty reduction being overestimated. Caution is therefore counseled, especially when extrapolating to a distant future (or past).

Improving Data on Poverty

Lack of funding and low capacity are often cited as main drivers for the data gaps in Africa. But middle-income status is not associated with the number of consumption surveys a country conducts, and countries receiving more development aid do not have more or higher-quality poverty data. In terms of capacity, the production of high-quality consumption surveys and statistics is technically complex, involving the mobilization of financial and human resources on a large scale and requiring the establishment of robust quality-control mechanisms. But many countries that do not conduct household surveys to measure poverty at the same time undertake other activities that are more or equally complex (delivering antiretroviral drugs to people with AIDS and conducting national elections, for example) (Hoogeveen and Nguyen 2015). Good governance is strongly correlated with higher-quality data (figure O.1). Countries that have better scores on safety and rule of law also have superior statistical capacity.

Many researchers have recently suggested that problems with the availability, comparability, and quality of data reflect the political preferences of elites (Carletto, Jolliffe, and Banerjee 2015; CGD 2014; Devarajan 2013; Florian and Byiers 2014; Hoogeveen and Nguyen 2015). Political elites may not favor good-quality statistics for several reasons. First, where clientelism and access to politics are limited, a record of achievement that can be supported by good-quality statistics is unnecessary because support from a small group of power brokers suffices. Second, maintaining a patronage network is costly, and high-quality statistics come at a high opportunity cost. Third, poor-quality statistics reduce accountability. The prevailing

FIGURE O.1   **Good governance and statistical capacity go together**

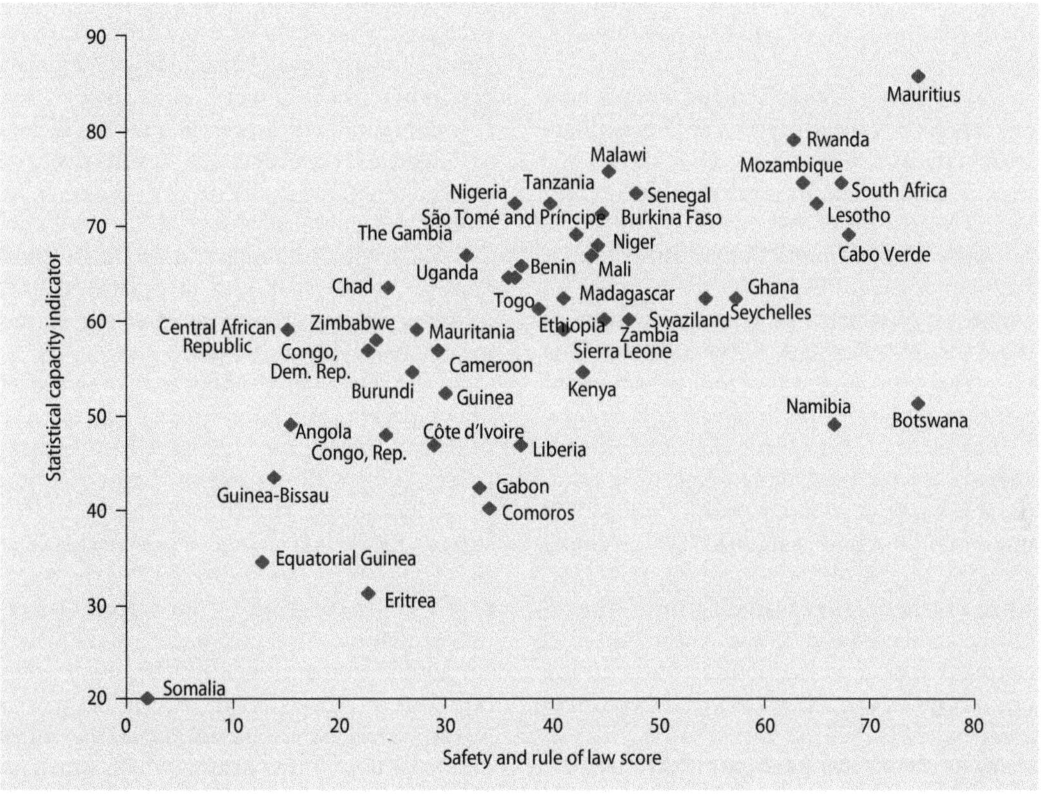

Source: Hoogeveen and Nguyen 2015.

political arrangements thus favor less (or less autonomous) funding for statistics because it represents one way to exercise influence over statistical agencies. In some countries donor financing has replaced domestic financing, but the interests of donors are not always aligned with the interests of governments. This problem highlights the need for alternative financing models, including cofinancing arrangements, preferably under a coordinated regional umbrella and with adequate incentives for quality improvements.

Politics and funding are not the only reasons statistics are inadequate. The evidence presented here suggests that better outcomes were possible even with the set of surveys that were conducted. African countries collected on average 3.8 consumption surveys in the past two decades, but many of them could not be used to track poverty reliably because of comparability and quality concerns caused

by failure to adhere to methodological and operational standards. While this problem partly reflects the lack of broader political support domestically, regional cooperation and peer learning, as well as clear international standards, could help improve technical quality and consistency. The Program for the Improvement of Surveys and the Measurement of Living Conditions in Latin America and the Caribbean (known by its acronym in Spanish, MECOVI) provides a compelling model for achieving better poverty data.

Revisiting Poverty Trends

Various technical approaches can be applied to address some of the data shortcomings in tracking regional poverty trends. They include limiting the sample to comparable surveys of good quality, using trends in other nonconsumption data rather than GDP to impute missing poverty estimates, and gauging inflation using alternative econometric techniques.

Taking these steps affects the view of how poverty has evolved in Africa. The estimate from PovcalNet in figure O.2 shows the now-familiar trend in poverty from surveys in the World Bank PovcalNet database. It provides the benchmark. These estimates are population-weighted poverty rates for the 48 countries, of which 43 countries have one or more surveys.[4] For years for which there were no surveys, poverty was estimated by imputation using GDP growth rates.

The estimate based on only comparable surveys shows the trends when only comparable surveys are used and the same GDP imputation method is applied. It largely mirrors the PovcalNet estimate. In contrast, when in addition to controlling for comparability, quality is taken into account, the 2012 estimate of poverty in Africa is 6 percentage points lower than the PovcalNet estimate

(37 percent instead of 43 percent). The series of comparable and good-quality surveys only excludes some of the surveys from Burkina Faso, Mozambique, Tanzania, and Zambia and replaces the poverty estimates of the two comparable but poorer-quality surveys of Nigeria (Nigeria Living Standards Surveys 2003/04 and 2009/10) with the estimate from the General Household Survey Panel 2010/11, which has been deemed of good quality. Poverty gap and severity measures follow similar trajectories, after correction for comparability and quality.

In the series depicted based on the subset of comparable and good-quality surveys, the information base for Nigeria, which encompasses almost 20 percent of the population of Africa, shifts. The 2003/04 and 2009/10 surveys showed no change in poverty in Nigeria. The poverty rate indicated by the alternative survey for 2010/11 (26 percent) is half the estimate obtained from the lower-quality survey (53 percent) in 2009/10. Given that only one survey is retained, the estimated poverty trend for Nigeria also relies more on the GDP growth pattern (which was high during the 2000s) as well as a lower poverty rate for 2010/11. Reestimating the poverty rate with only comparable surveys of good quality but without Nigeria indicates that Nigeria accounted for a large fraction of the additional decline observed using the corrected series (the red line). Without Nigeria, the corrected series declines from 55 percent to 40 percent (a 15 percentage point drop), compared with 57 percent to 43 percent (a 14 percentage point drop) in PovcalNet. Confidence in the revised regional series depends significantly on how reliable the trends in Nigeria's poverty obtained using the good-quality survey and greater dependence on GDP imputation are considered.

Consumption data gaps can also be filled by applying survey-to-survey (S2S) imputation techniques to nonconsumption survey data. In this method, at least one survey with consumption and basic household characteristics is combined with nonconsumption surveys with the same basic characteristics for different years. Consumption for the years

FIGURE O.2 Adjusting for comparability and quality changes the level of and trends in poverty

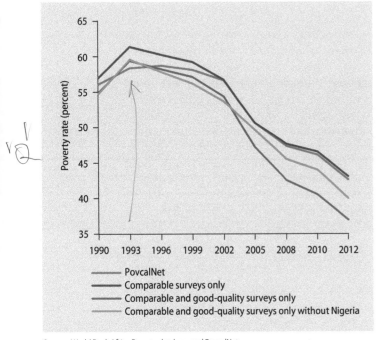

Sources: World Bank Africa Poverty database and PovcalNet.
Note: Poverty is defined as living on less than $1.90 a day (2011 international purchasing power parity).

with no survey is then estimated based on the evolution of the nonconsumption household characteristics as well as the relation between those characteristics and consumption, as estimated from the consumption survey. Where they have been tested, these prediction techniques perform mostly well in tracking poverty, although, as with GDP extrapolation, caution is counseled when predicting farther out in the past or the future (Christiaensen and others 2012; Newhouse and others 2014; World Bank 2015a). Applying this method to the 23 largest countries in Africa (which account for 88 percent of both the population and the poor) and keeping only good-quality and comparable consumption surveys suggests that poverty declined from 55 percent in 1990–94 to 40 percent in 2010–12 (figure O.3, blue line). This decline is slightly larger than the one obtained from the World Bank's PovcalNet for the same 23 countries (which showed the poverty rate falling from 57 percent to 43 percent) (green line) but smaller than the 19 percentage point reduction obtained using the comparable and good-quality surveys and GDP imputation for these countries (red line).

Another approach to addressing consumption data gaps is to forgo using consumption data entirely and examine changes in household assets. However, although changes in asset holdings may be indicative of some aspects of household material well-being, this approach does not yet serve well as a proxy or replacement for what consumption measures.

A final issue concerns how consumption data from a given survey year are adjusted to the year of the international poverty line, which is 2011. National CPIs are typically used to inflate/deflate nominal consumption to this benchmark year. To address concerns about applying CPI to adjust consumption of households, researchers can look for evidence of the potential level of CPI bias and the implications of any bias for poverty trends. An overestimated (underestimated) CPI will result in flatter (steeper) poverty trends.

One way to assess CPI bias is by using the Engel approach (Costa 2001; Hamilton 2001). It is based on the assumption that the

FIGURE O.3   Other estimates also suggest that poverty in Africa declined slightly faster and is slightly lower

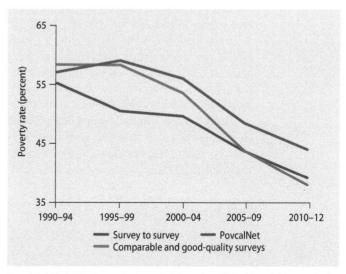

Source: World Bank Africa Poverty database; calculations using additional household surveys for the 23 largest countries in Africa.

Engel curve (which shows households' food budget share declining as real consumption rises) remains constant over time, so that deviations indicate over- or underestimation of the price deflator used. Application to urban households in 16 African countries with comparable surveys during the 2000s suggests that CPIs in Africa tend to overstate increases in the (urban) cost of living. Poverty in many African countries may have declined faster than the data indicate if the CPI is overestimated. Research on many more countries as well as rural areas and time periods is needed to confirm these results.

Taken together, this set of results suggests that poverty declined at least as much as reported using the World Bank database PovcalNet and that the poverty rate in Africa may be less than 43 percent. This news is encouraging. Nonetheless, the challenges posed by poverty remain enormous. As a result of rapid population growth, there are still substantially more poor people today (more than 330 million in 2012) than there were in 1990 (about 280 million), even under the most optimistic poverty reduction scenario (that is, using comparable and good-quality surveys only).

This exercise also underscores the need for more reliable and comparable consumption data to help benchmark and track progress toward eradicating poverty by 2030, as envisioned under the SDGs. More generally, it counsels against overinterpreting the accuracy conveyed by point estimates of poverty—or other region- or countrywide statistics of well-being. These estimates provide only an order of magnitude of levels and changes, albeit one that becomes more precise the more comparable and reliable is the underlying database.

Profiling the Poor

What distinguishes countries that have succeeded in reducing poverty from those that have failed? What are the effects of income status, resource richness, landlockedness, and fragility?

Not surprisingly, fragility is most detrimental to poverty reduction. Between 1996 and 2012, poverty decreased in fragile states (from 65 percent to 53 percent), but the decline was much smaller than in nonfragile economies (from 56 percent to 32 percent). The

gap in performance is 12 percentage points in favor of nonfragile countries. Conditional on the three other country traits, the difference in poverty reduction between fragile and nonfragile countries rises to 15 percentage points (figure O.4). Middle-income countries as a group did not achieve faster poverty reduction than low-income countries, and being resource rich was associated with poverty reduction that was 13 percentage points greater than in non-resource-rich countries after controlling for other traits. The main driver for the difference in poverty reduction in resource-rich and resource-poor countries, however, is corrections to the Nigeria data. More surprisingly, once resource richness, fragility, and income status are controlled for, landlocked countries did not reduce poverty less than coastal economies (the effect is not statistically significant and the point estimate is even negative). This finding contradicts the common notion that landlocked countries perform worse than coastal countries because transport costs impede trade and lower competitiveness (Bloom and Sachs 1998).

Although Africa is urbanizing rapidly, in the majority of countries, 65–70 percent of the population resides in rural areas (Canning, Raja, and Yazbeck 2015). Across countries rural residents have higher poverty rates (46 percent in rural areas in 2012 versus 18 percent in urban areas, using corrected data for all countries). But the gap between the poverty rate in rural and urban areas declined (from 35 percentage points in 1996 to 28 percentage points in 2012). Among the four geographic regions, only urban areas in West Africa halved poverty. Poverty among rural populations in West and Southern Africa declined about 40 percent.

Africa is distinguished by a large and rising share of female-headed households. Such households represent 26 percent of all households and 20 percent of all people in Africa. Southern Africa has the highest rate of female-headed households (43 percent). West Africa exhibits the lowest incidence (20 percent), partly reflecting the continuing practice of polygamy, together with high remarriage rates among widows. The poverty rates among people living in male-headed

FIGURE O.4   Fragility is associated with significantly slower poverty reduction

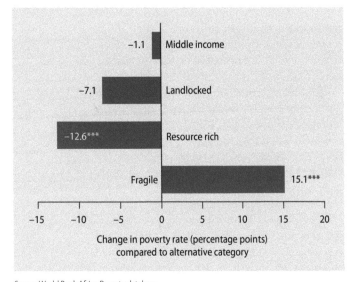

Source: World Bank Africa Poverty database.
Note: Figure shows results of a regression on the change in the poverty rate for 43 countries from 1996 to 2012 based on estimated poverty rates using comparable and good-quality surveys.
*** Statistically significant at the 1% level.

households (48 percent) are higher than in female-headed households (40 percent), except in Southern Africa, where poverty among female-headed households is higher (Milazzo and van de Walle 2015).

Two caveats are warranted. First, the smaller household size of female-headed households (3.9 people versus 5.1) means that using per capita household consumption as the welfare indicator tends to overestimate the poverty of male-headed households relative to female-headed households if there are economies of scale among larger households (Lanjouw and Ravallion 1995; van de Walle and Milazzo 2015). But household composition also differs: the dependency ratio is 1.2 among households headed by women and 1.0 among households headed by men. Counting children as equivalent to adults can lead to an underestimation of poverty in male versus female-headed households. Understanding the differences in poverty associated with the gender of the household head is intertwined with how one defines the consumption indicator used in measuring poverty. Second, woman household heads are a diverse group. Widows, divorced or separated women, and single women frequently head households that are relatively disadvantaged , as opposed to households with a temporarily absent male head (van de Walle and Milazzo 2015).

The evidence examined above captures snapshots of poverty. Looking at the body of evidence on the evolution of households' poverty over time (that is, taking movies of people's poverty status) reveals large variation across countries. Panel data estimates of chronic poverty (the share of households staying poor throughout) range from 6 percent to almost 70 percent. Countries with similar poverty rates can also be quite dissimilar in terms of their poverty dynamics. A systematic assessment using synthetic two-period panels (which are less prone to measurement errors) constructed for 21 countries reveals that about 58 percent of the poor population was chronically poor (poor in every period), with the remaining poor being poor only transiently (in only one period) (Dabalen and Dang 2015). Chronic poverty remains pervasive in the region.

Taking a Nonmonetary Perspective

Many aspects of well-being cannot be properly priced or monetarily valued (Sandel 2012; Sen 1985), such as the ability to read and write, longevity and good health, security, political freedoms, social acceptance and status, and the ability to move about and connect. Recognizing the irreducibility of these aspects of well-being, the Human Development Index (HDI) and the Multidimensional Poverty Index (MPI) (Alkire and Santos 2014) focus on achievements in education, longevity and health, and living standards (through income, assets, or both), which they subsequently combine into a single index.

This study expands the scope to include freedom from violence and freedom to decide (a proxy for the notion of self-determination that is critical to Sen's capability approach).[5] It also examines jointness in deprivation, by counting the share of people deprived in one, two, or more dimensions of poverty. This approach achieves a middle ground between a single index of nonmonetary poverty (which requires weighting achievements in the various dimensions) and a dashboard approach (which simply lists achievements dimension by dimension, ignoring jointness in deprivation) (Ferreira and Lugo 2013).

The focus in selecting indicators was on outcomes (not inputs) that are measured at the individual (not the household) level. Information on these indicators is now much more widely available than it once was, although some of the comparability and quality issues highlighted above also apply (see, for example, UNESCO 2015 for a review of data challenges in tracking adult literacy).

Overall, Africa's population saw substantial progress in most nonmonetary dimensions of well-being, particularly health and freedom from violence. Between 1995 and 2012, adult literacy rates rose by 4 percentage points. Gross primary enrollment rates increased dramatically, and the gender gap in education shrank. Life expectancy at birth rose 6.2 years, and the prevalence of chronic malnutrition among children under 5 fell by 6 percentage points. The number of deaths from politically motivated violence declined by 75 percent, and both the incidence and tolerance of gender-based domestic violence dropped. Scores on voice and accountability indicators rose slightly, and there was a trend toward greater participation of women in household decision-making processes.

These improvements notwithstanding, the levels of achievement remain low in all domains, and the rate of progress is leveling off.[6] Despite the increase in school enrollment, today still more than two out of five adults are unable to read or write. About three-quarters of sixth graders in Malawi and Zambia cannot read for meaning—just one example of the challenge of providing good-quality schooling. The need to reinvigorate efforts to tackle Africa's basic educational challenge is urgent.

Health outcomes mirror the results for literacy: progress is happening, but outcomes remain the worst in the world. Increases in immunization and bednet coverage are slowing. Nearly two in five children are malnourished, and one in eight women is underweight.

At the other end of the spectrum, obesity is emerging as a new health concern.

Africans enjoyed considerably more peace in the 2000s than they did in earlier decades, but the number of violent events has been on the rise since 2010, reaching four times the level of the mid-1990s (map O.2). Violence is increasingly experienced in terms of political unrest and terrorism rather than large-scale civil conflicts.

Africa also remains among the bottom performers in terms of voice and accountability, albeit with slightly higher scores than the Middle East and North Africa and East Asia and the Pacific. Tolerance of domestic violence (at 30 percent of the population) is still twice as high as in the rest of the developing world (figure O.5), and the incidence of domestic violence is more than 50 percent higher. Higher tolerance of domestic violence and less empowered decision making among younger (compared with older) women suggest that a generational shift in mindset is still to come.

Around these region-wide trends there is also remarkable variation across countries

MAP O.2   The number of violent events against civilians is increasing, especially in Central Africa and the Horn

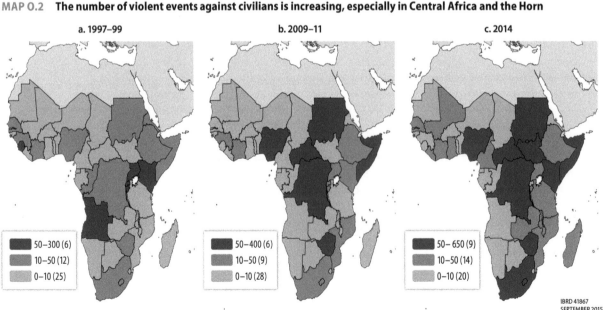

a. 1997–99   b. 2009–11   c. 2014

■	50–300 (6)
■	10–50 (12)
■	0–10 (25)

■	50–400 (6)
■	10–50 (9)
■	0–10 (28)

■	50–650 (9)
■	10–50 (14)
■	0–10 (20)

IBRD 41867
SEPTEMBER 2015

Sources: Armed Conflict Location and Events Dataset (ACLED); Raleigh and others 2010.
Note: Maps indicate annual number of violent events against civilians; number in parentheses indicates the number of countries. For the following countries there are no data: Cabo Verde, Comoros, Mauritius, São Tomé and Príncipe, and the Seychelles.

Acceptance of domestic violence is twice as high in Africa as in other developing regions

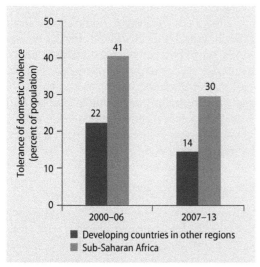

Source: Data from Demographic and Health Surveys 2000–13.
Note: Figures are population-weighted averages of 32 African and 28 non-African developing countries.

and population groups. Literacy is especially low in West Africa, where gender disparities are large. High HIV prevalence rates are holding life expectancy back in Southern Africa. Conflict events are more concentrated in the Greater Horn of Africa and the Democratic Republic of Congo.

Rural populations and the income poor are worse off in all domains, although other factors, such as gender as well as the education of women and girls, often matter as much or more (at times in unexpected ways). Women, for example, can expect to live in good health 1.6 years longer than men; and, among children under 5, boys, not girls, are more likely to be malnourished (by 5 percentage points).[7] At the same time, illiteracy remains substantially higher among women, women suffer more from violence (especially domestic violence), and they are more curtailed in their access to information and decision making. Multiple deprivation characterizes life for a sizable share of African women (data on men are not available).

Several groups—including orphans, the disabled, and refugees and internally displaced persons—have traits that may make them particularly vulnerable. In 2012, 3.5 million children in Africa were two-parent orphans (had lost both parents), and another 28.6 million children were single-parent orphans, bringing the total number of orphans to 32.1 million. The prevalence of orphanhood is particularly high in countries in or emerging from major conflict and in countries severely affected by HIV/AIDS. Because it can be correlated with wealth and urban status, orphanhood does not always confer a disadvantage on children in terms of schooling. Data on school enrollment among 10- to 14-year-olds in the most recent Demographic and Health Surveys show that in half of the countries surveyed, orphans were less likely to be enrolled than nonorphans.

In a sample of seven African countries for which comparable data are available, almost 1 working-age adult in 10 faces severe difficulties in moving about, concentrating, remembering, seeing or recognizing people across the road (while wearing glasses), or taking care of him- or herself. People with disabilities are more likely to be in the poorest 40 percent of the population, largely because of their lower educational attainment (Filmer 2008). They score 7.2 percent higher on the multidimensional poverty index than people without disabilities (Mitra, Posärac, and Vick 2013). Not unexpectedly, disability rates show a statistically significant correlation with HIV/AIDS and conflict.

Africa had an estimated 3.7 million refugees in 2013, down from 6.7 million in 1994 but up from 2.8 million in 2008. In addition, there were 12.5 million internally displaced people, bringing the number of people displaced by conflict to 16.2 million in 2013, or about 2 percent of Africa's population (Maystadt and Verwimp 2015). The main source of refugees is the Greater Horn of Africa, although the number of refugees from Central Africa is still about 1 million, about half of them from the Democratic Republic of Congo.

Although the suffering associated with displacement is tremendous, the displaced are not necessarily the poorest; and fleeing often helps them mitigate the detrimental effects of conflict (Etang-Ndip, Hoogeveen, and Lendorfer 2015). Refugee status is also not always associated with weaker socioeconomic outcomes. Finally, local economies often also benefit from the influx of refugees (Maystadt and Verwimp 2015) through increased demand for local goods (including food) and services, improved connectivity (as new roads are built and other transport services provided to refugee camps), and entrepreneurship by refugees themselves.

Three overarching aspects stand out from a review of the nonmonetary dimensions of poverty in Africa. First, fragile countries tend to perform worse and middle-income countries better. This unsurprising finding confirms the pernicious effects of conflict and is consistent with the widely observed associations with overall economic development.

Second, controlling for these factors, there is a worrisome penalty to residing in a resource-rich country: people in resource-rich countries tend to be less literate (by 3.1 percentage points), have shorter life expectancy (by 4.5 years) and higher rates of malnutrition among women (by 3.7 percentage points) and children (by 2.1 percentage

points), suffer more from domestic violence (by 9 percentage points), and live in countries that rank low in voice and accountability measures (figure O.6).

Third, better-educated women (secondary schooling and above) and children in households with better-educated women score decisively better across dimensions (health, violence, and freedom in decision). More rapid improvement in female education and women's socioeconomic opportunities will be game changing in increasing Africa's capability achievement.

Measuring Inequality

Although not all aspects of inequality are necessarily bad (rewarding effort and risk taking can promote growth), high levels of inequality can impose heavy socioeconomic costs on society. Mechanically, higher initial inequality results in less poverty reduction for a given level of growth. Tentative evidence also suggests that inequality leads to lower and less sustainable growth and thus less poverty reduction (Berg, Ostry, and Zettelmeyer 2012) (if, for example, wealth is used to engage in rent-seeking or other distortionary economic behaviors [Stiglitz 2012]). The pathway by which inequality evolves thus matters for poverty reduction and growth.

The report measures inequality using the Gini index, which ranges from 0 (perfect equality) to 1 (perfect inequality). It shows that inequality is especially high in Southern Africa (Botswana, Lesotho, Namibia, South Africa, Swaziland, and Zambia), where Gini indices are well above 0.5 (map O.3).

Of the 10 most unequal countries in the world today, 7 are in Africa. Excluding these countries (five of which have populations of less than 5 million and most of which are in Southern Africa) and controlling for country-level income, Africa has inequality levels comparable to developing countries in other parts of the world. Inequality levels do not differ significantly between coastal and landlocked, fragile and nonfragile, or resource-rich and resource-poor countries, controlling for subregion.

FIGURE O.6   **Residents in resource-rich countries suffer a penalty in their human development**

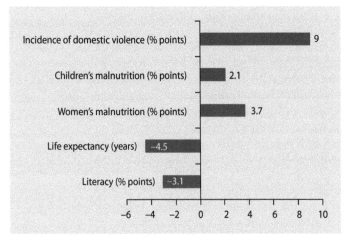

Source: Staff calculations based on World Health Organization and multiple Demographic and Health Surveys.
Note: Figure shows the gap between resource-rich and other countries in Africa. Results control for demographic factors, education, poverty, and other country characteristics (income, fragility, landlockedness).

MAP O.3   Inequality in Africa shows a geographical pattern

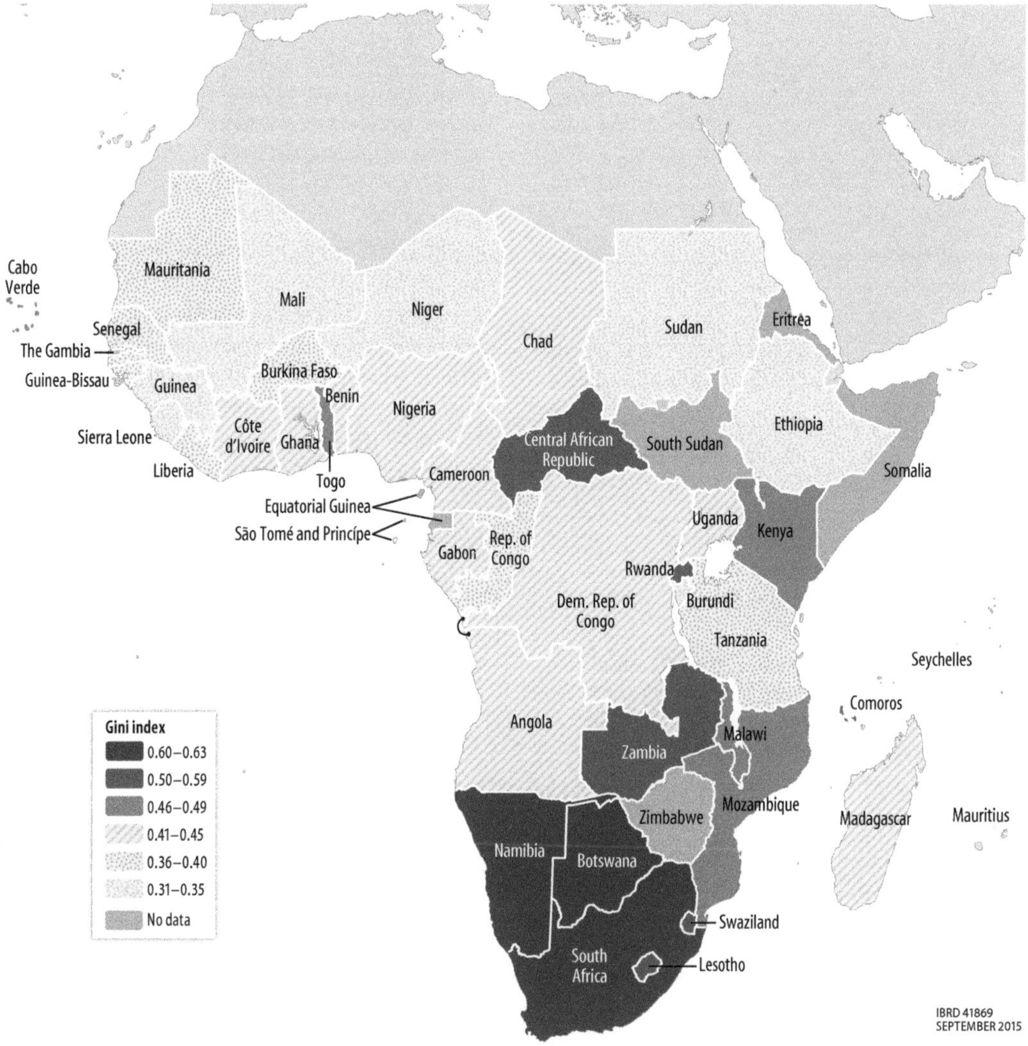

Gini index
- 0.60–0.63
- 0.50–0.59
- 0.46–0.49
- 0.41–0.45
- 0.36–0.40
- 0.31–0.35
- No data

IBRD 41869
SEPTEMBER 2015

Source: World Bank Africa Poverty database.

For the subset of 23 countries for which comparable surveys are available with which to assess trends in inequality, half the countries experienced a decline in inequality and the other half saw an increase. No clear patterns are observed by countries' resource status, income status, or initial level of inequality. While one might have expected a more systematic increase in inequality given Africa's double decade of growth and the role the exploitation of natural resources played in that growth, the results presented here do not provide strong evidence for such a trend.

Although declines in inequality are associated with declines in poverty, poverty fell, despite increasing inequality, in many countries (figure O.7, quadrant 1).

For Africa as a whole, ignoring national boundaries, inequality has widened. The Africa-wide Gini index increased from 0.52 in 1993 to 0.56 in 2008. A greater share of African inequality is explained by gaps across countries, even though within-country inequality continues to dominate. These results stand in contrast to changes in global inequality (Lakner and Milanovic

FIGURE O.7 **Declining inequality is often associated with declining poverty**

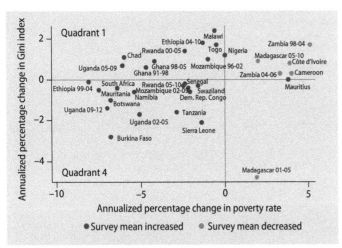

Source: Countries in World Bank Africa Poverty database with comparable surveys.
Note: Ethiopia 1995–99, an outlier, is excluded. Survey years are indicated for countries with more than one pair of comparable surveys.

2015). Not surprisingly, the wealthiest African households are much more likely to live in countries with higher per capita GDP.

Inequality can be decomposed into two parts: inequality between groups (horizontal inequality) and inequality within groups (vertical inequality). Among the range of groups one can examine, geography, education, and demography stand out as groups for which a large share of overall inequality is explained by the group to which one belongs. From the decomposition method, spatial inequalities (by region, urban or rural, and so forth) explain as much as 30 percent of total inequality in some countries. Perhaps a more straightforward approach to assessing spatial inequality is simply to look at mean consumption per capita across geographic domains. The ratio of mean consumption between the richest and the poorest regions is 2.1 in Ethiopia (regions), 3.4 in the Democratic Republic of Congo (provinces), and more than 4.0 in Nigeria (states). Price differences across geographic areas drive some of this gap; adjusted for price differences, spatial inequalities are lower but are still large.

Education of the household head is associated with even larger consumption gaps between households. In Rwanda, South Africa, and Zambia, educational attainment of the household head explains about 40 percent of overall inequality. Countries with higher inequality tend to have a high share of their inequality driven by unequal education, which is an association that is not observed for most of the other socioeconomic groupings.

The demographic composition of the household also explains a large share of inequality (30 percent in Senegal and 32 percent in Botswana). In countries for which data are available to study trends in horizontal inequality from the mid-1990s to the present, the main drivers—geography, education, and demographics—have not changed, though some variations exist at the country level.

Inequality in Africa is the product of many forces. The circumstances in which one is born (for example, in a rural area, to uneducated parents) can be critical. Inequality of opportunity (what sociologists call *ascriptive inequality*)—the extent to which such circumstances dictate a large part of the outcomes among individuals in adulthood—violates principles of fairness.

The evidence on inequality of economic opportunity in Africa has been limited. This report draws on surveys of 10 African countries to explore the level of inequality of economic opportunity by looking at such circumstances as ethnicity, parental education and occupation, and region of birth. The share of consumption inequality that is attributed to inequality of opportunity is as high as 20 percent (in Malawi) (because of data limitations, this estimate is a lower bound). But inequality of opportunity is not necessarily associated with higher overall inequality.

Another approach to measuring inequality of opportunity is to examine persistence in intergenerational education and occupation. Does the educational attainment of a child's parents affect a child's schooling less than it did 50 years ago? Is a farmer's son less likely to be a farmer than he was a generation ago?

Among recent cohorts, an additional year of schooling of one's parents has a lower association with one's own schooling than it did for older generations, suggesting more equal educational opportunities for younger cohorts. Intergenerational mobility trends are comparable to trends estimated for other developing countries. For occupation the findings are more mixed for the five countries for which data are available. Intergenerational occupational mobility has been rising rapidly in the Comoros and Rwanda. In contrast, it remains rigid in Guinea. The shift in the structure of occupations in the economy (sometimes called structural change) is not the sole reason for changes in intergenerational occupational mobility. Other factors, such as discrimination, social norms, and impediments to mobility (poor infrastructure, conflict, and so forth), are also changing in ways that can affect mobility.

These results tell only part of the story because household surveys are not suited to measuring extreme wealth. Data on holders of extreme wealth are difficult to collect, but such people are increasingly on the radar in discussions of inequality around the globe.

Africa had 19 billionaires in 2014 according to the Forbe's list of "The World's Billionaires." Aggregate billionaire wealth increased steadily between 2010 and 2014 in Nigeria (from 0.3 percent to 3.2 percent of GDP) and South Africa (from 1.6 percent to 3.9 percent). The number of ultra-high-net-worth individuals (people with a net worth of at least $30 million) also rose. Few detailed studies explore the level of extreme wealth of nationals. One exception comes from Kenya, where 8,300 people are estimated to own 62 percent of the country's wealth (New World Wealth 2014). The share of extreme wealth derived from areas prone to political capture, including extractives, has been declining, while the share derived from services and investment has been increasing. Between 2011 and 2014, 4 out of 20 billionaires in Africa derived their wealth mainly or partially from telecommunications. Data limitations make it difficult to draw conclusions about whether the emergence of extreme wealth in Africa is driven less by political connections than it used to be.

Notes

1. Throughout this report, *Africa* refers to Sub-Saharan Africa.
2. The focus is on a range of measurement issues, including the limited availability, comparability, and quality of consumption data and the remedies used to overcome these constraints. For a range of other measurement issues—including the measurement of service flows from housing and durable goods, the conversion of household into individual consumption measures (to account for differential needs and economies of scale), and methodological differences in constructing poverty lines—the report adopts standard approaches.
3. An additional aspect to measuring cross-country poverty is converting local currency measures into a common currency. This report adopts the new international poverty line of $1.90/day in 2011 based on the latest round of the purchasing power parity (PPP) exercise and discusses the complicated set of issues that PPPs entail.
4. The five countries for which no survey data are available to estimate poverty (Eritrea, Equatorial Guinea, Somalia, South Sudan, and Zimbabwe) were assigned the regional poverty rate based on the other 43 countries.
5. Sen's capability approach provides the philosophical foundations for the nonmonetary perspective.
6. Below-average performance in Africa's three most populous countries (Nigeria, the Democratic Republic of Congo, and Ethiopia) partly drives the high levels of nonmonetary poverty in the region.
7. Higher life expectancy for women is possible even in an environment that is disadvantageous to them, given that women are genetically predisposed to live longer (Sen 2002; World Bank 2011).

References

ACLED (Armed Conflict Location and Event Data Project) http://www.acleddata.com/about-acled/.

Alkire, Sabina, and Maria Emma Santos. 2014. "Measuring Acute Poverty in the Developing World: Robustness and Scope of the Multidimensional Poverty Index." *World Development* 59: 251–74.

Berg, Andrew, Jonathan D. Ostry, and Jeromin Zettelmeyer. 2012. "What Makes Growth Sustained?" *Journal of Development Economics* 98 (2): 149–66.

Bloom, David, and Jeffrey Sachs. 1998. "Geography, Demography, and Economic Growth in Africa." *Brookings Papers on Economic Activity* 2: 207–95.

Canning, David, Sangeeta Raja, and Abdo Yazbeck, eds. 2015. *Africa's Demographic Transition: Dividend or Disaster?* Africa Development Forum Series. Washington, DC: World Bank.

Carletto, Calogero, Dean Jolliffe, and Raka Banerjee. 2015. "From Tragedy to Renaissance: Improving Agriculture Data for Better Policies." *Journal of Development Studies* 51 (2):133–48.

CGD (Center for Global Development). 2014. *Delivering on the Data Revolution in Sub-Saharan Africa*. Final Report of the Data for African Development Working Group. Center for Global Development and African Population and Health Research Center, Washington, DC.

Christiaensen, Luc, Peter Lanjouw, Jill Luoto, and David Stifel. 2012. "Small Area Estimation-Based Prediction Methods to Track Poverty: Validation and Applications." *Journal of Economic Inequality* 10 (2): 267–97.

Costa, Dora L. 2001. "Estimating Real Income in the United States from 1888 to 1994: Correcting CPI Bias Using Engel Curves." *Journal of Political Economy* 109 (6): 1288–310.

Dabalen, Andrew, and Hai-Anh Dang. 2015. "The Transition of Welfare over Time for Africa: Evidence from Synthetic Panel Analysis." Background paper prepared for this report, World Bank, Washington, DC.

de la Briere, Benedicte, Deon Filmer, Dena Ringold, Dominic Rohner, Karelle Samuda, and Anastasiya Denisova. 2015. *From Mines to Minds: Turning Sub-Saharan's Mineral Wealth into Human Capital*. Washington, DC: World Bank.

Demographic and Health Surveys. 2015. Calverton, MD: ICF International.

Devarajan, Shantayanan. 2013. "Africa's Statistical Tragedy." *Review of Income and Wealth* 59 (S1): S9–S15.

Etang-Ndip, Alvin, Johannes Hoogeveen, and Julia Lendorfer. 2015. "Socioeconomic Impact of the Crisis in North Mali on Displaced People." Policy Research Working Paper 7253, World Bank, Washington, DC.

Ferreira, Francisco H. G., and María Ana Lugo. 2013. "Multidimensional Poverty Analysis: Looking for a Middle Ground." *World Bank Research Observer* 28 (2): 220–35.

Filmer, Deon. 2008. "Disability, Poverty, and Schooling in Developing Countries: Results from 14 Household Surveys." *World Bank Economic Review* 22 (1): 141–63.

Florian, Krätke, and Bruce Byiers. 2014. "The Political Economy of Official Statistics: Implications for the Data Revolution in Sub-Saharan Africa." PARIS21 Discussion Paper 5.

Hamilton, Bruce W. 2001. "Using Engel's Law to Estimate CPI Bias." *American Economic Review* 91 (3): 619–30.

Hoogeveen, Johannes, and Nga Thi Viet Nguyen. 2015. "Statistics Reform in Africa: Aligning Incentives with Results." Working Paper, World Bank, Poverty and Equity Global Practice, Washington, DC.

IMF (International Monetary Fund). 2003. *Ghana: First Review under the Three-Year Arrangement under the Poverty Reduction and Growth Facility*. IMF Country Report 03/395, Washington, DC.

———. 2007. *Ghana: Article IV Consultation: Staff Report*. IMF Country Report 07/210, Washington, DC.

Jerven, Morten. 2013. "Comparability of GDP Estimates in Sub-Saharan Africa: The Effect of Revisions in Sources and Methods since Structural Adjustment." *Review of Income and Wealth* 59 (S1): S16–S36.

Lakner, Christoph, and Branko Milanovic. 2015. "Global Income Distribution: From the Fall of the Berlin Wall to the Great Recession." *World Bank Economic Review*. Advance access published September 26, 2015.

Lanjouw, Peter, and Martin Ravallion. 1995. "Poverty and Household Size." *Economic Journal* 105 (433): 1415–34.

Loayza, Norman V., and Claudio Raddatz. 2010. "The Composition of Growth Matters for Poverty Alleviation." *Journal of Development Economics* 93 (1): 137–51.

Maystadt, Jean-François, and Philip Verwimp. 2015. "Forced Displacement and Refugees in Sub-Saharan Africa: An Economic Inquiry." Policy Research Working Paper 7517, World Bank, Washington, DC.

Milazzo, Annamaria, and Dominique van de Walle. 2015. "Women Left Behind? Poverty and Headship in Africa." Policy Research Working Paper 7331, World Bank, Washington, DC.

Mitra, Sophie, Aleksandra Posärac, and Brandon Vick. 2013. "Disability and Poverty in Developing Countries: A Multidimensional Study." *World Development* 41: 1–18.

New World Wealth. 2014. *Wealth in Kenya: The Future of Kenyan HNWIs.* Johannesburg.

Newhouse, David, S. Shivakumaran, Shinya Takamatsu, and Nobuo Yoshida. 2014. "How Survey-to-Survey Imputation Can Fail." Policy Research Working Paper 6961, World Bank, Washington, DC.

Raleigh, Clionadh, Andrew Linke, Håvard Hegre, and Joakim Karlsen. 2010. "Introducing ACLED-Armed Conflict Location and Event Data." *Journal of Peace Research* 47 (5).

Oxfam. 2015. "Wealth: Having It All and Wanting More." Oxfam Issue Briefing, January. Oxford.

Sandel, Michael J. 2012. *What Money Can't Buy: The Moral Limits of Markets.* New York: Farrar, Straus and Giroux.

Sen, Amartya. 1985. *Commodities and Capabilities.* Amsterdam: North-Holland.

———. 2002. "Why Health Equity?" *Health Economics* 11 (8): 659–66.

Stiglitz, Joseph E. 2012. *The Price of Inequality: How Today's Divided Society Endangers Our Future.* New York: W. W. Norton.

UN (United Nations). 2015. *The Millennium Development Goals Report 2015.* New York: United Nations.

UNESCO (United Nations Educational, Scientific and Cultural Organization). 2015. *Education for All 2000–2015: Achievements and Challenges.* EFA Global Monitoring Report. Paris: UNESCO.

van de Walle, Dominique, and Annamaria Milazzo. 2015. "Are Female-Headed Households Poorer? New Evidence for Africa." mimeo, DECRG. World Bank, Washington, DC.

World Bank. 2007. "Underreporting of Consumer Price Inflation in Tanzania 2002–2006." World Bank Policy Note, Washington, DC.

———. 2011. *World Development Report 2012: Gender and Development.* Washington, DC: World Bank.

———. 2012. *Niger: Investing for Prosperity: A Poverty Assessment.* Washington, DC: World Bank.

———. 2013. "Burkina Faso: A Policy Note: Poverty Trends and Profile for 2003–2009." World Bank, Washington, DC.

———. 2015a. *A Measured Approach to Ending Poverty and Boosting Shared Prosperity: Concept, Data, and the Twin Goals.* Policy Research Report. Washington, DC: World Bank.

———. 2015b. "Tanzania Mainland Poverty Assessment." World Bank, Washington, DC.

Introduction

Africa has experienced a dramatic turnaround since the mid-1990s. Following 20 years of economic decline in the 1970s and 1980s, it grew at a robust pace of 4.5 percent a year, a more rapid pace than in the rest of the developing world, excluding China. Thanks to a sharp decline in large-scale conflicts during the 1990s, better macroeconomic fundamentals and governance, a commodity supercycle, and discoveries of new natural resources, the narrative of Africa as a "growth tragedy" has shifted to one of Africa rising.

Despite this growth, a large share of the African population continues to live below the international poverty line of $1.90 a day. Africa's poverty rate declined from 57 percent in 1990 to 43 percent in 2012, according to the latest estimates from the World Bank's PovcalNet database. Because of population growth, however, the number of poor people implied by these estimates increased, from 288 million in 1990 to 389 million in 2012.

Poverty reduction in Africa significantly lags other developing regions. East Asia and South Asia started out with poverty rates that were about as high as Africa's in the 1990s; their poverty rates are much lower today (figure I.1). According to the latest Millennium Development Goal (MDG) report (UN 2015), Africa remains the only developing region where the MDG 1 target of halving extreme poverty by 2015 will not be attained.

Understanding and addressing poverty is complicated by the fact that poverty statistics in the region are often limited and sometimes of poor quality. Poverty estimates are based on data from a patchwork of household surveys that are conducted at irregular intervals, and that are sometimes incomparable and of questionable quality. Concerns about the availability, comparability, and quality of poverty data are not unique to Africa, but the challenges in Africa are perceived as much greater than in other regions.

Some researchers have used alternative data and methods to estimate poverty. They find that substantially more people have been lifted out of poverty than the traditional estimates suggest (Pinkovskiy and Sala-i-Martín 2014; Young 2012). Others are more cautious and question such optimism (Chen and Ravallion 2010; Harttgen, Klasen, and Vollmer 2013).

The lack of reliable and timely statistics in Africa across a range of areas, including poverty, is increasingly recognized as a matter demanding greater international attention (Devarajan 2013; Garcia-Verdu 2013; Jerven 2013). The United Nations' post-MDG

FIGURE I.1   **Poverty reduction in Africa lags other regions**

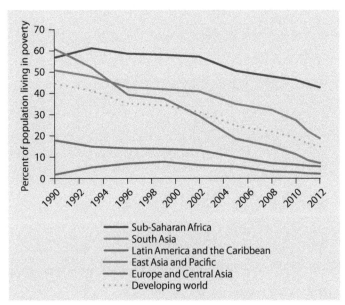

Source: World Bank 2016.

it examines five classifications of countries (table I.1). The literature has identified these groupings as capturing deep currents that determine Africa's performance in poverty reduction and growth.

The report consists of four chapters. Chapter 1 maps out the availability, comparability, and quality of the data needed to track monetary poverty (consumption, price, gross domestic product, and census data); reflects on the governance and political processes that underpin the current situation with respect to data production; and describes some approaches to addressing the data gaps. It is unique in that studies of poverty in Africa typically overlook the important yet mundane details of the data on hand.

TABLE I.1   **Classification of countries in Africa**

Classification	Number of countries
Resource-rich[a]	17
Fragile[b]	17, including 6 that are also resource rich
Income[c]	
Low	26
Lower-middle	14
Upper-middle- and high	8
Landlocked	16
Subregion	
Central Africa	9
East Africa	18
Southern Africa	5
West Africa	16

Note: Countries are classified into subregions according to the UN DESA classification, with the exception of Sudan, which is classified in that system as North Africa. Central Africa includes Angola, Cameroon, the Central African Republic, Chad, the Democratic Republic of Congo, the Republic of Congo, Equatorial Guinea, Gabon, and São Tomé and Príncipe. East Africa includes Burundi, Comoros, Eritrea, Ethiopia, Kenya, Madagascar, Malawi, Mauritius, Mozambique, Rwanda, Seychelles, Somalia, South Sudan, Sudan, Tanzania, Uganda, Zambia, and Zimbabwe. Southern Africa includes Botswana, Lesotho, Namibia, South Africa, and Swaziland. West Africa includes Benin, Burkina Faso, Cabo Verde, Côte d'Ivoire, The Gambia, Ghana, Guinea, Guinea-Bissau, Liberia, Mali, Mauritania, Niger, Nigeria, Senegal, Sierra Leone, and Togo.

a. Resource-rich countries include countries that had average rents from natural resources (excluding forests) that exceeded 10 percent of GDP in 2006–11; countries with diamonds (Botswana, Liberia, Namibia, and Sierra Leone); and Niger (which has uranium). The group does not include Somalia, for which inadequate data are available for classification.

b. Fragile countries are countries that appear on the World Bank's 2015 harmonized list of fragile situations, which classifies countries as fragile if they (a) had an average Country Policy and Institutional Assessment (CPIA) rating of 3.2 or less or (b) hosted a UN or regional peace-keeping or peace-building mission in the previous three years.

c. Country income categories are from World Development Indicators.

frameworks calls for a "data revolution" (UN 2014) to provide timely and reliable household surveys and other statistics (such as indicators from national accounts). If it occurs, such a revolution will surely change the terms of the debate about living standards in Africa, which is now often dominated by data and methodological aspects. Data quality considerations remain very much at the forefront of any assessment of poverty in Africa.

Given the state of the data, what is the best way to study poverty in Africa and put forth an agenda to accelerate poverty reduction? This report is the first of two reports that seek to improve the understanding of poverty reduction in Africa (report 1) and articulate policies to accelerate it (report 2). It reassesses trends in poverty and inequality in Africa by examining the primary data sources and identifying potential biases in them. Careful evaluation of the data for monitoring poverty in Africa will help sharpen the focus on data issues in Africa in general and on consumption data in particular.

A regional report like this cannot provide in-depth analysis for each country. Instead,

Chapter 2 evaluates the robustness of the estimates of poverty in Africa. It concludes that poverty reduction in Africa has not been overestimated and in fact may be slightly greater than traditional estimates suggest, although even the most optimistic estimates of poverty reduction imply that more than 330 million people were living in poverty in 2012. The chapter also presents a very broad-stroke profile of poverty and trends in poverty in the region.

Chapter 3 broadens the view of poverty by considering nonmonetary dimensions of well-being, such as education, health, and freedom, using Sen's (1985) capabilities and functionings approach. In contrast to the dearth of good-quality and comparable surveys on household expenditures, there has been a surge in survey-based information on these and related nonmonetary dimensions of poverty.

Chapter 4 reviews the evidence on inequality in Africa. In addition to patterns of monetary inequality, it examines other dimensions, including inequality of opportunity and intergenerational mobility in occupation and education. Viewing inequality from beyond the realm of household surveys, this work also explores extreme wealth (billionaires and millionaires) in Africa.

References

Chen, Shaohua, and Martin Ravallion. 2010. "The Developing World Is Poorer Than We Thought, but No Less Successful in the Fight against Poverty." *Quarterly Journal of Economics* 125 (4): 1577–625.

Devarajan, Shantayanan. 2013. "Africa's Statistical Tragedy." *Review of Income and Wealth* 59 (S1): S9–S15.

Garcia-Verdu, Rodrigo. 2013. "The Evolution of Poverty and Inequality in Sub-Saharan Africa over the Period 1980–2008: What Do We (and Can We) Know Given the Data Available?" International Monetary Fund, Washington, DC.

Harttgen, Kenneth, Stephan Klasen, and Sebastian Vollmer. 2013. "An African Growth Miracle? Or: What do Asset Indices Tell Us about Trends in Economic Performance?" *Review of Income and Wealth* 59 (S1): S37–S61.

Jerven, Morten. 2013. "Comparability of GDP Estimates in Sub-Saharan Africa: The Effect of Revisions in Sources and Methods since Structural Adjustment." *Review of Income and Wealth* 59 (S1): S16–S36.

Pinkovskiy, Maxim L., and Xavier Sala-i-Martín. 2014. "Africa Is on Time." *Journal of Economic Growth* 19 (3): 311–38.

Sen, Amartya. 1985. *Commodities and Capabilities*. Amsterdam: North-Holland.

UN (United Nations). 2014. *A World that Counts: Mobilising the Data Revolution for Sustainable Development*. Independent Expert Advisory Group on a Data Revolution for Sustainable Development, New York.

———. 2015. *The Millennium Development Goals Report 2015*. New York: UN.

World Bank. 2016. *Global Monitoring Report 2015/2016: Development Goals in an Era of Demographic Change*. Overview booklet. Washington, DC: World Bank.

Young, Alwyn. 2012. "The African Growth Miracle." *Journal of Political Economy* 120 (4): 696–739.

The State of Data for Measuring Poverty | 1

Africa has grown robustly for two decades—performance that lies in stark contrast to the "growth tragedy" of the 1980s (Easterly and Levine 1997). The statistics suggest that Africa's people are faring better and that poverty has come down. But scrutiny of these statistics has raised doubts about the quality of the underlying data and the exact magnitude of Africa's progress. The World Bank's Bulletin Board on Statistical Capacity indicator gave Africa a regional score of 59 in 2014, well below the world average of 66 and low even relative to the average for the low-income category of countries. The lack of good-quality and accessible data to assess socioeconomic changes now regularly features in discussions of the development agenda for Africa (Devarajan 2013; Jerven 2013).

There is no doubt that Africa needs better data to monitor the evolution of both the monetary and nonmonetary dimensions of living conditions. Progress on this front will also be crucial to monitor the post-2015 Sustainable Development Goals (SDGs). To be sure, there have been improvements in data availability in Africa in recent years. The

number of household surveys, particularly surveys that collect data on the nonmonetary dimensions of poverty, has increased, thanks to donor-funded programs such as the Demographic and Health Surveys (DHS) and the Multiple Indicator Cluster Surveys (MICS). The frequency and coverage of data on citizen opinions on a wide range of topics, including governance, political leadership, democracy, and corruption, have increased, and data tracking salient events, such as conflict and weather events, are now widely available. In addition to national statistical offices, the actors in data collection now include nongovernmental organizations (NGOs), polling firms, and universities.

These improvements notwithstanding, major concerns remain. Problems with the availability, comparability, and quality of the data, combined with different approaches and methods to correct for these shortcomings, are at the center of the divergent views regarding the direction and magnitude of poverty reduction in Africa over the past two decades (Chen and Ravallion 2010; Harttgen, Klasen, and Vollmer 2013; Pinkovskiy and Sala-i-Martín 2014; Young 2012).

Consider the measurement of monetary poverty, for example. The share of Africa's population consuming less than $1.90 a day

---

This chapter was written with Rose Mungai, Nga Thi Viet Nguyen, and Shinya Takamatsu.

(in 2011 international purchasing power parity [PPP] dollars) declined, according to the World Bank's PovcalNet, falling from 57 percent in 1990 to 43 percent in 2012.[1] However, this estimate is based on surveys in a subsample of countries that cover only one-half to two-thirds of the population. For the remaining population, the poverty rate was imputed from surveys that were often several years old. For five countries (Equatorial Guinea, Eritrea, Somalia, South Sudan and Zimbabwe), which together represent 5 percent of the African population, no data were available with which to measure poverty.

Equally if not even more important are concerns about the comparability and quality of the underlying household survey and price data. Guinea and Mali, for example, each fielded four surveys since the mid-1990s, but no two of these surveys is considered comparable for measuring poverty.

Against this background and as a starting point in revisiting estimates of poverty in Africa, this chapter takes stock of the data available to measure the evolution of monetary poverty in the region. It focuses on household-level consumption and price data but also briefly reviews auxiliary data sources needed to estimate poverty.

The cornerstone of poverty estimates in Africa (and most other developing regions) are consumption data from household surveys that are representative of the population.[2] By themselves, consumption data are not sufficient to analyze changes in living standards. Monitoring changes in real terms requires data on inflation at the country level—such as a consumer price index (CPI)—to adjust nominal consumption into real values. Estimating global or regional poverty levels requires setting a common poverty line, such as the international poverty line of $1.90 per capita per day, and converting local currency units to a common reference currency. Auxiliary data sources also have a bearing on Africa's poverty estimates. Population censuses are needed to derive population statistics from sample surveys and, when used jointly with a consumption survey,

estimate poverty for small areas in a country. Gross domestic product (GDP) from national income accounts is used to fill gaps between surveys to provide annual poverty estimates.

This chapter reviews the state of these data in Africa. It reflects on the governance and political incentives that influence data production, in order to help understand why multiple challenges beset the data for poverty measurement, and discusses some approaches for addressing data shortfalls.

Types of Data for Measuring Monetary Poverty

Estimating poverty requires consumption or income data from household surveys, but other data are also needed. This includes price data to adjust nominal consumption values for changes in price levels over time, census data to estimate the population, and national accounts data to impute poverty in years in which no household survey was conducted.

Household Survey Data

Household surveys are essential for obtaining the socioeconomic data necessary to understand the welfare of populations across the world. Some 50 years ago, regular household surveys were virtually nonexistent in developing countries. Although both the number of surveys conducted in Africa and their comparability and quality have improved, substantial gaps remain.

Frequency and scope of data collection
Only a handful of household surveys were collected in Africa in the 1980s. The number grew modestly for almost a decade, expanding rapidly in the mid-1990s, partly as a result of growing interest among governments and the international community in monitoring the Millennium Development Goals (MDGs). The first decade of the 2000s was one of the most productive for household data collection in Africa. By 2010 the number of national household surveys in Africa was the second highest in the developing world,

after South Asia (Demombynes and Sandefur 2014; Garcia-Verdu 2013) (figure 1.1).[3]

The breadth of the socioeconomic data that surveys cover has also increased. A majority of African countries collect data on welfare and key MDG indicators from multiple survey sources, including integrated household surveys, often with a focus on consumption; the DHS, which focus on women's fertility decisions, health, and nutrition; the MICS, which are designed to monitor human development outcomes, particularly among women and children; the Core Welfare Indicators Questionnaire (CWIQ) Surveys, which emphasize poverty-related indicators and service-delivery outcomes; population and housing censuses; and labor force surveys. In addition, specialized surveys conducted outside the national statistical system (Barometer, Gallup, the World Values Surveys) solicit citizens' opinions on governance, leadership, political stability, corruption, and a range of social issues, including crime, social capital, and religious practices (box 1.1).

The impressive improvement in survey data collection depicted in figure 1.1 has arisen almost entirely because of the expansion of surveys that do not collect consumption data.[4] Figure 1.2 provides a breakdown of the types of surveys conducted in Africa in five-year periods since the 1990s. It shows steady growth in the number of nonconsumption surveys during the 1990s. The number of such surveys peaked in 2000–04 but still numbered 92 in 2010–14.

The increase in the number of nonconsumption surveys has enriched knowledge of nonincome dimensions of poverty, such as child nutrition, women's empowerment, and access to services in many sectors as well as on joint deprivation across dimensions. Many of these indicators are collected at the individual level and hence provide information on differences in the experiences of poverty and deprivation of men and women, insights that cannot be gained from household-level consumption data. Chapter 3 makes extensive use of these datasets to conduct an

FIGURE 1.1   All regions have increased the number of household surveys they conduct

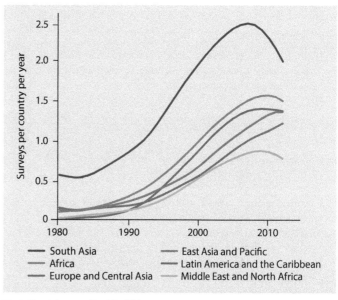

Source: Demombynes and Sandefur 2014.

analysis that would not have been possible even a decade ago.

Consumption surveys, the building blocks for measuring monetary poverty and inequality, have not witnessed similar growth. There are not more surveys available today to measure monetary poverty than there were in the early 1990s. The average number of consumption surveys per five-year period has been just under 40 since 1990, with only small variations around the mean.

An average of 40 consumption surveys every five years for Africa results in less than one survey per country every five years with which to measure poverty. Even more troublesome is the uneven coverage across countries. Between 1990 and 1999, there is not a single survey with consumption data to monitor poverty for 18 of 47 countries in Africa (figure 1.3). Among the remaining 29 countries, 16 each have just a single survey. As a result, for 34 of 47 countries in the region (covering 42 percent of the population), there are no data on changes in poverty or consumption for an entire decade. Coverage has improved since. Data are unavailable for only

BOX 1.1 **Sources outside the national statistical system provide valuable information on well-being**

Impressive large-scale household survey efforts are being conducted outside the national statistical system. They elicit data on nonconsumption aspects of well-being and perceptions.[a]

Afrobarometer

Afrobarometer is a nonpartisan research project that gathers data on social, political, and economic attitudes. It has conducted surveys in more than 30 African countries. A key feature of these surveys is the harmonized set of questions, which allows comparison across countries and within countries over time. Survey questions probe attitudes toward democracy, governance, elections, macroeconomics and markets, poverty, social capital, conflict and crime, participation, and national identity. The latest round introduced modules on corruption, access to justice, the role of China in Africa, pan-Africanism and regional integration, energy supply, tolerance, and citizenship. Data from these surveys are used to construct the lived poverty index (LPI), which is based on experiential measures, such as how often households go without basic necessities (Dulani, Mattes, and Logan 2013). Barometer surveys are also conducted in other regions of the world.

Gallup World Poll

Since 2005 the Gallup World Poll has tracked issues such as economic confidence; life satisfaction; employment; confidence in the leadership, military, and police; religion; access to food; the environment; migration; media freedom; human suffering; and corruption. Surveys are standardized to allow comparisons across countries and within countries over time. Gallup recently added a question about self-reported household income to measure poverty (Phelps and Crabtree 2013).

World Value Surveys

The World Values Survey, established in 1981, is a global research project that explores people's values and beliefs and their social and political impact in almost 100 countries. Topics include support for democracy, tolerance of foreigners and ethnic minorities, support for gender equality, the role of religion and changing levels of religiosity, work, family, politics, national identity, culture, diversity, insecurity, attitudes toward the environment, the impact of globalization, and subjective well-being.

Each wave has covered a wider range of topics, some of which are harmonized across countries. Eleven African countries have been included, some with multiple rounds.

Nonsurvey Methods of Data Collection

Satellites, run mostly by the U.S. National Aeronautics and Space Administration (NASA), collect data on metrics such as night lights, vegetation cover, and precipitation. The unique features of these datasets are their high resolution and geo-referencing. The data are collected from small areas at high frequency.

The use of satellite data is flourishing. They have been used to study urbanization, the accuracy of GDP information, deforestation, and impending drought or crop failure. There have also been attempts to extend their use to understand the evolution of poverty and inequality (Elvidge and others 2009; Mveyange 2015; Noor and others 2008; Pinkovskiy and Sala-i-Martín 2015).

a. Like household surveys conducted by national statistics offices, these surveys rely on face-to-face interviews with household members. Widespread cell phone ownership in Africa has opened up opportunities for collecting data by phone, obviating the need for face-to-face interviews. If executed well, phone surveys can collect representative data on a wide range of topics more frequently and at lower cost than traditional face-to-face surveys (Hoogeveen and others 2014). This approach generally relies on a baseline survey of face-to-face household interviews. The World Bank's Listening to Africa Initiative, for example, combines a face-to-face baseline household survey with follow-up phone interviews of selected respondents. This approach allows the collection of a rich dataset at baseline and a few selected questions about specific issues (education, health, labor markets, and so on) at higher frequency (monthly, twice a week) and at later points in order to gauge changes in the fundamental dimensions of well-being. In addition to collecting data for policy analysis and research, cell phone surveys have proven to be effective tools for monitoring service delivery failures, corruption, and the breakout of conflict and epidemics. Cell phone surveys have been used to monitor the impacts of Ebola in Guinea, Liberia, and Sierra Leone (World Bank 2015c) and the welfare of refugees in Mali (Etang-Ndip, Hoogeveen, and Lendorfer 2015).

three countries over the period 2000–09, 23 countries conducted one survey and another 21 had at least two surveys.

A wave of consumption surveys was conducted in the region between 2011 and 2015. Many fragile states, including Chad, the Democratic Republic of Congo, Sierra Leone, and Togo, were part of this wave. Twenty seven countries have done a survey since 2011 (map 1.1).

Conducting a survey does not necessarily mean that the data collected are available. If the microdata collected in a survey are not included in the World Bank database, the data are deemed inaccessible in this report. This definition of accessibility is a narrow one, because it does not address access by the general public or whether users have to pay for the data, two important factors that significantly curb the usefulness of household survey data to the public and hence undermine knowledge about poverty trends and drivers in Africa.

For three countries (Equatorial Guinea, South Sudan, and Zimbabwe), recent data are not available even though surveys were

FIGURE 1.2 **Africa conducts more nonconsumption surveys than consumption surveys**

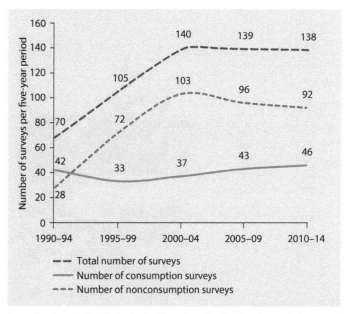

Sources: Data from the World Bank microdata library, PovcalNet, World Development Indicators, and the International Household Survey Network.
Note: Consumption surveys include surveys that may not be the source of the official poverty estimates. Nonconsumption surveys include Demographic and Health Surveys (DHSs), Multiple Indicator Cluster Surveys (MICSs), labor force surveys, and other ad hoc surveys.

FIGURE 1.3 **Many African countries lack surveys with which to gauge changes in poverty**

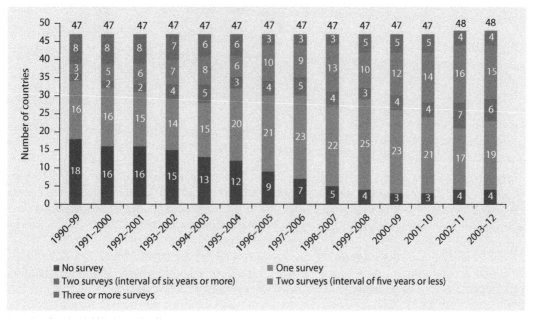

Source: Data from the World Bank microdata library.
Note: In 2011 the number of countries increased from 47 to 48 with the independence of South Sudan. Surveys for which microdata could not be accessed are counted as not available. Four countries (rather than five) have no data for the period 2003–12. Although the Zimbabwe 2007–08 survey is available, its consumption data cannot be used for monetary measures of poverty because it was conducted at a time of hyperinflation. See also endnote 5.

MAP 1.1   More than half of African countries completed a consumption survey between 2011 and early 2015

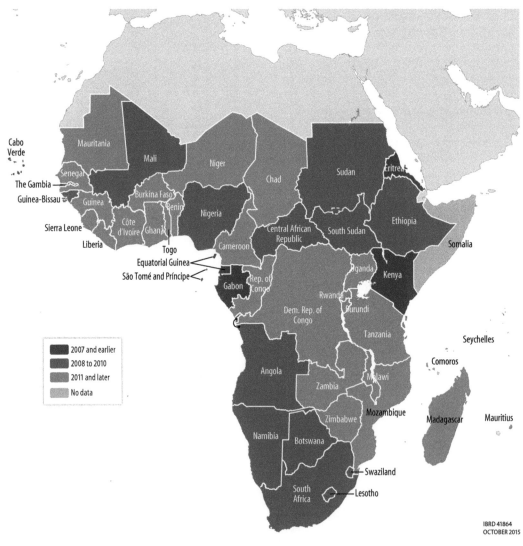

Source: Data from the World Bank microdata library.

conducted.[5] Eritrea and Somalia have not fielded national consumption surveys over the past 20 years. These five countries represent 5 percent of the region's population.

Comparability of consumption data

The lack of consumption surveys is an obvious impediment to monitoring poverty, but problems with consumption data do not end there. Even where multiple surveys are available for a country, they are often not comparable with one another (or with those of other countries). Tracking poverty trends is difficult when changes in measured consumption partly reflect changes in survey design or implementation.

The survey design literature documents multiple ways in which two surveys can be rendered noncomparable. For this report, household consumption surveys are considered comparable if the following features are consistent across surveys:[6]

- *Nationally representative sample*: A nationally representative sample is necessary to obtain statistics that apply to the whole population, not merely a subgroup. Comparability is obviously impossible if one round covers only urban households and the next covers only rural areas.
- *Seasonality*: Many consumption patterns vary over the year, which has implications for measuring poverty (Kaminski, Christiaensen, and Gilbert 2014; Muller 2008). In Africa, for instance, food and cash income among farmers is plentiful after harvests and dwindles during the lean season. Comparability may be lost if survey rounds are conducted during different months.
- *Reporting instrument and period*: Consumption data can be collected either by asking household members to recall their purchases and consumption from own production (farm harvest) (in the past seven days, past two weeks, the last month, and so on) or to keep a diary of such activities (for two weeks, a month, or longer). A body of evidence shows that the method used matters (see Beegle and others 2012). Both the reporting period and the instrument (recall or diary form) should remain consistent.

Based on these three criteria, 148 consumption surveys conducted in Africa between 1990 and 2012 were reviewed for comparability.[7] Figure 1.4 displays the results. Blue dots indicate surveys that are comparable within the country; solid black diamonds indicate noncomparable surveys. Dotted lines connect comparable surveys. Hollow black diamonds indicate surveys that are not available. In some instances two or more cross-sections in a country with four or more cross-sections are comparable but the other two or more are not. (South Africa, for example, has two pairs of surveys that are comparable with each other, but it does not have four comparable surveys).

Several observations emerge from the findings presented in figure 1.4. First, many consumption surveys are not comparable.

Between 1990 and 2012, only 27 of 48 countries conducted two or more comparable surveys (map 1.2). As a result, even some countries that have multiple surveys are unable to track poverty reliably over time. Guinea and Mali, for example, each conducted four surveys, but none of them is comparable (box 1.2).

Second, there was a slight improvement in comparability between 2000 and 2014. More surveys were implemented after 2000, and more of them were comparable than before 2000.

The picture of comparability would appear even bleaker if a more stringent definition of comparability had been adopted. For instance, the list of consumption items on which household members are asked to report can be long (a list of specific foods) or short (if foods are grouped). It is not unusual for surveys in the same country to change these lists dramatically from one round to the next (from well under 100 to well over 100).[8] In general, respondents recall more when presented with a more disaggregated list, so that reported consumption is generally higher; a condensed list may lead to more reporting errors. Changing the list over time thus compromises consistency. If other factors—such as the quality of fieldwork and supervision—are also taken into consideration, even fewer household surveys in Africa would be considered comparable.

Lack of comparability, combined with the long gap between surveys (often five years or more) hampers the ability to understand changes in welfare over time. Although Africa is doing well in terms of the number of countries on which data are available and compares reasonably well with other poor regions in the number of surveys per country, the region trails most other country groupings in terms of comparable surveys, falling in the bottom half of the World Bank's regional grouping of countries (table 1.1). Since 1990 the average African country conducted only 3.8 consumption surveys (about one survey every six years), 2.2 fewer than the developing world average. The average developing country conducts one survey every four

FIGURE 1.4 Comparability of consumption surveys has improved, but it remains a major problem

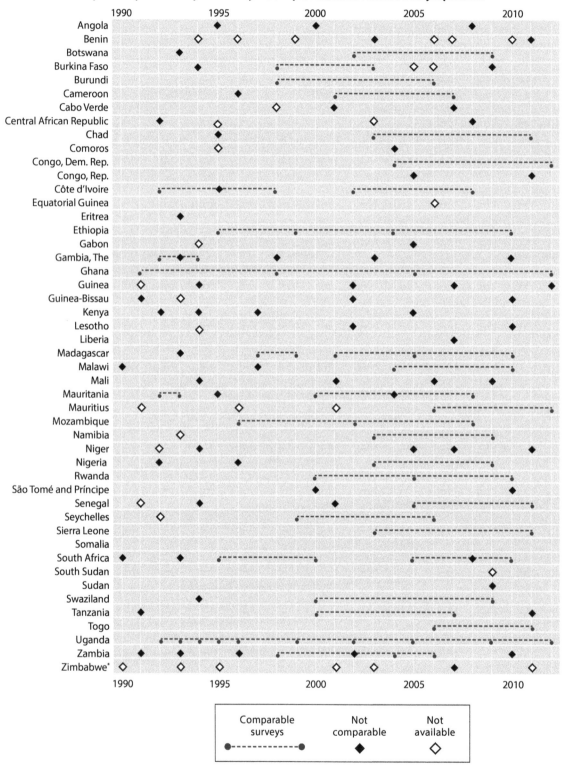

Note: Figure is based on all household surveys conducted in Africa between 1990 and 2012. It excludes consumption surveys not used for official poverty monitoring. Not available refers to surveys for which the microdata and/or documentation could not be accessed.

MAP 1.2   Lack of comparable surveys in Africa makes it difficult to measure poverty trends

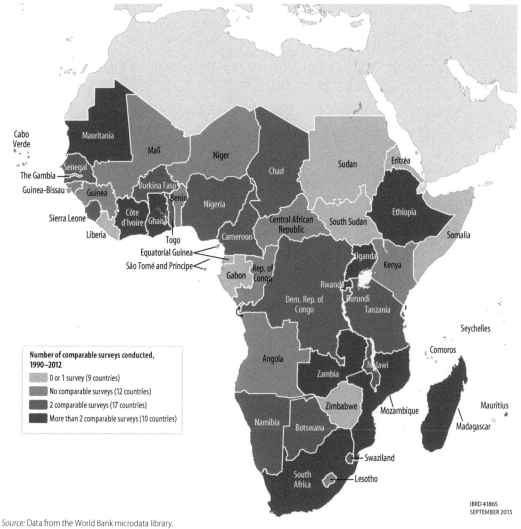

Source: Data from the World Bank microdata library.

years, and the average Latin American country conducts at least one survey every two years. If comparability is taken into account, the picture is even worse, with African countries producing just 1.6 comparable poverty estimates per country between 1990 and 2012.

Does noncomparability matter? Survey experiments show that changes in questionnaire design can matter a lot. According to Beegle and others (2012), use of diary versus recall, shorter versus longer reporting periods, and changes in the number of consumption items drastically affect poverty and inequality measures. Using methods other

than the benchmark method of personal diary with daily visits yielded poverty rates that were 7–19 percentage points higher. Most instruments, including household-level diaries or recall questionnaires of different granularity, thus underreport consumption compared with the supervision-intensive personal diary. Backiny-Yetna, Steele, and Djima (2014) show that poverty estimates in Niger are sensitive to the reporting period, with estimates of 51 percent, 47 percent, and 43 percent depending on the approach. Results from the 2005/06 survey in Kenya also point to significant differences in poverty calculations depending on whether the recall or

BOX 1.2 How did poverty change in Guinea and Mali? Lack of comparable data makes it difficult to know

Guinea conducted four household surveys between 1994 and 2012. The 1994/95 and the 2002/03 surveys were conducted over 12 months, the 2007 survey was conducted in July–October 2007, the 2012 survey was conducted in February–March 2012. In 1994/95 each household was visited 11 times, one visit every three days for a month. Food consumption data were collected from visit 2 to visit 11, using a three-day recall period. A 12th of the sample was visited each month. In 2002/03 each household was visited three times, or once every four months (the survey is thus a panel of three observations). During each visit, food consumption data were collected using a three-day recall period in urban areas and two-day recall in rural areas. In the 2007 and 2012 surveys, each household was visited once. Food consumption data were collected by asking about typical monthly consumption (not actual consumption, such as consumption the previous week). The 2007 and 2012 surveys were conducted in different seasons. The number of consumption items also differed: the 1994/95 questionnaire included 116 food and 110

nonfood items, the 2002/03 survey included 240 food and 425 nonfood items, and the 2007 and 2012 surveys included 110 food and 130 nonfood items.

Mali implemented four surveys between 1994 and 2012; the surveys vary in a number of ways. The 1994/95 survey included 10 food and 34 nonfood items, the fewest among the surveys, and a 15-day food recall period. In 2001/02 every household was interviewed every quarter. Food consumption data were collected through a seven-day diary; in theory each household was visited 7 times a quarter, for a total of 28 visits during the year. The 2006 and 2010 surveys were Core Welfare Indicators Questionnaire (CWIQ)–type surveys fielded in July–November 2006 and December 2009–August 2010. Food consumption data were collected using the usual-month approach. The number of items on the questionnaires was similar, although some types of expenditures (food eaten away from home, beverages, cigarettes) were reported by each individual household member using an open list.

TABLE 1.1 Africa lags in the number of comparable surveys per country, conducted between 1990 and 2012

Region	Developing countries that conducted at least one consumption survey			Median year of most recent survey	Average number of surveys per developing country	Average number of comparable surveys per developing country
	Number of countries	Country coverage (percent)	Population coverage (percent)			
East Asia and Pacific	15	63	96	2010	3.9	2.8
Europe and Central Asia	21	100	100	2011	10.0	6.4
Latin America and the Caribbean	22	85	98	2011	11.1	6.3
Middle East and North Africa	12	92	98	2007	3.2	1.8
South Asia	8	100	100	2010	4.1	2.8
Africa	47	98	99	2010	3.8	1.6
World	125	89	98	2010	6.0	3.5

Sources: Data from the World Bank microdata library, PovcalNet, and World Development Indicators.
Note: The table includes low-income, lower-middle-income, and upper-middle-income countries, with the exception of Equatorial Guinea, which is a high-income country.

---

diary approach to consumption was used (Dabalen and others 2015).[9]

In Nigeria two household surveys were conducted the same year. The Nigeria Living Standards Survey (NLSS) was fielded in 2009/10. It overlapped with the first wave of

the General Household Survey-Panel (GHS-Panel), which was launched in the last quarter of 2010. The NLSS, which relied on the diary approach, reported much lower consumption than the GHS-Panel, which used the recall approach (figure 1.5). The surveys

FIGURE 1.5 Different survey designs can result in very different consumption estimates

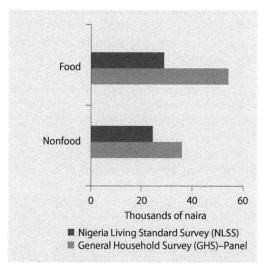

Sources: Data from the NLSS and GHS-Panel for overlapping months in 2010.

were also different in other salient ways, in particular with respect to field supervision and field team composition, both of which may affect quality.

At the country level, noncomparability between survey rounds is often a concern; country-level poverty reports are replete with discussions of survey comparability (see World Bank 2013 for Burkina Faso; World Bank 2012 for Niger; World Bank 2015b for Tanzania). These differences are often overlooked at the regional level, partly because databases such as PovcalNet do not vet surveys on the basis of comparability.

Lack of survey comparability within countries across time is not unique to consumption measures. It has been reported in the measurement of literacy, for example (see box 3.2 in chapter 3). Although more systematic documentation of these differences in a metadatabase would not resolve these issues, it would be helpful to analysts.

Quality of consumption data

The closest approximation of a broad definition of good-quality data involves fitness for use: data should be accurate, rich in detail, relevant, timely, and likely to achieve the purposes for which the survey was intended

(Biemer and Lyberg 2003; Gryna and Juran 1980). At the core of data quality problems is often a process failure.[10] Interviewers may fail to make contact with respondents and subsequently report fake data, perhaps because supervision was lax or insufficient (as Finn and Ranchhod [forthcoming] document in a survey in South Africa). Enumerators may not have been given sufficient training to probe for the responses intended by the questions. Respondents may refuse to participate, or they may provide false information. Modes of data collection—computers, phones, paper—could also be compromised because the infrastructure needed was not planned appropriately. Errors may be introduced in entering (or keying) data. Poor data quality can undermine comparability over time because process failures that occur one year may not be repeated in another.

Misreported data are clearly the most serious way data quality can be compromised. There is little value in all the other dimensions of data (such as timeliness, richness of detail, relevance, availability, and even comparability), if the data are erroneous and hence cannot be used for the purposes for which they were designed (Biemer and Lyberg 2003).

The systematic detection of poor quality is challenging. Judge and Schechter (2009) apply Benford's law—a statistical method for reviewing the digits in reported statistics for abnormal patterns as a sign of fraudulence—to surveys in Bangladesh, Ghana, Mexico, Pakistan, Paraguay, Peru, South Africa, the United States, and Vietnam. They find widespread evidence of fake crop and livestock production data. Among the surveys reviewed, data quality was far worse in surveys in developing countries. Consumption data for almost 40 percent of households surveyed in the Malawi 1997/98 household survey were incomplete or inaccurate, and the data were unusable in poverty analysis (Benson, Machinjili, and Kachikopa 2004).

One commonly observed manifestation of poor quality is deterioration in reporting over the survey period that cannot be explained by seasonality. In Tanzania average household size fell significantly over the course of surveys

FIGURE 1.6 **Data errors may account for some of the reported change in consumption**

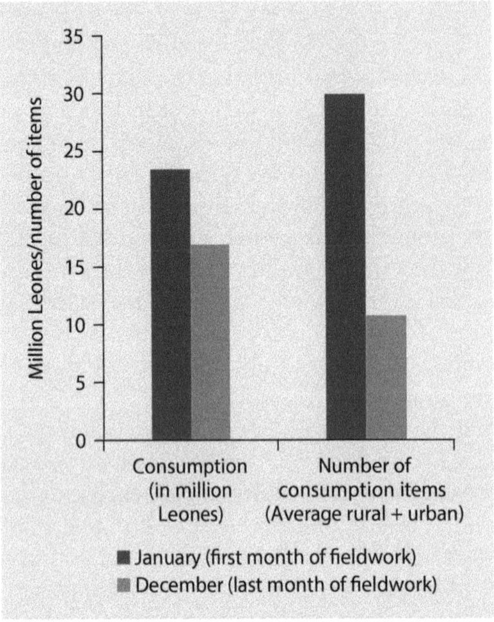

Source: Data from the 2011 Sierra Leone Integrated Household Survey.

over 12 months, specifically for the Household Budget Surveys 2000/01 and 2007, most likely reflecting enumerator fatigue (NBS 2009). In Sierra Leone, where households were randomly interviewed, both the number of food items and the level of consumption fell steadily during the 12 months of fieldwork (figure 1.6). The number of reported food purchases among urban respondents fell by one-third over the course of the survey, a drop that is explained only partly by seasonality. The reported urban-rural gap also narrowed, possibly because of data quality issues.

Price Data

Price data are indispensable to poverty measurement. Global poverty estimates reported in PovcalNet rely on two types of price indexes: national CPIs to deflate nominal consumption to a common base year and PPP exchange rates to convert local currencies into a common currency.

Because people living in different countries face different prices, comparison of living standards between countries calls for the use of PPP exchange rates to achieve parity in the purchasing power of people's incomes. The same principle applies within countries, where consumers in rural and urban areas often face different prices, but the evidence for Africa is scant. Empirical studies for developing countries in other regions suggest that within-country price variation can be important, at least in larger countries (Deaton and Dupriez 2011; Majumder, Ray, and Sinha 2012).

Despite the importance of adjusting for differences in the cost of living across regions in a country for capturing true living standards, such adjustments are not widespread. In Africa, PovcalNet, which has the largest collection of consumption data from household surveys across countries of the world, adjusts for spatial price differences only in Angola, Burkina Faso, and South Africa. There is no explanation for why the adjustment is made only in these countries. Outside of Africa, PovcalNet data on consumption are adjusted for within-country spatial price differences in countries in Latin America and the Caribbean, China, India, Indonesia, and, for food only, in countries in Europe and Central Asia. This report uses the consumption measure used in PovcalNet for Africa, meaning that for most countries it has not been adjusted for spatial price differences.[11]

Adjusting for price changes using the CPI

The CPI is used to track inflation in consumer prices. This core economic indicator is used to index pensions, wages, taxes, and social security benefits and to anchor monetary policy.

The largest consumer price data collection exercise in Africa is conducted by Statistics South Africa, which regularly collects 65,000 price quotations from 27,000 outlets (ILO 2013). In other African countries, the number of CPI price quotations ranges from 1,150 (São Tomé and Príncipe) to 51,170 (Ethiopia).

CPI calculation requires weights to aggregate the price data across items into an index. These weights typically come from budget share estimates from household surveys.

Combining the price data with weights to construct the CPI is a complex process that often differs significantly across countries. Partly because of these variations and partly because the CPI is not designed specifically to apply to the measurement of poverty, CPIs may not always accurately depict changes in the cost of living experienced by the average household or (particularly) the poor.

CPIs suffer from several potential sources of bias. *Commodity substitution bias* relates to the use of an imperfect indexing formula and outdated weights. The most common index for CPIs is the Laspeyres index, which uses weights from a base (reference) period. This index disregards substitution behavior that may stem from inflation itself—that is, it ignores the fact that when the prices of some goods rise more quickly than the prices of others, households shift consumption to similar but cheaper items. It therefore overestimates inflation and underestimates poverty reduction.

Updating weights can address this problem, but CPI weights are often many years old. As of July 2012, for example, 13 percent of the African population was living in countries in which the CPI basket was based on data from the 1990s (or earlier), and data on 11 percent of the population were missing altogether (figure 1.7).

Outlet substitution bias is related to changes in the retail landscape. Price data for the CPI are often collected from a fixed set of stores or markets. With the advent of discount retail stores in some countries in Africa, failure to adjust where the price data are collected is expected to lead to an overestimation of inflation and underestimation of poverty reduction.

Quality change bias reflects the fact that the quality of a product can change (typically, improve) while the price remains unchanged. Evidence from the developed world suggests that quality change bias generally leads to an overestimation of inflation (Hausman 2003). Overestimating inflation thus understates poverty reduction.

New products bias is similar to quality change bias. The introduction of new products

FIGURE 1.7 The weights used to construct consumer price indexes in Africa are outdated

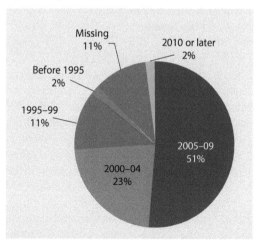

Source: ILO 2013.
Note: Figures indicate the share of Africa's population in 2013 living in countries in which the weights used to calculate the consumer price index (CPI) in July 2012 came from each time period.

and brands increases living standards. Econometric techniques seek to estimate the gains that occur as a result. Hausman (1996, 1999) measures the consumer gains resulting from the introduction of new breakfast cereals and mobile phone services by estimating virtual (reservation) prices. Whether such techniques should find their way into the estimation of the CPI remains controversial.[12] New product bias is by definition positive. It leads to an overestimation of inflation in the CPI and therefore an underestimation of poverty reduction.

Plutocratic bias arises because CPI weights are computed in a way that implicitly weights households in proportion to their total consumption (so-called plutocratic weights) and are hence more representative of wealthier households (Deaton 1998; Ley 2005; Oosthuizen 2007). Plutocratic weights are the natural choice in the deflation of economic aggregates, such as national accounts, but generally not the first choice for measuring poverty and welfare. The alternative would be weighting all households equally (Prais 1959). If consumption patterns and rates of inflation differ among poor, average, and better-off households, the CPI will not accurately track the changes in prices experienced by the poor.

In Africa and other developing regions, there is empirical evidence that inflation inequality can be important—that is, the poor and the nonpoor may experience different inflation rates. Whether these differences result in over- or underestimation of the inflation faced by the poor is less clear. In Burkina Faso in 1994–98, food crop prices increased much more quickly than the prices of other consumer items (Günther and Grimm 2007). Because the poor spend a larger share of their budgets on food, they experienced higher inflation than other consumers. Inflation inequality has also been documented in Brazil, Colombia, Indonesia, Mexico, Peru, South Africa, Tanzania, and Uganda (Goñi, López, and Servén 2006; McCulloch, Weisbrod, and Timmer 2007; Mkenda and Ngasamiaku 2009; Okidi and Nsubuga 2010; Oosthuizen 2007). While some studies find that the inflation poor households experience is higher, in some countries it is better-off households that face higher rates of inflation. Even within the same country, the direction of bias can change. In Burkina Faso, for example, the poor encountered

lower inflation than the better off between 1998 and 2003.

Urban bias arises because many CPIs in Africa are based on prices collected only in urban areas. Some countries also base weights only on urban consumption patterns. Urban-based prices and weights are significantly more prevalent in Africa than elsewhere (figure 1.8). There is reason to believe that the *urban bias* in prices and weights is even more common than suggested by the data of the International Labour Organization (ILO). For instance, Kenya, which is listed as having nationwide coverage in the ILO database, reports, in its CPI publication, that, outside of Nairobi, urban centers were selected to represent each province (KNBS 2010). Whether urban bias matters in measuring poverty depends on whether rural inflation does or does not track urban inflation.

Bias from the treatment of own consumption stems from the practice of including only market purchases in the CPI weights, excluding consumption from food grown by the household. One-quarter of Africa's

FIGURE 1.8 **Both the prices and weights used to construct consumer price indexes in Africa reflect a strong urban bias**

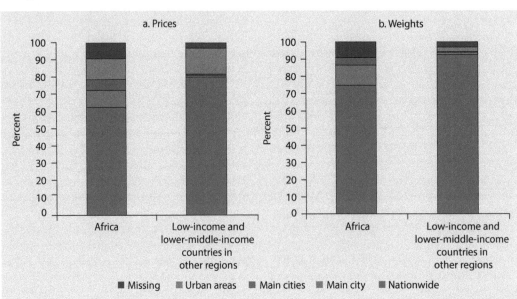

Source: ILO 2013.
Note: Figures are weighted using the population in 2013.

population lives in countries that exclude home production from weights; for another third, it is not clear whether the weights include home production. The CPI guidelines issued by the United Nations (UN 2009) leave the decision on the inclusion of own production in weights to the discretion of countries, because the decision depends partly on what the index is used for. For the purpose of poverty analysis, where own-consumed goods are typically included in the consumption aggregate and valued at (proximate) market prices, the weights for price indexes should include consumption of own production. As with urban and plutocratic bias, whether this bias matters in measuring poverty depends on whether the inflation associated with these goods differs from the inflation associated with other items.

Biases arising from computational and similar errors also reduce the accuracy of the CPI. In Tanzania, for instance, the CPI underestimated inflation in 2002–05 because of defective protocols for removing outliers and other computational errors. The mistakes were eventually corrected and the CPI series revised, though concerns remained that the series continued to underestimate inflation (Adam and others 2012; World Bank 2007). Similar evidence is reported for Ghana in 1999–2001 (IMF 2003, 2007).

In situations where price changes are politically sensitive, governments may have an incentive to exert pressure on statistical agencies to misreport inflation or strategically time methodological changes to reduce measured inflation. If statistical agencies are not independent, CPI-measured inflation may be biased downward, leading to an overestimation of poverty reduction (Barrionuevo 2011; Berumen and Beker 2011). Although the notion of *political economy bias* is plausible, political influence on the computation of the rate of inflation is difficult to document.

Because of these shortcomings of the CPI, poverty estimates at the national level often use alternative approaches to adjust for spatial or temporal price differences. Some statistical agencies and academic studies reweight CPI subcomponents to reflect the consumption patterns of the poor or construct survey-based price deflators so that prices and weights are computed directly from household surveys. Since there is little agreement or technical guidance on how to adjust nominal consumption data for price changes, countries often use ad hoc and context-specific methods.

Another approach is the Engel curve method, pioneered by Costa (2001) and Hamilton (2001). It is based on the notion that changes in food budget shares over time reflect changes in real incomes. Chapter 2 takes a closer look at what this method suggests about the magnitude and direction of the CPI bias and the implications for measuring poverty in Africa.

Despite the caveats, national CPIs are applied almost uniformly for across-survey price adjustment in the context of global poverty measurement (although in cases where CPI-measured inflation rates appear highly implausible, alternative inflation estimates are occasionally used).

Using purchasing power parities to measure global poverty

For cross-country analysis, it is necessary to convert local currency values into a common currency. The approach has typically involved using PPP rather than traditional currency exchange rates to compare both poverty and GDP across countries.

The PPP exchange rate is based on a large-scale effort to collect and compare prices for a set of items across all countries (see World Bank 2014 for a detailed discussion of PPPs). The International Comparison Program (ICP), which is in charge of the PPP calculations, is a massive global undertaking that covers thousands of goods and services in 200 countries.[13] About 199 countries, with 97 percent of the world's population and 90 percent of the world's economy, participated in the latest round (2011). In Africa 45 of 48 countries (all but Eritrea, Somalia, and South Sudan) participated, up from 19 in 1993 and 44 in 2005.

A controversy erupted in 2014 following the release of the 2011 PPPs. The debate revolved around whether the world has become more or less equal and whether it has become less poor relative to the United States, whose currency is taken as the benchmark when calculating these exchange rates. Such debates have become routine with every round of ICP PPP releases (see the discussion in Almås 2012; Ciccone and Jarociński 2010; Deaton 2010), partly because in each round major revisions have been made to methods, the number of countries participating, and coverage (rural and urban) within countries, so that some reranking becomes inevitable. In the latest release, the consumption and income of the average developing country rose by 25 percent (Inklaar and Rao 2014). The new PPPs project large declines in poverty and a shift in the geography of the poor from Asia to Africa (Dykstra, Kenny, and Sandefur 2014; Jolliffe and Prydz 2015).

Experts are divided over whether the 2005 or the 2011 PPP better describes the world. Supporters of the 2011 round (Deaton and Aten 2014) argue that the methodological changes introduced in 2011, in particular the use of a core global list of goods rather than 18 ring countries in 2005, undid some of the mistakes made in the 2005 PPP, which inflated the price ratios for Africa, Asia (without Japan), and western Asia by 20–30 percent. On the other side of the debate, Ravallion (2014) finds that the 2011 PPP places more weight on strongly internationally traded goods than do past ICP rounds, seen through a convergence of price levels and exchange rates, especially in Asia. He argues that these results are inconsistent with expectations from the methodological changes introduced in the 2011 ICP round.

Lanjouw, Massari, and van der Weide (2015) use a multiple imputations approach that avoids the use of PPPs entirely to rank poverty rates of countries. Their method generates multiple imputed consumption and poverty rates for each country (so for a sample of five countries, there are five estimates per country), each corresponding to the estimate obtained when a particular country is used as the reference in the model. They then rank countries on the basis of these poverty rates and compare these ranks to ranks obtained using 2005 PPP and 2011 PPP. For a sample of five African countries, the 2011 PPP ranking followed the ranking from this imputation approach more closely than the 2005 PPP did. In contrast, there was no major difference in the rankings of the 2011 and 2005 PPP on the one hand and the ranking based on the imputation approach for a sample of countries in Europe and Central Asia and Latin America and the Caribbean.

What do the latest PPPs say about the change in national income levels (GDP per capita) in Africa? The region remains the world's poorest, even though its share of global income inched higher, from 3.3 percent in 2005 to 4.5 percent in 2011. All 10 of the world's poorest economies were in Africa. Country rankings within Africa remained fairly stable, but there were some changes in rank, such as Botswana and Gabon at one end and Ghana and Zambia in the middle (figure 1.9).

Population Census and GDP Data

Surveys and price data are not the only data needed for estimating poverty. Census data are needed both to select the sample for a survey and to estimate the size of the population. GDP data from the system of national accounts are used to estimate poverty in years with no survey.

Census data

A census is essential for measuring and monitoring monetary and nonmonetary poverty, for several reasons. First, it is the basis for the sample frame for surveys and the selection of the primary sampling units (communities) from which households are sampled. At the back end of surveys, censuses—specifically the population projections from the past census to the survey year—are needed to obtain the population statistics from the survey estimates. The absence of an up-to-date census introduces significant uncertainty into population-level statistics on living standards

FIGURE 1.9   **Adoption of the 2011 purchasing power parity values increased GDP per capita figures across Africa**

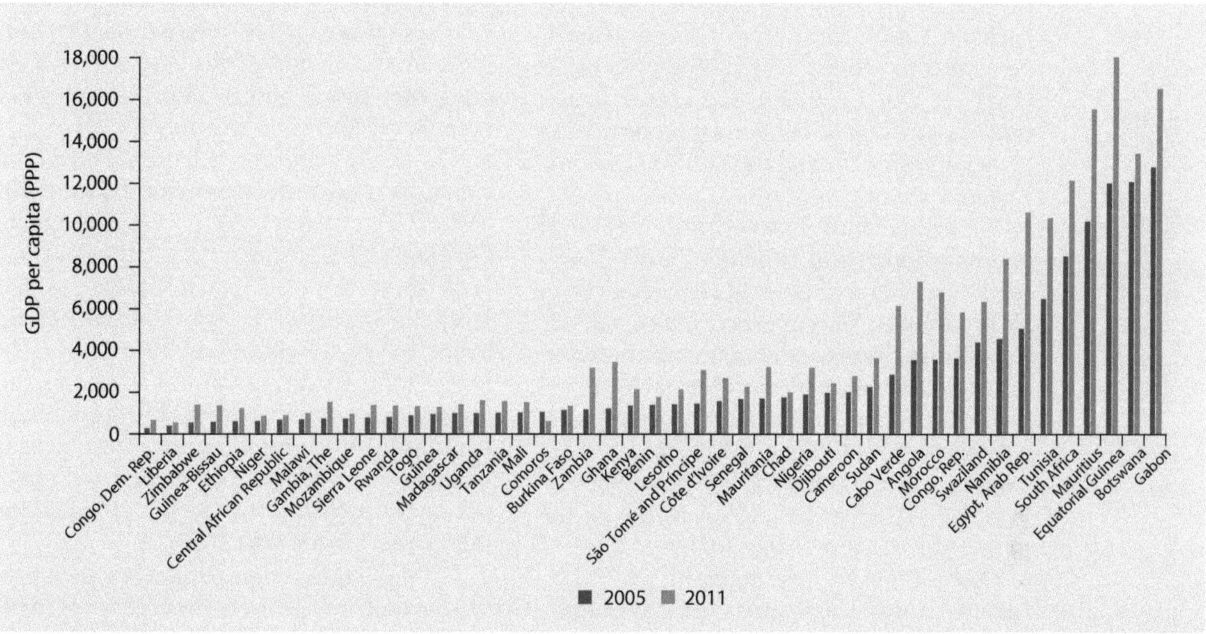

Source: World Bank 2014.
Note: Countries are ranked by their 2005 PPP estimate of GDP per capita. GDP per capita of Equatorial Guinea using 2011 PPP was $39,440; in the figure it is capped at $18,000, so that incomes for the other countries are distinguishable.

(or any measures from household surveys) (World Bank 2015a). Second, census data have been used to estimate poverty rates and poverty counts at the smallest possible jurisdiction, through poverty mapping techniques (Elbers, Lanjouw, and Lanjouw 2003). Third, census data are useful for understanding a number of nonmonetary dimensions of living standards, such as housing conditions and educational attainment.

Because of the enormous financial, personnel, and managerial demands of censuses, they are ideally conducted once every 10 years. The coverage of population censuses in Africa improved significantly in the last two rounds. In the 2000 round (1995–2004), 33 of 47 countries participated; only 8 countries had no census in the 2010 round (2005–14).[14] The eight countries represent about 13 percent of Africa's population. The Democratic Republic of Congo has not conducted a census since 1984. Because it is estimated to be the third most populous country in Africa, obtaining the

correct count of the poor there is critical for regional estimates.

Only a handful of countries make their census data sets available to the public. The Integrated Public Use Microdata Series (IPUMS)—the world's largest collection of public use census microdata files—currently includes 19 African countries.[15]

National accounts data

National accounts are the comprehensive economic statistics that measure economic activity in a country. They are also important for estimating poverty in years in which no survey has been conducted. Rather than assume a steady rate of change in poverty between survey rounds, researchers apply per capita growth rates of GDP or private consumption (referred to as household final consumption expenditure in the World Development Indicators) to the household survey means to interpolate the pattern of poverty between two surveys or extrapolate it beyond the survey range (when no other survey is available).[16] For a country with only one survey, the survey mean is adjusted forward and backward using the real growth rate of GDP per capita to give poverty estimates in other years (see World Bank 2015a). These calculations assume that GDP per capita or private consumption per capita grows at the same rate for everyone.

When used to interpolate, national accounts imputation is preferred over assuming a steady rate of poverty change between survey rounds. This approach helps capture possible downturns and upswings between surveys. The assumption that each household's consumption expands uniformly at the rate of the overall economy becomes more tenuous when extrapolating beyond the surveys, especially farther into the future (or the past).

One reason why the reliability of GDP-imputed poverty estimates declines the farther away the estimate is from the actual survey is that the structure of the economy changes over time. Every year statistical agencies collect proxy information on the level of production in various sectors. They aggregate these values assuming the structure of the economy in the base year. As the structure of the economy changes (for example, the agricultural sector shrinks and the service sector

grows), the base year becomes less and less representative of the economy and therefore requires updating. The international recommendation is to update the base year at least every five years. This process of replacing the base year is known as *rebasing*.

Thanks to rebasing, a national economy can grow statistically overnight (figure 1.10). The GDP rebasing exercise carried out by Ghana in 2010, for example, caused such a large increase in GDP that Ghana jumped from low-income to low-middle-income country status. Rebasing in Nigeria in 2014 propelled it to surpass South Africa as the biggest economy in Africa. The announcement drew much attention from the media, business community, economists, and international organizations (BBC 2014; Economist 2014; Magnowski 2014).

Only 22 countries in Africa (less than half of all countries) use base years that are more recent than 2004. Growing sectors may thus be undercounted, leading to underestimation of GDP, GDP growth, and poverty reduction. Given that rebasing typically gives greater weight to nonagricultural sectors, which are not as powerful at reducing extreme poverty as agricultural growth, underestimation of poverty reduction is likely to be smaller than underestimation of GDP (Christiaensen, Demery, and Kuhl 2011; Loayza and Raddatz 2010).

Of the 14 countries that rebased their GDP in the last 10 years, only 3 reported a decline in GDP. Some of the upward revisions were large, partly because the base year had not been changed in many years.

Interpolation and extrapolation are necessary to estimate poverty in years in which no survey data are available. Should the imputations be based on GDP or private consumption data from national accounts? Private consumption is preferred, because it captures a set of goods and services that more closely mirrors consumption from household surveys (see Deaton 2005 for a critique of private consumption as a proxy for household survey consumption). In practice, however, considerations such as the availability and quality of GDP and private consumption data and the strength of correlations between data from

FIGURE 1.10 **Rebasing increased GDP values in many African countries**

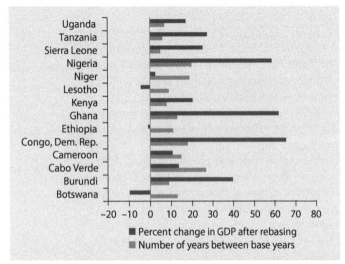

■ Percent change in GDP after rebasing
■ Number of years between base years

Source: Data from national statistical agencies for each country.

national accounts and household surveys typically influence the choice. PovcalNet uses private consumption per capita for interpolations, except in Africa, where it uses GDP per capita.

For 1991–2012 the average ratio of average consumption per capita from household surveys to average private consumption per capita from national accounts (based on 83 household surveys in Africa) was 0.86. This figure is similar to the global average but less than the ratio of 1.0 for Africa estimated in Deaton (2005). The ratio of average consumption per capita from household surveys to GDP per capita for the same sample of surveys was 0.61. This figure is two-thirds of the global average (0.9) and 60 percent of the 1.0 ratio reported in Deaton (2005). The lower ratio when using GDP is expected, because GDP includes more than private household consumption.

What about growth rates? For a subset of countries for which two comparable surveys are available, annual per capita growth rates from the household consumption surveys can be compared with the corresponding annual per capita growth of GDP and private consumption from national accounts. Annual growth rates are 0.41 percentage points higher for private consumption per capita and 1.2 percentage points higher for GDP per capita than estimates of consumption per capita growth from household surveys (based on a simple country average for each period for which comparable pairs of survey data are available). For Africa overall, without restricting to years with comparable surveys, GDP and private consumption per capita growth rates from national accounts are very close, with the GDP per capita growth rate higher by only 0.02 percentage points on average. This finding suggests that the performance of GDP in tracking consumption from surveys is worse in the subset of countries for which comparable surveys are available. Overall, using private consumption from national accounts rather than GDP to impute poverty when surveys are lacking does not appear to make a significant difference. Both sources lead to overestimation of the decline in poverty.

In Kenya, for example, where the last household survey was conducted in 2005, the poverty rate associated with the $1.90 poverty line was 34 percent. Extrapolating from the 2005 survey using a real average GDP per capita growth rate of 2.3 percent yields a poverty estimate of 26 percent for 2012. Reducing the growth rate by 0.5 percentage point a year increases the estimate to 28 percent. The larger the measurement error in GDP growth rates and the older the survey data the projections rely on, the larger the difference between the "true" and the estimated poverty rate using projections.

The Political Economy of Data Production

After years of investment in statistics by African governments and the international development community, a feeling of disappointment is noticeable in recent discussions about the absence of adequate data for poverty measurement, let alone high-quality data. The issues are not unique to consumption data (box 1.3). Explanations for the delays in the availability of data and quality improvements point to inadequate funding, the limited capacity of national statistical offices, the lack of strategic planning, and administrative cultures. The response of some supporters of statistics in the region has been to ask for more money and more capacity building. But there is increasing recognition that the problem may be more deeply seated than lack of money or technical expertise.

Country-Level Factors Associated with the Availability, Comparability, and Openness of Data

Do richer countries in Africa tend to have more surveys and more surveys that are comparable? Are countries that receive more aid doing a better job of collecting data, perhaps because donors have an interest in showing results? Which countries collect more frequent and comparable consumption survey data and make the data available to the public?[17]

BOX 1.3   Many kinds of data in Africa are unreliable

Poor quality and lack of comparability affect many kinds of data in Africa, not just consumption data. One telling sign is the wide variance in indicators such as health care use, educational enrollment, adult literacy, child mortality, and access to water and sanitation for the same country from different surveys (box 3.2, in chapter 3, shows the challenge of tracking adult literacy). Another is the divergence between survey and administrative data (see, for example, Gaddis and Hoogeveen 2015). Although political incentives to show positive results may drive some of the differences between surveys and administrative data (Sandefur and Glassman 2015), data quality problems also play a role. Estimates of maize yields for Malawi for 2006/07, for example, range from 1,700 kilograms per hectare to more than 2,500 (a difference of almost 50 percent) (Carletto, Jolliffe, and Banerjee 2015).

This section groups countries in four ways—by income level, natural resource endowment, geographical location (landlocked versus coastal), and fragility—to identify patterns. Besides these broad groupings, the analysis draws attention to the role of governance and development aid in data production. The upper panel in table 1.2 reports results for Africa, whereas the bottom panel shows results for developing countries in other regions.

Lack of financial resources is generally considered as a major constraint to statistics in Africa. Surprisingly, this is not supported by the results. In Africa, middle-income countries neither collect more consumption surveys than low-income countries, nor are the surveys they collect more likely to be comparable or open to the public. Outside of Africa, middle-income countries collect more consumption surveys than low-income countries, but the relationship turns insignificant after controlling for the share of aid in the budget, political freedoms, and government effectiveness.

African countries that are rich in natural resources conduct fewer consumption surveys than non-resource-rich countries in the region. Both in Africa and in other regions, fragile countries collect fewer consumption surveys than nonfragile countries, although in Africa, the statistical significance disappears after controlling for the share of aid in the budget, political freedoms, and government effectiveness. Unexpectedly, in some specifications, the share of surveys that are comparable and open to the public is higher in fragile than in nonfragile countries in Africa.

Countries receiving more development aid (as a share of the government budget) might be expected to have more and higher-quality poverty data (defined narrowly as having consumption surveys that are comparable), in part because donors are presumably interested in collecting data with which to assess whether their aid is having an impact. There is no strong evidence that they do. In the non-African sample, there is a negative correlation between aid and the number of consumption surveys. In the African sample, there is no statistically significant relationship between aid and the number of consumption surveys or the share of comparable surveys. In fact, the more aid a country in Africa receives, the less likely it is to open its surveys to the public.

The lack of positive correlation between aid and data production in Africa is puzzling. It may be that donors do not explicitly or implicitly demand more or better data. Alternatively, the incentives of donors and governments could be misaligned. An example of such misaligned interests is the case in which donors ask and are willing to pay for data that are high in quality (small sample, multi-topic surveys) though less frequently collected, whereas governments prefer larger samples that are representative at lower administrative levels (CGD 2014). National statistical agencies can be caught between the preferences of donors and those of their governments.

TABLE 1.2 **Only a few country characteristics are correlated with the number and share of comparable and open consumption surveys**

Country characteristic	Number of consumption surveys		Share of consumption surveys that are comparable		Share of consumption surveys that are open	
	(1a)	(1b)	(2a)	(2b)	(3a)	(3b)
Africa						
Middle-income	−0.781	−0.343	−0.072	−0.141	0.068	0.069
Resource-rich	−0.869*	−1.115*	−0.096	0.075	0.016	−0.079
Landlocked	0.794	1.093	0.047	−0.268*	−0.056	0.015
Fragile	−1.963***	−0.823	−0.084	0.396*	0.169***	−0.010
Log of aid share of government budget		−0.146		0.031		−0.076*
Worldwide Governance Indicators						
— government effectiveness index		0.363		0.581***		−0.280**
Political rights freedom index		−0.165		0.101*		−0.022
Outside Africa						
Middle–income	4.107**	2.360	0.090	0.146	0.094	0.160
Resource-rich	−0.954	−2.755	0.233**	0.166	0.050	−0.067
Landlocked	1.349	3.675**	0.189**	0.122	0.046	−0.001
Fragile	−6.236***	−4.766***	0.025	0.156	0.020	−0.094
Log of aid share of government budget		−1.707***		0.020		−0.003
Worldwide Governance Indicators						
— government effectiveness index		−1.371		−0.018		−0.073
Political rights freedom index		−0.895		0.026		0.009
Number of observations	133	93	133	93	132	93
R–squared	0.251	0.432	0.098	0.390	0.096	0.189

Sources: Survey counts: International Household Survey Network, World Bank microdata library, and PovcalNet. Government effectiveness variable: Worldwide Governance Indicators. Freedom index: Freedom House. Other control variables: World Development Indicators.
Note: The data set consists of one observation per country. In columns 1a and b, the dependent variable is the total number of consumption surveys conducted between 1990 and 2012. In columns 2a and b, the dependent variable is the share of consumption surveys that are comparable. In columns 3a and b, the dependent variable is the number of surveys that are open (that is, available to the public). The freedom index is Freedom House's freedom of political rights and civil liberties. It ranges from 1 to 7, where 1 is the most free and 7 is the least free. Regressions control for population and land area. Standard errors are clustered at the country level. The constant term is not shown. The R-squared is for a pooled regression (African and non-African countries) with interaction terms.
Significance level: * = 10 percent, ** = 5 percent, *** = 1 percent.

Unlike aid, good governance is positively correlated with higher-quality data in Africa. The government effectiveness indicator—one of six dimensions of governance tracked in the Worldwide Governance Indicators (WGI) database—is highly correlated with greater comparability of surveys. However, the indicator is negatively correlated with the share of household surveys that are open. Political openness is (measured by the freedom index) also positively correlated with a greater share of comparable surveys.

Alternative indicators of statistical capacity and governance yield stronger results. There is a strong positive correlation between a country's score on the statistical capacity indicator (which measures a country's data collection, data availability, and data practices) and a country's safety and rule of law score (one of the governance indicators tracked in the Ibrahim Index of African governance) (figure 1.11). Countries with better scores on safety and rule of law also have higher statistical capacity scores.

Political Aspects of the Lack of Good-Quality Data

The production of statistics is a technically complex task. It involves mobilizing financial

FIGURE 1.11 **Good governance and statistical capacity go together**

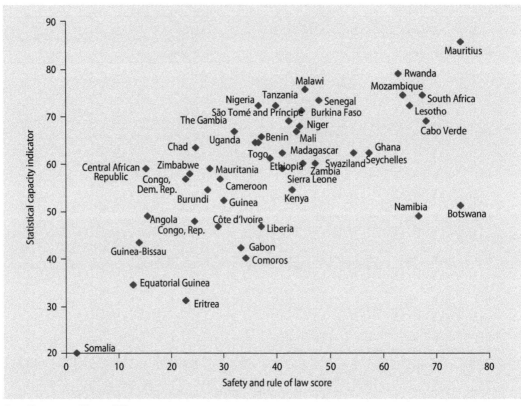

Source: Hoogeveen and Nguyen 2015.

and human resources on a large scale and establishing robust quality control mechanisms. Pervasive asymmetries of information, which create difficulties if users or buyers seek to verify the quality of the product, render the task even more complicated.

These challenges partly explain the lack of high-quality consumption surveys. But governments in Africa have been able to meet their capacity needs in performing other activities that are more or equally complex technically, such as delivering antiretroviral drugs to people with AIDS and conducting national elections (Hoogeveen 2015). Why have they failed to produce more and better data on living standards?

Several recent reports and papers advance the proposition that data are weak because of the political preferences of elites (Carletto, Jolliffe, and Banerjee 2015; CGD 2014; Devarajan 2013; Krätke and Byiers 2014; Hoogeveen 2015; Jerven 2013). According to

these studies, autonomous statistical agencies fail to emerge even where legislation mandates them because the norms and procedures for making decisions remain informal (personalized), centralized, and even ad hoc (Krätke and Byiers 2014). As a consequence, statistical agencies are unable to produce timely, good-quality data that are free of bias. This failure leaves the agencies vulnerable to pressure from local political and well-organized advocacy groups (CGD 2014). In addition, where outside financiers tie funding to specific indicators (such as school enrollment), both statistical offices and local politicians may have incentives to exaggerate achievements—and produce unreliable data to support them.

The political environment in many African countries is characterized by ethnic divisions, fractious alliances, high degrees of competition for political leadership and economic resources, and vague rules of the game. Many elites in such contexts may take a hostile attitude toward reliable and timely data collection, which they consider a partisan audit of their performance. This tendency creates strong incentives to establish competing and politicized statistical units, which in turn leads to fragmentation, duplication, wastage, and, ultimately, ineffective agencies.

Political elites may not favor good-quality statistics for other reasons as well. First, where clientelism exists and opportunities to engage politically are limited, as is the case in most African countries, a record of achievement that can be supported by good-quality data is unnecessary, because support from a small group of power brokers suffices

(Hoogeveen 2015). Second, because supporting the patronage network is costly, the opportunity costs of funding high-quality statistics are high in terms of political survival. Third, poor-quality statistics allow elites to escape accountability, because they can contest bad outcomes. This lack of demand by and support from the top of the political hierarchy may be the most important constraint to changing the poverty data landscape in Africa. However, experiences from other regions (notably Latin America and the Caribbean) suggest that regional cooperation and peer learning, together with international standards and technical guidelines, can still go a long way in improving the quality and consistency of existing data (box 1.4).

BOX 1.4   Can donors improve the capacity of national statistics offices? Lessons learned from MECOVI

The Program for the Improvement of Surveys and the Measurement of Living Conditions in Latin America and the Caribbean (known as MECOVI, its acronym in Spanish) was a coordinated effort led by the Inter-American Development Bank, the United Nations Economic Commission for Latin America and the Caribbean, and the World Bank to provide technical assistance to national statistical offices to increase their capacity to produce high-quality household surveys in a sustainable manner. Launched in 1996, the program was active until 2005. The concept and framework it developed still influence household surveys in the region.

The program has been widely recognized as successful in building the capacity of participating countries' statistical agencies, encouraging regional cooperation and peer learning, and establishing the foundations for the sustainability of household survey programs. Several lessons emerge from the program's success:

- Planning for the medium term was crucial. The minimum timeframe for all activities was four years.
- Concentrating on a limited and focused set of activities related specifically to household surveys helped obtain objectives. Clearly allocating local funds to surveys and outside resources to technical assistance rather than data collection led to sustainability.

- Commitment and ownership were key. The national statistical office in each country clearly defined its resources, activities, and work plans.
- Defining the governance structures of the three sponsoring institutions was important.
- Regional training and experience-sharing activities focused on South-South exchanges were critical.

The focused nature of MECOVI's support for household surveys created "islands of efficiency" in some of the least-developed statistical offices. Survey departments became the "favorite child"—with the most funding and the best resources—but the technical nature of the support allowed for significant spillovers to other departments, which benefited from improvements in areas such as data quality control, questionnaire design, sampling, and data entry.

Is MECOVI replicable? Some factors that contributed to its success (such as significant interest in household surveys to measure poverty) cannot be reproduced. Others, however, can be. They include close coordination among donors, cooperation between countries, a long-term view, clearly defined and limited goals, heavy involvement of national statistical offices, well-focused objectives, and secure funding.

Contribution by Jose Antonio Mejia-Guerra.

Reappraising the Information Base on Poverty

The ability to track poverty accurately in Africa hinges on overcoming the many data challenges identified in this chapter. Among these challenges, one set of issues concerns the availability, comparability, and quality of consumption data. A second involves the quality and possible biases in the most commonly used price data (the CPI) used to monitor real standards of living.

Filling in Years with No Consumption Survey

One major data challenge is that consumption surveys are not conducted every year. Global or regional poverty estimates fill in gaps between surveys by relying on GDP or private consumption data as an approximation of consumption growth. Additionally, some consumption surveys may be noncomparable or of dubious quality. If comparability and quality concerns result in excluding some surveys, greater reliance will need to be placed on GDP-based imputations.

The alternative to using GDP imputations to fill in missing data is to use survey-to-survey (S2S) imputations. This approach relies on at least one survey with consumption (the reference survey), which is used to build a model that can be used to estimate consumption in other surveys based on other household traits. The fact that this approach can make use of many types of nonconsumption surveys, such as the DHS and the MICS, is one of its main attractions. The approach can be used to address multiple data problems, including low frequency, lack of comparability, and poor quality. If the model eschews regressors that require adjustments in the cost of living, concerns about the CPI bias can be addressed simultaneously (because the imputation is effectively in real terms). The model's success depends on the stability of the estimated relationship between consumption and the household traits tracked. The evidence mostly suggests that this method does not pose major issues, at least when there are no dramatic turnarounds in the economy or the predictions are not too far in the future (Christiaensen and others 2012; Douidich and others 2013; Kijima and Lanjouw 2003).

Using the Engel Curve Approach to Avoid the Biases Inherent in the CPI

Engel's Law is based on the observation that the share of food in households' consumption declines as income increases. The Engel curve method exploits this empirical regularity to estimate changes in real incomes based on changes in food budget shares over time, controlling for other factors that affect the household's allocation of its budget between food and nonfood items (for example, the demographic composition of the household and the relative prices of food and nonfood items) (Costa 2001; Hamilton 2001). Inconsistencies between changes in real incomes estimated by the Engel curve method and measured changes in real incomes (for instance, CPI-deflated nominal incomes) are regarded as evidence of measurement bias in the CPI. A drift of Engel curves to the left, so that over time a given food budget share is associated with a smaller level of real income, is an indication that the CPI overstates increases in the "true" cost of living and that real incomes are increasingly underestimated (Hamilton 2001).

The key identifying assumption of this approach is that no unobserved factors affect the share of the budget spent on food (that is, there are no changes in preferences or price changes beyond the broad factors for which the model controls). This assumption is not trivial and can be violated (because of shifts in preferences toward specific consumer durables, such as mobile phones, for example). For this reason, although the method can provide useful indications of CPI bias, especially when applied to a large number of countries, the results should not be overinterpreted for any specific country.

Recognizing Other Challenges in Measuring Poverty

Several other challenges make measuring poverty difficult.[18] First, it is difficult to monetize the consumption of many goods and services. For example, the market price of food grown and consumed by the household (or given as a gift or wage payment) must be estimated in order to monetize the value of that food. The use value of housing and durable goods, when included in the consumption measure, must also be estimated. Although econometric techniques can be used to estimate the rental price when a home is owned by a household, for example, the estimates are reliable only if a robust rental market exists, which is not the case in many rural areas of Africa. The problem of imputing a use value is complicated by the fact that the typical data collected in surveys do not always reflect the information needed to calculate use values. For instance, many surveys collect information on whether families own specific consumer durables, but few collect information on the (current or past) value of these items. Many consumption measures include expenditures on education and health, but they understate the "true" consumption value if those services are subsidized or publicly provided.

Second, the global monitoring of poverty uses consumption per capita as the measure of welfare comparisons, dividing total household consumption by the number of household members. Such a practice ignores differences in consumption across household members and economies of scale in household consumption. Failure to address both issues may affect poverty comparisons across groups within and across countries.

Third, having chosen consumption as the welfare measure, a standard needs to be set to determine who is poor and who is not; different approaches exist to determine such a poverty line (box 1.5).

BOX 1.5   What is the threshold for being poor?

Measuring poverty requires setting a level of consumption below which people are defined as poor. Most developing countries define a national poverty line based on the cost of a "basic needs" food basket, with some allowance for fundamental nonfood requirements (such as clothing and housing). Although these national lines have the advantage of measuring poverty according to country-specific standards and circumstances, they are not comparable across countries. For instance, Uganda's national poverty lines are based on a minimum daily calorie intake of 3,000 kcal per adult, which is much higher than the norms used in neighboring Kenya (2,250 kcal) and Tanzania (2,200 kcal). Many other salient differences also undermine cross-country comparisons of national poverty lines.

To measure poverty at the global or regional level and to compare poverty across countries, it is common practice to apply the same absolute standard in each country to estimate the number of poor. The World Bank's international poverty line has historically been defined as a line that is representative of national poverty lines in the poorest countries, after conversion into a common currency using PPP exchange rates (World Bank 1990; Ravallion, Datt, and van de Walle 1991; Chen and Ravallion 2010). In 2008 this international line was estimated at $1.25 per capita per day at 2005 prices. In 2015 the line was updated to $1.90 at 2011 prices based on results from the 2011 PPP round, the value used in this report.

Several researchers have proposed alternative poverty lines. Ravallion and Chen (2011) and Chen and Ravallion (2013) propose "weakly relative" poverty lines, which combine features of an absolute poverty line for the poorest countries with the notion that once a country has passed a certain income threshold the poverty line should increase with rising per capita income. Klasen and others (forthcoming) propose an international poverty line of about $1.70 in 2011 prices, derived using a method that is similar to the one used by Jolliffe and Prydz (2015).

Concluding Remarks and Recommendations

The production of social and economic statistics in Africa has been improving over the past 20 years. More household surveys are being conducted. Participation in decennial census rounds is rising. More countries are updating their GDP base years. Participation by African countries in the latest International Comparison Program round reached the highest level ever. Data on governance, political attitudes, and other nonmonetary aspects of poverty are being collected in greater volume, as are gender-disaggregated data on health, violence, and empowerment-related issues. These data have helped researchers examine poverty from a broader perspective.

These improvements are welcome, but there is cause for concern, for three main reasons. First, data production has increased from a very low base. A sustained effort in producing data will continue to be important if the region hopes to catch up with other regions.

Second, many of the data that have been produced, especially consumption data, are of poor quality; in the worst cases, they are unusable. For instance, of the 148 surveys reviewed, only 78 were comparable to another survey in order to track poverty. Only 11 countries rely on GDP base years that are no more than five years old, the recommended frequency of updating.

Third, data problems are more than technical. An important, often underappreciated reason for low investment in statistics in Africa is that frequent and high-quality statistics do not enjoy strong support from politicians and policy makers. Once produced, its use does not preclude another person's use of it. As such they can be used by independent researchers, advocacy groups, and rival politicians to illuminate progress but also to audit performance of incumbents.

Because of these problems, the foundation on which to make policy and demand accountability for results is weak. What can be done?

Rethink the financing model. The most desirable and sustainable arrangement for financing a country's statistical needs is through domestic resources. Doing so requires elites to embrace the benefits of evidence-based decision making and make the collection of statistics the responsibility of an autonomous agency, run by an independent governance board and professionalized staff. The agency should have a clear mandate regarding the types of data it is to collect, dedicated funding from general appropriations, and clear reporting arrangements to institutions that represent the electorate, such as parliament. Current political arrangements often favor limited funding for statistics, perhaps to exercise influence over statistical agencies. The replacement of domestic financing by donor financing has not always been effective because the interests of donors are not always aligned with the interests of governments.

Alternative financing models are therefore needed. One model would require donors, such as the World Bank, to finance statistical production in perpetuity through grant programs in countries that are unwilling to produce good-quality statistics. This model would be akin to the model the U.S. Agency for International Development (USAID) follows with the DHS. Where there is domestic interest in improving the volume and quality of statistics but financing is a constraint, a cofinancing arrangement could be pursued. For instance, donors could finance a larger share of the costs in the early stages of data production. As domestic resources expand and institutional capacity grows, that share would decline. Additional incentives to increase demand through open data access, participation in regional programs for standard setting, and additional capacity support could be built into the compact.

Focus on results and open data access. Too many statistical support programs focus on inputs and outputs rather than results. There is also weak demand for data production. Opening data to public access could address both problems. Public scrutiny by users and policy makers could help improve quality and increase accountability. Knowledge production externalities would follow, as research using the data expands.

Develop and enforce methodological and operational standards. The ultimate aim of improving the capacity of national statistical offices should be to enable them to collect more frequent and higher-quality data. But better outcomes are possible even without more frequent data collection. The average African country implemented four consumption surveys in the past two decades, but many of them cannot be used because of comparability and quality concerns. Had survey methods been consistent, the data collected could have been useful. Developing consensus on international standards for measuring monetary poverty would help guide countries on international best practices for measuring monetary poverty.

Notes

1. PovcalNet is the World Bank's online analysis tool. It is available at http://iresearch.world bank.org/PovcalNet/.

2. Latin American and some Europe and Central Asian countries traditionally use income instead of consumption to measure poverty. Measuring household income in economies dominated by subsistence agriculture and informal self-employment, which includes most African countries, is complicated. For this reason, consumption is generally the preferred indicator of monetary living standards and poverty.

3. This result is based on reviews of the inventory in the International Household Survey Network, a voluntary association of development partners and member countries that aims to improve the availability, accessibility, and quality of household surveys.

4. Consumption surveys collect data on more than just consumption. If they are carried out as integrated surveys, they provide information on income sources, labor, use of education and health care services, remittances, social assistance, and other socioeconomic dimensions of households.

5. Data from the Zimbabwe 2007–08 Income Consumption Expenditure Survey are available, but that survey was conducted during a period of hyperinflation, making it very challenging to use any monetary measures. The survey has been used to measure other aspects of well-being.

6. Other survey design and implementation features can also render survey-based consumption estimates incomparable. The focus here is on the most common types of comparability problems.

7. Even though 180 surveys were identified, only 148 were available in the World Bank's microdata library and could be included in the review. Not all of these 148 surveys were available for use by the report team, however. Some surveys do not include a consumption aggregate with which to measure poverty. Some include consumption measures but have not gone through a vetting process used by the World Bank. Others (such as South Africa 2000) have consumption aggregates that are available only as grouped data. The team was able to use 113 of the 148 surveys for the analysis of poverty trends.

8. In Kenya, for instance, the number of food items increased from about 80 in the 1997 Welfare Monitoring Survey to more than 150 in the 2005/06 Kenya Integrated Household Budget Survey. In Zambia the number of food items rose from less than 40 to more than 130 between the 2006 and 2010 rounds of the Living Conditions Monitoring Survey.

9. The Kenya and Niger studies do not offer a benchmark for consumption that is taken as true consumption. The Tanzania study proposes that the intensive personal diary is such a benchmark. Both the Kenya and the Niger studies find that diary consumption is lower than recall consumption, but it is not clear whether the finding indicates underreporting in the diary survey or overestimation in the recall survey.

10. Poor questionnaire design (flow and question wording or content) is an important aspect of quality that is not related to process.

11. Using spatially deflated consumption measures does not change the overall story in chapter 2. Some poverty estimates are lower, some are higher, and many show no change when consumption is adjusted for price differences. Likewise, the inequality analysis in chapter 4 is robust to using spatially deflated consumption measures.

12. An influential National Research Council report (Schultze and Mackie 2002) argues against including the virtual price reduc-

tions associated with the introduction of new goods in the U.S. CPI.

13. Unlike national CPIs, PPPs are not intended for assessing changes in country-level prices over time (Feenstra, Inklaar, and Timmer 2015).

14. The 14 countries that failed to participate in the 2000 round were Angola, Burundi, Cameroon, Chad, the Democratic Republic of Congo, Eritrea, Ethiopia, Guinea Bissau, Liberia, Madagascar, Nigeria, Somalia, Sudan, and Togo. The 8 countries that did not participate in the 2010 round were the Central African Republic, Comoros, the Democratic Republic of Congo, Equatorial Guinea, Eritrea, Madagascar, Sierra Leone, and Somalia. Sierra Leone conducted a census in late 2015.

15. See https://international.ipums.org /international/.

16. To calculate the poverty rate for years between two surveys, one can take the first survey and apply the GDP growth rate forward to the interim year, take the second survey and apply the GDP growth backward to the interim year, and take the average of the two poverty estimates, weighted by the number of years to the first and second survey. This weighting gives a survey closer to the interim year more weight.

17. Openness in this section is defined as access to the public and hence differs from the concept of availability in the previous discussion, which considers only whether data are accessible to the report team.

18. These challenges feature prominently not only in cross-country poverty measurement but also in poverty measurement for a single country using national poverty lines.

References

Adam, Christopher, David Kwimbere, Wilfred Mbowe, and Stephen O'Connell. 2012. "Food Prices and Inflation in Tanzania." Working Paper, International Growth Centre, London.

Almås, Ingvild. 2012. "International Income Inequality: Measuring PPP Bias by Estimating Engel Curves for Food." *American Economic Review* 102 (2): 1093–117.

Backiny-Yetna, Diane Steele, and Ismael Yacoubou Djima. 2014. "The Impact of Household Food Consumption Data Collection Methods on Poverty and Inequality Measures in Niger." Policy Research Working Paper 7090, World Bank, Washington, DC.

Barrionuevo, Alexei. 2011. "Inflation, an Old Scourge, Plagues Argentina Again." *New York Times*, February 5.

BBC. 2014. "How Nigeria Will Become Africa's Biggest Economy." April 4. http://www.bbc .com/news/world-africa-26873233.

Beegle, Kathleen, Joachim De Weerdt, Jed Friedman, and John Gibson. 2012. "Methods of Household Consumption Measurement through Surveys: Experimental Results from Tanzania." *Journal of Development Economics* 98 (1): 3–18.

Benson, Todd, Charles Machinjili, and Lawrence Kachikopa. 2004. "Poverty in Malawi, 1998." *Development Southern Africa* 21 (3): 419–41.

Berumen, Edmundo, and Victor A. Beker. 2011. "Recent Developments in Price and Related Statistics in Argentina." *Statistical Journal of the IAOS* 27 (1–2): 7–11.

Biemer, Paul, and Lars E. Lyberg. 2003. *Introduction to Survey Quality.* Wiley Series in Survey Methodology. Hoboken, NJ: John Wiley & Sons.

Carletto, Calogero, Dean Jolliffe, and Raka Banerjee. 2015. "From Tragedy to Renaissance: Improving Agricultural Data for Better Policies." *Journal of Development Studies* 51 (2):133–48.

CGD (Center for Global Development). 2014. *Delivering on the Data Revolution in Sub-Saharan Africa.* Final Report of the Data for African Development Working Group, Center for Global Development and African Population and Health Research Center, Washington, DC.

Chen, Shaohua, and Martin Ravallion. 2010. "The Developing World Is Poorer Than We Thought, but No Less Successful in the Fight Against Poverty." *Quarterly Journal of Economics* 125 (4): 1577–625.

———. 2013. "More Relatively-Poor People in a Less Absolutely-Poor World." *Review of Income and Wealth* 59 (1): 1–28.

Christiaensen, Luc, Lionel Demery, and Jesper Kuhl. 2011. "The (Evolving) Role of Agriculture in Poverty Reduction: An Empirical Perspective." *Journal of Development Economics* 96 (2): 239–54.

Christiaensen, Luc, Peter Lanjouw, Jill Luoto, and David Stifel. 2012. "Small Area

Estimation-Based Prediction Methods to Track Poverty: Validation and Applications." *Journal of Economic Inequality* 10 (2): 267–97.

Ciccone, Antonio, and Marek Jarociński. 2010. "Determinants of Economic Growth: Will Data Tell?" *American Economic Journal: Macroeconomics* 2 (4): 222–46.

Costa, Dora L. 2001. "Estimating Real Income in the United States from 1888 to 1994: Correcting CPI Bias Using Engel Curves." *Journal of Political Economy* 109 (6): 1288–310.

Dabalen, Andrew, Paul Gubbins, Johan Mistiaen, and Ayago Wambile. 2015. "Diary versus Recall in Food Consumption: Example from Kenya." World Bank, Poverty and Equity Global Practice, Washington, DC.

Deaton, Angus. 1998. Getting Prices Right: What Should Be Done? *Journal of Economic Perspectives* 12 (1): 37–46.

———. 2005. "Measuring Poverty in a Growing World (or Measuring Growth in a Poor World)." *Review of Economics and Statistics* 87 (1): 1–19.

———. 2010. "Price Indexes, Inequality, and the Measurement of World Poverty." *American Economic Review* 100 (1): 5–34.

Deaton, Angus, and Bettina Aten. 2014. "Trying to Understand the PPPs in ICP2011: Why Are the Results So Different?" NBER Working Paper 20244, National Bureau of Economic Research, Cambridge, MA.

Deaton, Angus, and Olivier Dupriez. 2011. "Spatial Price Differences within Large Countries." Working Paper 1321, Woodrow Wilson School of Public and International Affairs, Research Program in Development Studies, Princeton University, Princeton, NJ, and World Bank, Washington, DC.

Demombynes, Gabriel, and Justin Sandefur. 2014. "Costing a Data Revolution." Working Paper 383, Center for Global Development, Washington, DC.

Devarajan, Shantayanan. 2013. "Africa's Statistical Tragedy." *Review of Income and Wealth* 59 (S1): S9–S15.

Douidich, Mohamed, Abdeljaouad Ezzrari, Roy van der Weide, and Paolo Verme. 2013. "Estimating Quarterly Poverty Rates Using Labor Force Surveys: A Primer." Policy Research Working Paper 6466, World Bank, Washington, DC.

Dulani, Boniface, Robert Mattes, and Carolyn Logan. 2013. "After a Decade of Growth in Africa, Little Change in Poverty at the Grassroots." Afrobarometer Policy Brief 1. http://www.afrobarometer.org/publications/pp1-after-decade-growth-africa-little-change-poverty-grassroots.

Dykstra, Sarah, Charles Kenny, and Justin Sandefur. 2014. "Global Absolute Poverty Fell by Almost Half on Tuesday." Center for Global Development, Washington, DC. http://www.cgdev.org/blog/global-absolute-poverty-fell-almost-half-tuesday.

Easterly, William, and Ross Levine. 1997. "Africa's Growth Tragedy: Policies and Ethnic Division." *Quarterly Journal of Economics* 112 (4): 1203–50.

The Economist. 2014. "Nigeria's GDP. Step Change: Revised Figures Show that Nigeria Is Africa's Largest Economy." April 12. http://www.economist.com/news/finance-and-economics/21600734-revised-figures-show-nigeria-africas-largest-economy-step-change.

Elbers, Chris, Jean O. Lanjouw, and Peter Lanjouw. 2003. "Micro-Level Estimation of Poverty and Inequality." *Econometrica* 71 (1): 355–64.

Elvidge, Christopher D., Paul C. Sutton, Tilottama Ghosh, Benjamin Tuttle, Kimberly E. Baugh, Budhendra Bhaduri, and Edward Bright. 2009. "A Global Poverty Map Derived from Satellite Data." *Computers & Geosciences* 35 (8): 1652–60.

Etang-Ndip, Alvin, Johannes Hoogeveen, and Julia Lendorfer. 2015. "Socioeconomic Impact of the Crisis in North Mali on Displaced People." Policy Research Working Paper 7253, World Bank, Washington, DC.

Feenstra, Robert, Robert Inklaar, and Marcel Timmer. 2015. "The Next Generation of the Penn World Table." *American Economic Review* 105 (10): 3150–82.

Finn, Arden, and Vimal Ranchhod. Forthcoming. "Genuine Fakes: The Prevalence and Implications of Data Fabrication in a Large South African Survey." *World Bank Economic Review*.

Gaddis, Isis, and Johannes Hoogeveen. 2015. "Primary Education in Mainland Tanzania: What Do the Data Tell Us?" In *Preparing the Next Generation in Tanzania: Challenges and Opportunities in Education,* edited by Arun Joshi and Isis Gaddis. Washington, DC: World Bank.

Garcia-Verdu, Rodrigo. 2013. "The Evolution of Poverty and Inequality in Sub-Saharan Africa over the Period 1980–2008: What Do We (and Can We) Know Given the Data Available?" International Monetary Fund, Washington, DC.

Goñi, Edwin, Humberto López, and Luis Servén. 2006. "Getting Real about Inequality: Evidence from Brazil, Colombia, Mexico, and Peru." Policy Research Working Paper 3815, World Bank, Washington, DC.

Gryna, Frank, and Joseph Juran. 1980. *Quality Planning and Analysis*, 2nd ed. New York: McGraw-Hill.

Günther, Isabel, and Michael Grimm. 2007. "Measuring Pro-Poor Growth When Relative Prices Shift." *Journal of Development Economics* 82 (1): 245–56.

Hamilton, Bruce W. 2001. "Using Engel's Law to Estimate CPI Bias." *American Economic Review* 91 (3): 619–30.

Harttgen, Kenneth, Stephan Klasen, and Sebastian Vollmer. 2013. "An African Growth Miracle? Or: What Do Asset Indices Tell Us about Trends in Economic Performance?" *Review of Income and Wealth* 59 (S1): S37–S61.

Hausman, Jerry. 1996. "Valuation of New Goods under Perfect and Imperfect Competition." In *The Economics of New Goods*, edited by Timothy F. Bresnahan and Robert J. Gordon, 209–48. Chicago: University of Chicago Press.

———. 1999. "Cellular Telephone, New Products, and the CPI." *Journal of Business and Economic Statistics* 17 (2): 188–92.

———. 2003. "Sources of Bias and Solutions to Bias in the Consumer Price Index." *Journal of Economic Perspectives* 17 (1): 23–44.

Hoogeveen, Johannes, and Nga Thi Viet Nguyen. 2015. "Statistics Reform in Africa: Aligning Incentives with Results." Working Paper, World Bank, Poverty and Equity Global Practice, Washington, DC.

Hoogeveen, Johannes, Kevin Croke, Andrew Dabalen, Gabriel Demombynes, and Marcelo Giugale. 2014. "Collecting High-Frequency Panel Data in Africa Using Mobile Phone Interviews." *Canadian Journal of Development Studies* 35 (1): 186–207.

ILO (International Labour Organization). 2013. *All Countries CPI Descriptions: Methodologies of Compiling Consumer Price Indices*. 2012 ILO Survey of Country Practices. Geneva: ILO.

IMF (International Monetary Fund). 2003. *Ghana: First Review under the Three-Year Arrangement under the Poverty Reduction and Growth Facility: Staff Report*. IMF Country Report 03/395. Washington, DC: IMF.

———. 2007. *Ghana: Article IV Consultation: Staff Report*. IMF Country Report 07/210. Washington, DC: IMF.

Inklaar, Robert, and D. S. Prasada Rao. 2014. "Cross-Country Income Levels over Time: Did the Developing World Suddenly Become Much Richer?" Groningen Growth and Development Centre, University of Groningen, Netherlands.

Jerven, Morten. 2013. "Comparability of GDP Estimates in Sub-Saharan Africa: The Effect of Revisions in Sources and Methods since Structural Adjustment." *Review of Income and Wealth* 59 (S1): S16–S36.

Jolliffe, Dean Mitchell, and Espen Beer Prydz. 2015. "Global Poverty Goals and Prices: How Purchasing Power Parity Matters." Policy Research Working Paper 7256, World Bank, Washington, DC.

Judge, George, and Laura Schechter. 2009. "Detecting Problems in Survey Data Using Benford's Law." *Journal of Human Resources* 44 (1): 1–24.

Kaminski, Jonathan, Luc Christiaensen, and Christopher L. Gilbert. 2014. "The End of Seasonality? New Insights from Sub-Saharan Africa." Policy Research Working Paper 6907, World Bank, Washington, DC.

Kijima, Yoko, and Peter Lanjouw. 2003. "Poverty in India during the 1990s: A Regional Perspective." Policy Research Working Paper 3141, World Bank, Washington, DC.

Klasen, Stephan, Tatyana Krivobokova, Friederike Greb, Rahul Lahoti, Syamsul Pasaribu, and Manuel Wiesenfarth. Forthcoming. "International Income Poverty Measurement: Which Way Now?" *Journal of Economic Inequality*.

KNBS (Kenya National Bureau of Statistics). 2010. *The New Consumer Price Index (CPI) Users' Guide*.

Krätke, Florian, and Bruce Byiers. 2014. "The Political Economy of Official Statistics: Implications for the Data Revolution in Sub-Saharan Africa." PARIS21 Discussion Paper 5.

Lanjouw, Peter, Renzo Massari, and Roy van der Weide. 2015. "International Poverty Comparisons: An Imputation-Based Approach." World Bank, Washington, DC.

Ley, Eduardo. 2005. "Whose Inflation? A Characterization of the CPI Plutocratic Gap." *Oxford Economic Papers* 57 (4): 634–46.

Loayza, Norman, and Claudio Raddatz. 2010. "The Composition of Growth Matters for Poverty Alleviation." *Journal of Development Economics* 93 (1): 137–51.

Magnowski, Daniel. 2014. "Nigerian Economy Overtakes South Africa's on Rebased GDP." April, Bloomberg.

Majumder, Amita, Ranjan Ray, and Kompal Sinha. 2012. "Calculating Rural-Urban Food Price Differentials from Unit Values in Household Expenditure Surveys: A Comparison with Existing Methods and A New Procedure." *American Journal of Agricultural Economics* 94 (5): 1218–35.

McCulloch, Neil, Julian Weisbrod, and Peter Timmer. 2007. "Pathways out of Poverty during an Economic Crisis: An Empirical Assessment of Rural Indonesia." Policy Research Working Paper 4173, World Bank, Washington, DC.

Mkenda, Adolf F., and Wilhelm Ngasamiaku. 2009. "An Analysis of Alternative Weighting System on the National Price Index in Tanzania: The Implication to Poverty Analysis." *Botswana Journal of Economics* 6 (10): 50–70.

Muller, Christophe. 2008. "The Measurement of Poverty with Geographical and Intertemporal Price Dispersion: Evidence from Rwanda." *Review of Income and Wealth* 54 (1): 27–49.

Mveyange, Anthony. 2015. "Night Lights and Regional Income Inequality in Africa." Department of Business and Economics, University of Southern Denmark, Odense, Denmark.

NBS (National Bureau of Statistics). 2009. *Household Budget Survey 2007: Final Report.* Dar es Salaam, Tanzania.

Noor, Abdisalan M., Victor A. Alegana, Peter W. Gething, Andrew J. Tatem, and Robert W. Snow. 2008. "Using Remotely Sensed Night-Time Light as a Proxy for Poverty in Africa." *Population Health Metrics* 6: 5. http://www.biomedcentral.com/content/pdf/1478-7954-6-5.pdf.

Okidi, John, and Vincent Nsubuga. 2010. *Inflation Differentials among Ugandan Households: 1997–2007.* Research Series 72, Economic Policy Research Centre, Kampala, Uganda.

Oosthuizen, Morné. 2007. "Consumer Price Inflation across the Income Distribution in South Africa." Development Policy Research Unit Working Paper 07–129, University of Cape Town, Rondebosch, Cape Town, South Africa.

Phelps, Glenn, and Steve Crabtree. 2013. "More Than One in Five Worldwide Living in Extreme Poverty." Gallup. http://www.gallup.com/poll/166565/one-five-worldwide-living-extreme-poverty.aspx.

Pinkovskiy, Maxim, and Xavier Sala-i-Martín. 2014. "Africa Is on Time." *Journal of Economic Growth* 19 (3): 311–38.

———. 2015. "Lights, Camera…, Income! Estimating Poverty Using National Accounts, Survey Means, and Lights." Staff Report 669, Federal Reserve Bank of New York.

PovcalNet. Database. http://iresearch.worldbank.org/PovcalNet/.

Prais, Sigbert. 1959. "Whose Cost of Living?" *Review of Economic Studies* 26 (2): 126–34.

Ravallion, Martin. 2014. "An Exploration of the International Comparison Program's New Global Economic Landscape." NBER Working Paper 20338, National Bureau of Economic Research, Cambridge, MA.

Ravallion, Martin, and Shaohua Chen. 2011. "Weakly Relative Poverty." *Review of Economics and Statistics* 93 (4): 1251–61.

Ravallion, Martin, Gaurav Datt, and Dominique van de Walle. 1991. "Quantifying Absolute Poverty in the Developing World." *Review of Income and Wealth* 37 (4): 345–61.

Sandefur, Justin, and Amanda Glassman. 2015. "The Political Economy of Bad Data: Evidence from African Survey and Administrative Statistics." *Journal of Development Studies* 51 (2): 116–32.

Schultze, Charles, and Christopher Mackie. 2002. *At What Price? Conceptualizing and Measuring Cost-of-Living and Price Indexes.* Washington, DC: National Academy Press.

UN (United Nations). 2009. *Practical Guide to Producing Consumer Price Indices.* New York: United Nations. http://www.unece.org/fileadmin/DAM/stats/publications/Practical_Guide_to_Producing_CPI.pdf.

World Bank. 1990. *World Development Report 1990: Poverty.* Washington, DC: World Bank.

———. 2007. "Underreporting of Consumer Price Inflation in Tanzania 2002–2006." World Bank Policy Note, Washington, DC.

———. 2012. *Niger: Investing for Prosperity, a Poverty Assessment.* Washington, DC: World Bank.

———. 2013. "Burkina Faso: A Policy Note: Poverty Trends and Profile for 2003–2009." World Bank, Washington, DC.

———. 2014. *Purchasing Power Parities and the Real Size of World Economies: A Comprehensive Report of the 2011 International Comparison Program*. Washington, DC: World Bank.

———. 2015a. *A Measured Approach to Ending Poverty and Boosting Shared Prosperity: Concepts, Data, and the Twin Goals*. Policy Research Report. Washington, DC: World Bank.

———. 2015b. "Tanzania Mainland Poverty Assessment." World Bank, Washington, DC.

———. 2015c. *The Socio-Economic Impacts of Ebola in Sierra Leone: Results from a High-Frequency Cell Phone Survey: Rounds 1–3*. Washington, DC: World Bank.

Young, Alwyn. 2012. "The African Growth Miracle." *Journal of Political Economy* 120 (4): 696–739.

Revisiting Poverty Trends

2

This chapter examines trends in poverty in Africa using household consumption, generally the variable of choice for tracking poverty there.[1] In many African countries, such data are collected infrequently, are of poor quality, or are not comparable across surveys. How these data challenges are dealt with often underlies differing views about Africa's progress toward reducing poverty, including the Millennium Development Goal (MDG) target of halving poverty by 2015.[2]

The chapter is divided into five sections. The first section looks at whether correcting for the comparability and quality of data changes the view of how poverty has evolved in Africa. It focuses on region-wide trends, with specific countries featured only for illustrative purposes. The results are benchmarked against the World Bank's PovcalNet, the most comprehensive repository for poverty data for calculating regional and global trends. Scrutiny of data quality and comparability entails excluding some data, which leads to reliance on imputations to obtain long-term trends. The second section checks whether these imputations drive the alternative trends reported here, by reporting poverty trends using alternative methods and assumptions.

The third section provides a brief profile of the poor, based on country typology, location within a country (urban/rural), and gender. The fourth section examines the dynamics of poverty—the movement of people into and out of poverty. The last section summarizes the chapter's main findings.

Trends Using Comparable and Better-Quality Data

According to the latest estimates in PovcalNet, the share of Africa's population living below the international poverty line of $1.90 declined from 57 percent in 1990 to 43 percent in 2012. This rate of poverty reduction was the slowest among the major regions of the world.

Consensus about the accuracy of these figures is lacking, because of debate over the quality of the data (Pinkovskiy and Sala-i-Martín 2014; Young 2012). What does the trend in poverty look like if known data comparability issues across surveys within countries and quality problems are addressed?[3]

Figure 2.1 shows four trends. The PovcalNet line shows changes in poverty based on all surveys in its database. These estimates are population-weighted poverty rates from 47 of Africa's 48 countries. Of the 47 countries for which poverty estimates

---

This chapter was written with Nga Thi Viet Nguyen and Shinya Takamatsu.

FIGURE 2.1 **Adjusting for comparability and quality changes the level, depth, and severity of poverty**

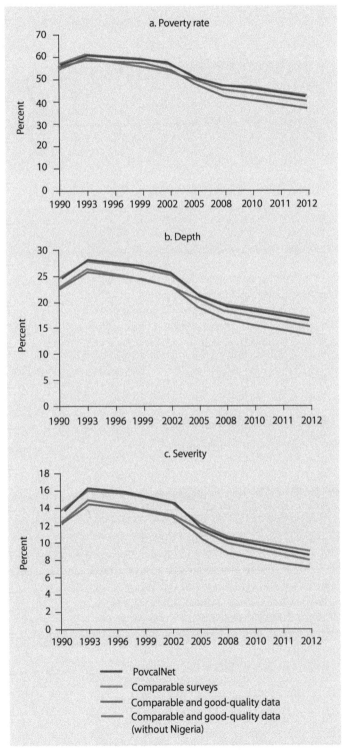

a. Poverty rate

b. Depth

c. Severity

— PovcalNet
— Comparable surveys
— Comparable and good-quality data
— Comparable and good-quality data (without Nigeria)

Source: World Bank Africa Poverty database.

have been computed, one or more surveys are available for 43.[4] For each of these countries, a poverty rate is estimated from actual survey data (regardless of comparability or quality). For years without surveys, per capita growth in gross domestic product (GDP) is used to simulate consumption growth between survey years (see World Bank 2015b for a discussion of the method).

Additional estimates are based on only comparable surveys, comparable and good-quality surveys (as described in chapter 1, and henceforth referred to as corrected data), and comparable and good-quality surveys without Nigeria.[5] For the subset of comparable surveys identified in each country, the imputation methodology used in PovcalNet, which relies on growth in GDP per capita, was applied to fill gaps between surveys. By design, this method relies on fewer surveys and more imputed estimates of poverty.

Another set of estimates goes a step farther by taking quality as well as comparability into account. Starting from the subset of surveys deemed comparable, this estimate drops surveys of poor quality. This step affected five countries (Burkina Faso, Mozambique, Nigeria, Tanzania, and Zambia), which together represent 30 percent of Africa's population. Detailed descriptions of the quality of the surveys were used to determine which to exclude (Alfani and others 2012; World Bank 2012, 2013, 2014b, 2015c). For Nigeria, home to 18 percent of the population of Africa, this implied dropping the two comparable surveys (both of poor quality), and replacing them by one deemed of good quality (at the expense of greater reliance on imputation). The last set of estimates is based on a sample that corrects for comparability and quality and excludes Nigeria.

Correcting only for comparability shows slightly higher regional poverty rates between 1990 and 1999 but little change in trends compared with the PovcalNet estimates. Correcting for quality and comparability leads to a change in level after about 2002. Using these surveys only, the estimate of poverty in Africa is 6 percentage points lower

(37 percent instead of 43 percent) than the PovcalNet estimate in 2012. Nigeria accounts for a large fraction of this change. The fourth estimate, based on surveys that were both comparable and of good quality and excludes Nigeria, shows that poverty declined from about 55 percent to 40 percent (15 percentage points), compared to the 14 percentage-point decline (from 57 percent to 43 percent) revealed by the PovcalNet data.

The headcount poverty rate is a simple measure of the share of the population living below the poverty line; it does not distinguish among the poor. Depth of poverty captures the amount of shortfall in consumption among the poor as a share of the poverty line. Severity of poverty adds more weight to the shortfall of the poorest and thus captures inequality among the poor.

Measures of the depth and severity of poverty follow trajectories similar to the poverty rate (see panels b and c of figure 2.1). In 1990 the depth of poverty was 25 percent using PovcalNet (compared to 23 percent using corrected data), indicating that resources equivalent to 25 percent of the value of the poverty line per person would have been needed to eliminate the shortfall in consumption among the poor. By 2012 this share had fallen to 14–17 percent, depending on the sample used. The severity of poverty also declined, falling from about 12 percent in 1990 (compared to 14 percent using PovcalNet) to 7–8 percent using corrected data (9 percent with PovcalNet).[6]

The trends based on corrected data raise two major concerns, both of which potentially bias the results in a way that may

---

BOX 2.1   Adjusting the data for Nigeria has a huge effect on estimates of poverty reduction

Nigeria is home to 18 percent of Africa's population. As a result, it has a major effect on regional levels and trends in poverty.

Nigeria has conducted household budget surveys since the early 1990s, but design changes made them noncomparable. Since 2003 it has measured poverty by conducting two Nigeria Living Standard (NLSS) and two General Household Survey Panel (GHS-Panel) surveys. Official national poverty measures and PovcalNet use the NLSS 2003/04 and 2009/10.

The NLSS and GHS-Panel are not comparable, and they differ in the quality of implementation (World Bank 2014c). The poverty estimates and trends from the two sources also differ sharply. At the $1.90 poverty line (2011 PPP), poverty rates from the NLSS 2009/10 (53 percent) are twice as high as rates obtained from the GHS-Panel 2010/11 (26 percent). The NLSS shows no change in poverty between 2003/04 and 2009/10, whereas the GHS-Panel suggests a decline from 26 percent in 2009/10 to 23 percent in 2012/13. Using the GHS-Panel instead of the NLSS changes poverty levels in Nigeria—and therefore the region.

Nigeria's GDP growth rates were higher in the 2000s than in the 1990s. Because GDP is used to fill in data gaps for years when there are no surveys, this

difference also affects changes in poverty. The combination of using imputations and the GHS-Panel instead of the NLSS leads to significant changes in Nigeria and regional poverty trends.

The confidence one can attach to the revised regional series depends crucially on the acceptance of the trends in poverty in Nigeria that are obtained based on the GHS-Panel and GDP growth projections. The recent exercise in rebasing the GDP lends support to the use of the GHS-Panel data, which better describe the link between growth and poverty, urban and rural gaps, the spatial distribution of poverty (World Bank 2014b), and Nigeria's performance relative to its peers. The implied poverty rates in the GHS-Panel suggest that Nigeria is no longer the poorest country in West Africa (as implied by the NLSS).

Additional evidence in support of the corrected data comes from the use of survey-to-survey (S2S) imputations (discussed later in the chapter) rather than GDP projections to look at trends. The imputations using GDP growth suggest that the poverty rate in Nigeria dropped by 12 percentage points between 2004 and 2012. The S2S imputations using GHS-Panel consumption suggest a 10 percentage point decline for the same period (Corral, Molini, and Oseni 2015).

TABLE 2.1 **Addressing quality and comparability reduces the surveys available for poverty monitoring**
(percent of total data points available from surveys)

Estimates	1990–94	1995–99	2000–04	2005–09	2010–12
PovcalNet	13.5	11.6	15.3	16.7	17.8
Comparable surveys only	1.4	4.7	9.3	13.5	14.7
Comparable and good-quality surveys only	1.4	3.7	7.0	12.1	17.1

Note: Number of data points needed in all periods was 215, except in 2010–12, when 129 were needed because there are 3 instead of 5 years in the period.

exaggerate poverty reduction. One is the influence of the adjustments for poor-quality surveys in Nigeria (box 2.1), which affects the level of poverty. The other is the extent to which GDP imputations are used to fill in gaps, which has the potential to influence trends.

The number of survey-based estimates for annual poverty rates in Africa is small (table 2.1). Between 1990 and 1994, for example, only 13 percent of the 215 data points needed for 43 countries were based on a survey estimate under PovcalNet—and the share is much smaller if comparability and quality are taken into account. Coverage rates are low in other periods as well, although since 2005 the share of actual data used in PovcalNet and the adjusted data has converged. Restricting the revised poverty estimates to comparable surveys of reasonable quality reduces the number of surveys used from 143 to 74. By design, the removal of noncomparable and poor-quality data increases the number of imputations and reliance on GDP.

 Relying on GDP estimates to fill survey data gaps entails several important assumptions. First, models assume that all aggregate income growth is consumed. This assumption may overestimate the magnitude of a decrease in poverty during periods of high growth (when savings result) or overestimate the increase during periods of major downturns (when people can draw on savings to smooth consumption). Second, they take for granted that growth is shared equitably across households, either nationwide or within sectors of activity, an assumption that is not always supported by empirical evidence. Third, GDP data are prone to their own quality and measurement problems (Jerven 2013; Deaton 2005).

Robustness to Reliance on GDP Imputation

To check the robustness of alternative estimates of poverty trends to the reliance on GDP imputations, we present three illustrative sources of evidence on trends. The first is the selection of a sample of countries in which two or more comparable and relatively good-quality surveys are available. The second approach, survey-to-survey (S2S) imputations, also entails imputations, but of a type that does not rely at all on GDP. The last illustration addresses one additional potential source of bias in the trends: the role that prices have played since 2002.

Comparable Spells Data as a Robustness Check

Between 1990 and 2012, very few countries in Africa conducted more than two consumption surveys that are comparable and of good quality. Having a large pool of countries with such data would have allowed us to assess the GDP-heavy imputation trends against actual data. Only three countries (Ethiopia, Ghana, and Uganda) have data that pass this test, which is too small a sample to make general conclusions. However, data for 24 countries—out of the 27 countries that conducted at least two comparable surveys during this period—are available.[7] Figure 2.2 shows the average annual percentage point reduction in poverty between comparable surveys for these countries.

Poverty reduction varied widely across countries. In four countries poverty increased,[8] in three it stagnated;[9] in the other two-thirds, it fell 0.3–4.9 percentage points a year. More than half of the countries

FIGURE 2.2 **Analysis based only on comparable surveys suggests that poverty reduction in Africa was faster than previously thought**

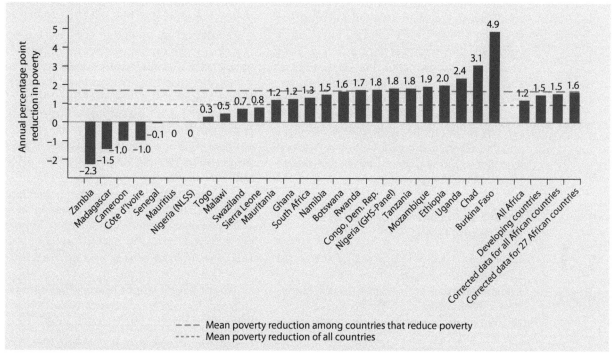

--- Mean poverty reduction among countries that reduce poverty
····· Mean poverty reduction of all countries

Source: Data for individual African countries are from World Bank Africa Poverty Database. Developing country data are from PovcalNet.

Note: Positive values denote a reduction in poverty, while negative values denote an increase. The survey years are as follows: Botswana (2002 and 2009), Burkina Faso (1998 and 2003), Cameroon (2001 and 2007), Chad (2003 and 2011), Democratic Republic of Congo (2004 and 2012), Côte d'Ivoire (2002 and 2008), Ethiopia (1999 and 2010), Ghana (1998 and 2005), Madagascar (2001 and 2010), Malawi (2004 and 2010), Mauritania (2000 and 2008), Mauritius (2006 and 2012), Mozambique (2002 and 2008), Namibia (2003 and 2009), Nigeria (2003 and 2009 [Nigeria Living Standards Survey] and 2010 and 2012 [GHS-Panel]), Rwanda (2000 and 2010), Senegal (2005 and 2011), Sierra Leone (2003 and 2011), South Africa (2005 and 2010), Swaziland (2000 and 2009), Tanzania (2000 and 2007), Togo (2006 and 2011), Uganda (1999 and 2012), and Zambia (1998 and 2006). Nigeria GHS-Panel data are shown but were not used to estimate averages. Data on all Africa and developing countries are for 1999–2012. "Corrected data for 27 African countries" reports poverty estimates based on comparable and good-quality data for countries with data from at least two comparable surveys, excluding Nigeria. "Corrected data for all African countries" shows average based on comparable and good-quality data for all of Africa.

reduced poverty by more than 1 percentage point a year. On average these 24 countries achieved an annual rate of poverty reduction of 0.92 percentage points. In contrast, the corrected data suggest an average annual poverty reduction rate of 0.8 percentage points between 1990 and 2012 for Africa. Annual poverty reduction for the developing world as a whole, using uncorrected data, is 1.5 percentage points.

Except for a few countries (Ethiopia, Ghana, and Uganda, where the earliest surveys started in the first half of the 1990s), most of these comparable surveys were conducted during the 2000s. Limiting the analysis to surveys in the 2000s does not change the results: the implied average poverty

reduction from actual data remains about 1 percentage point a year. By contrast, the rate of poverty reduction based on only comparable and good-quality surveys and GDP imputations to fill the data gaps for both all countries and the 27 countries for which comparable data are available is about 1.6 percentage point a year in the 2000s—a much higher rate of poverty reduction than the actual data imply. The corrected data are heavily influenced by the data on Nigeria. Excluding Nigeria reduces the implied poverty reduction obtained from corrected data to 1.2 percentage point a year, which is closer to the poverty reduction rate of 1 percentage point a year based on actual data if Nigeria is excluded for the entire period.

These 24 countries represent 75 percent of the total population of Africa and 83 percent of its poor. The list includes large and small countries, some that fell into conflict between surveys, coastal and landlocked countries, and countries with different levels of resource endowments. The experience of these countries arguably captures the experiences of countries in the region. The poverty estimates suggest that the average annual poverty reduction from these surveys is reasonably close to the rate obtained from an appropriate comparison of poverty estimates based on GDP imputations.

Survey-to-Survey Imputation as a Robustness Check

Instead of using GDP growth rates to fill gaps in consumption survey data, the S2S imputation takes advantage of nonconsumption household surveys. Survey-based imputation techniques have a long tradition in economics and statistics. They have been used to recover missing values of one or more variables because respondents did not provide the needed information, the data were corrupted, or errors that cannot be ignored arose during the measurement of variables. S2S imputations are attractive in Africa because they can address the challenges posed by the noncomparability of surveys, the poor quality of consumption data, the low frequency of consumption surveys and the paucity of poverty data points, and missing or poor-quality price data. Validation of S2S imputation against actual poverty trends based on reliable data suggests that the method can track poverty well, provided there are no major economic turnarounds and the periods are not too far apart (Christiaensen and others 2012; Douidich and others 2013).

Figure 2.3 illustrates how an S2S imputation can be used to estimate a poverty trend and why accounting for comparability is

FIGURE 2.3 **Survey-to-survey imputation and evidence from comparable surveys provide similar estimates of poverty**

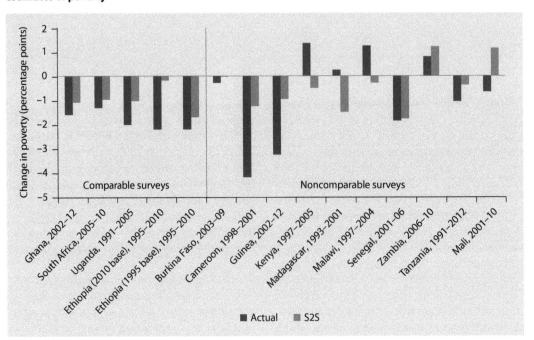

Source: World Bank Africa Poverty database.
Note: The end year is used to impute the start year, except in Ethiopia, where, because the imputation was sensitive to the choice of the base year, both results are reported. The set of covariates used to model consumption includes traits of the household head (education, occupation, employment status), household demographics, housing and asset ownership, location (rural and urban), and interactions with other variables. For S2S, the povimp stata command was used (for details see Dang and Nguyen 2014).

important. It presents poverty estimates for 10 countries in which surveys are not comparable and 4 in which the surveys are comparable. The results lead to two conclusions. First, for comparable surveys, imputed and actual changes are in the same direction, and the estimates are similar in magnitude (in 3 out of 5 spells). This finding provides some validation of the S2S method.

Second, trends derived from noncomparable surveys are not very reliable. Estimates based on the S2S imputation reverse the poverty trends in 4 of the 10 countries, and the size of the gap between actual and S2S predicted poverty is substantially larger for noncomparable surveys than for comparable surveys. These findings underscore the potential importance of the exercise underpinning figure 2.1, where comparability is taken into account.

We applied the S2S approach to the largest 23 countries in Africa in order to check the robustness of trends that are largely dependent on GDP imputations.[10] For these countries, the S2S model was calibrated on a recent good-quality consumption survey and the estimated parameters applied to the poverty predicting (nonconsumption) variables from other consumption and nonconsumption surveys (including, for example, from the Demographic and Health Surveys [DHS]). For each country, at least one data point was obtained for each of five periods: 1990–94, 1995–99, 2000–04, 2005–09, and 2010–15. Annual estimates were not possible, because of insufficient survey coverage. When there was no suitable survey in a period, the most recent available estimate in the preceding or subsequent period was used.[11] If neither was available, a regional average poverty rate from countries with available imputations was assigned.[12]

Figure 2.4 shows population-weighted average poverty rates for each period. Because there is only one data point per country in each period for the S2S, a period's point estimate is assumed to be the average for a country in that period. These averages were then used to obtain an average regional estimate for the period. These estimates are compared with the regional estimates for the largest 23

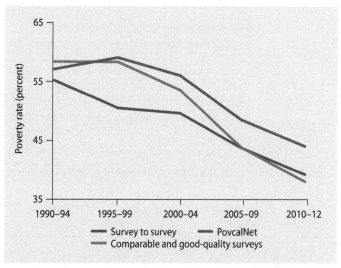

FIGURE 2.4 Survey-to-survey imputations suggest that poverty in Africa is lower than household survey data indicate

Source: World Bank Africa Poverty database.
Note: Sample includes the 23 largest countries in the region. The S2S line shows the estimate in the period based on available surveys and the S2S method described in the text. The comparable and good-quality line shows the trend using corrected data for these 23 countries, and PovcalNet line shows the PovcalNet estimate for these 23 countries.

countries obtained using five-year averages for each period using PovcalNet and data from comparable and good-quality surveys.[13]

The S2S approach suggests a 16 percentage point decline in the poverty rate (from 55 percent in 1990–94 to 39 percent in 2010–12), only slightly higher than the 13 percentage point reduction estimates from PovcalNet (from 57 percent to 44 percent) but lower than the 20 percentage point estimate based on the data corrected for comparability and quality.

The regional poverty estimates obtained from the S2S lead to two additional observations. First, the S2S imputation approach predicts lower poverty rates throughout the period. Second, discrepancies between the poverty rates estimated using S2S, the rates based on the PovcalNet and comparable and quality-corrected data are largest in the late-1990s; they narrow in the 2000s. The S2S results hint at the possibility that the results from both PovcalNet and the comparable and quality-corrected data provide a distorted picture of the extent of poverty reduction in the region—PovcalNet because it fails to account for the noncomparability and poor quality of surveys and the corrected data because they rely too heavily on GDP imputations.

The Role of Price Adjustments in Measuring Poverty

Consumer price indexes (CPIs), which are used to estimate real consumption in 2011 (the base year of the poverty line) may not have taken full account of the inflation

associated with the food and fuel crises that occurred during the period under study (1990–2012) (box 2.2).[14] CPI basket weights typically reflect the expenditure patterns of wealthier households, which spend a much smaller share of their budgets on food than the average poor family does. If food prices increase much more quickly than general consumer prices, CPIs may underestimate the true inflation experienced by the poor. In

---

BOX 2.2   How do spikes in food prices affect the measurement of poverty?

Poverty estimates indicate that poverty reduction accelerated beginning around 2002. One concern with this finding is that the CPIs in the 2000s may have understated the sharp rise in food prices, especially for major staples such as maize, wheat, and rice, observed in 2007/08 and 2011.

A comparison of trends in food prices and the overall CPI in African countries with long-run CPI series highlights the effect of the 2007/08 food price crisis. Most countries experienced significantly higher food price inflation over this period than over the 2000s as a whole. Between 2007 and 2009, food CPIs increased more quickly than general CPIs in seven of nine countries (figure B2.2.1, panel a).

For the longer period (2002–12, panel b), food CPIs increased more quickly than the general CPIs in Burkina Faso, Ethiopia, Mozambique, and Uganda and less quickly in Ghana, Malawi, and Zambia. In Nigeria—which, because of its large population, has a substantial effect on the regional trend—the two inflation rates almost coincide. It is possible that these patterns would look different if price deflators that are more tailored to the consumption patterns of the poor than the food CPIs had been used. But the evidence suggests that the broad increase in poverty reduction after 2002 is not merely a reflection of a failure to account for rapidly rising food prices.

FIGURE B2.2.1   Food inflation does not always exceed overall inflation

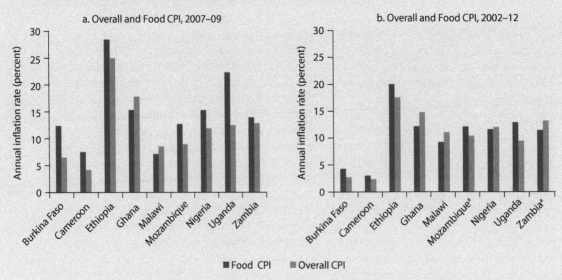

Sources: Databases of the International Labour Organization (http://laborsta.ilo.org/STP/guest) and the Food and Agriculture Organization (http://faostat3.fao.org/download/P/CP/E).
a. Series for Mozambique and Zambia run only through 2011.

this case, the rate of poverty reduction will be overstated. There are other reasons, outlined in chapter 1, why CPIs may not accurately depict the inflation experience of the poor. If CPIs do not adjust correctly for price increases, the measurement of poverty will be flawed. An underestimated (overestimated) CPI will overstate (understate) poverty reduction. In terms of the level of poverty, when adjusting a survey from before 2011 forward to 2011, if the CPI is overestimated, the poverty rate in the year before 2011 will be underestimated. When adjusting a survey from after 2011 back to 2011, an overestimated CPI will cause the poverty rate in the year after 2011 to be overestimated.

How does correcting for these biases affect poverty rates (and trends)? There are two broad approaches to investigating biases in the CPI and reassessing poverty rates and trends. One approach uses item-level price data (for example, unit record data from the consumer price collection) to check for aggregation errors, experiment with different weights, and perform more detailed demand estimations to approximate the relative contribution of various sources of CPI bias (see, for instance, Boskin and others 1996; Diewert 1998; Hausman 2003).

An alternative approach exploits the empirical regularity that food budget shares decline as consumption increases—that is, they act according to Engel's law.[15] Accordingly, provided that nominal consumption has been measured consistently over time, differences in the food budget share among demographically similar households with the same level of consumption at different points in time indicate the CPI's mismeasurement of the true change in cost of living (Costa 2001; Hamilton 2001). Any wedge between the estimated changes in real consumption derived from demand functions for food (that is, Engel curves) and measured changes in real consumption (that is, CPI-deflated nominal consumption) is attributed to CPI measurement bias in this approach.

The Engel approach is applied to comparable surveys from 16 countries to estimate the direction and magnitude of CPI bias.[16] Because CPI data collection is often restricted to urban areas, only urban households are used for these estimations, except for Ethiopia, Mauritius, Nigeria, and Rwanda.[17] The estimation of the CPI bias in Africa follows the methodology outlined in Gibson, Stillman, and Le (2008) (for a review of these methods, see also Gaddis 2015). This approach is based on the assumptions that (a) food and nonfood consumption are measured consistently across surveys and without serious measurement error and (b) preferences remain stable over time.

Unobserved time-varying factors that are correlated with the food budget share could also potentially bias the estimates. They may also explain why the Engel curve method has been shown to perform poorly when comparing cost of living differences across space—such as regions or provinces (Gibson, Le, and Kim 2014).

FIGURE 2.5 **Correcting for CPI bias suggests that poverty reduction is underestimated**

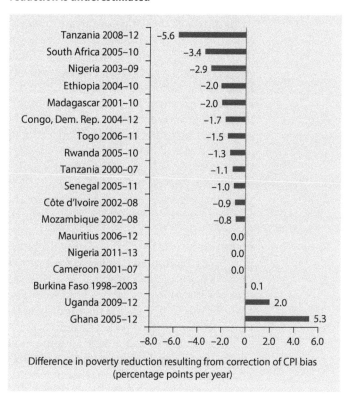

Difference in poverty reduction resulting from correction of CPI bias (percentage points per year)

Source: World Bank Africa Poverty database.
Note: A negative value indicates that the CPI underestimates the reduction in poverty (or in few cases, overestimates the increase in poverty). A positive value denotes the opposite.

Figure 2.5 displays estimates of the extent of CPI bias for pairs of surveys. The later year in each pair was used as the reference; the implied poverty rate that corrects for the size of the bias during the period of the surveys was computed for the other year. Estimates of poverty reduction from the Engel curve and the CPI are then compared.

The Engel curve estimates suggest that CPIs in Africa tend to overstate increases in the cost of living.[18] In 11 countries, the cost of living for an average urban household rose by less than what is suggested by the official CPI. (For a detailed discussion of the estimation see Dabalen, Gaddis, and Nguyen 2015). The difference in annualized poverty reduction between the Engel method and CPI updates ranges from about 5 percentage points in Ghana to almost −6 percentage points in Tanzania. Burkina Faso, Ghana, and Uganda are the three countries whose estimated differences are positive, although for Burkina Faso the difference is not statistically significant. This means that CPI updates in these countries understate the increase in the cost of living (and therefore overstate poverty reduction) for the period studied. The size of the divergence in Nigeria depends on which survey is used. The poorer-quality survey (Nigeria Living Standard Surveys 2003/04 and 2009/10) yields a 3 percentage point difference in poverty reduction between the CPI and Engel methods, implying that the CPI overstates cost of living and therefore understates poverty reduction; the higher-quality survey (Nigeria GHS-Panel 2011 and 2013) yields no difference between the two methods.

The 16 countries in figure 2.5 represent 70 percent of the African population. The results imply that on average, CPI updates understate poverty reduction by 1 percentage point a year.[19] They also provide prima facie evidence that poverty in many African countries may have declined more quickly than indicated by trends in international poverty rates.

These estimates come with an important caveat, however. The Engel curve estimates do not necessarily imply that CPIs provide biased estimates of general inflation. CPIs, by design, capture inflation faced by households in the 70th or even 80th percentile. By contrast, the Engel curve captures inflation rates of a household whose position in the distribution is unknown. Some of the measured difference in poverty reduction between the two methods may reflect differential growth in the inflation of the households represented by these deflators.[20] The large differences in poverty rates the two methods yield in some countries suggest that more work is needed to corroborate the Engel curve estimation results. Ideally, such work would extend these overall bias estimates by examining the CPI product list using the method suggested by Hausman (2003).

Asset Ownership as a Measure of Poverty Trends

Given the low frequency and measurement problems common to consumption surveys (discussed in chapter 1), might other sources of data offer a substitute for consumption? Some efforts have focused on using asset ownership as an alternative measure of consumption change and a means to track poverty.

Assets as a proxy for consumption or income have several advantages that have made them popular since the 1990s.[21] First, nonconsumption household surveys containing asset information covering many countries and years, such as the Demographic and Health Survey, have become available. Data on assets are easier to collect than data on consumption, which require detailed questionnaires. Second, the asset approach avoids the need to monetize values, which requires price data.

Although they find that assets have a robust correlation with nonincome dimensions of poverty (including nutrition, health care use, educational enrollment, fertility, and child mortality), Filmer and Scott (2012) show that the correlation between consumption and asset indexes is weak. Assets and asset indexes are more strongly correlated with consumption in urban areas and in settings in which transitory shocks are mild, measurement error in consumption is limited, and the share of privately consumed goods, such as food, in consumption is small.

These factors are likely to lead to a weaker correlation between assets and consumption in Africa than in other settings. Howe and others (2009) assess the correlation between asset indexes and expenditure in 36 data-sets and conclude that the indexes are a poor proxy for consumption data.

Assets have been frequently used to rank households in country-level analysis and then differentiate households in the poorest and richest quintiles. Can assets also be used to assess poverty levels and trends? There are several methodological concerns about using assets to monitor poverty. First, households may increase their assets in the absence of consumption growth ("asset drift") (Harttgen, Klasen, and Vollmer 2013). Second, the ability to accumulate assets varies substantially across countries for reasons that may have little to do with the ability to purchase them. Populations in two countries that are

equally poor may accumulate different levels of the same asset because of various factors, including conflict, trade restrictions on the asset, or poor provision of a public good that is highly complementary to the asset (unreliable electricity would reduce the acquisition of refrigerators, for example). Third, because assets are stocks, having more assets reflects both current and past consumption or income. Fourth, the extent to which households opt to accumulate assets may be a function of alternative means of saving or storing wealth, which varies across countries.

A fifth concern is the challenge of setting a poverty line based on asset indexes. For consumption measures, there is a cost-of-basic needs anchor. In contrast, there is no consensus on the minimum set of assets needed to meet basic needs. Moreover, there is no consensus on how to aggregate assets (box 2.3). The choice of which assets to include in the

---

BOX 2.3   Can wealth indexes be used to measure changes in poverty?

Three indexes measure asset ownership.

The DHS Wealth Index
The Demographic and Health Survey (DHS) wealth index is the most commonly used asset index. It is constructed from a large set of household assets and utility services in the DHS and includes country-specific items (Rutstein and Johnson 2004). This index is a standardized score with a mean of 0 and a standard deviation of 1. Principal component analysis is used to assign the indicator weights to each asset or service. Because the number of assets or utility services and the weights change over time and across countries, this index is not comparable across surveys within a country, over time, or between countries.

The International Wealth Index
To circumvent concerns about varying the assets included in an asset index across countries and years, the international wealth index is constructed from a small set of common assets. Principal component analysis is used to determine the asset weights (Smits and Steendijk 2015). Countries are weighted by the square root of population size; the weighted

wealth score is rescaled to range between 0 and 100. If a new asset or a new country is introduced, the index needs to be recalibrated. Although not identical, this index is highly correlated with the DHS wealth index. Its correlation with consumption is low (0.5) for the two countries for which it was evaluated (Malawi and Niger) for this report.

The Comparative Wealth Index
The comparative wealth index aims to make existing country-specific DHS wealth indexes comparable with one another, to enable trend analysis within and across countries (Rutstein and Staveteig 2014). The approach adjusts households' country-specific DHS wealth index based on the country-level relationship between some "unsatisfied basic needs" and ownership of four assets (car, refrigerator, fixed telephone, and television) relative to a reference country. For each survey, thresholds for ownership of the assets are determined using a logistic regression, and unsatisfied basic needs are estimated based on the cumulative distribution of unsatisfied needs. These thresholds are regressed against the thresholds for the reference country and the coefficients used to reweight the national wealth index for each survey.

index, how to weight them, and what weights to choose matters, because survey-specific asset indexes are tailored to the asset patterns in a particular country for a specific year. The most common index, the national wealth index (NWI), relies on statistical procedures (for example, principal component analysis) to determine weights. Even within countries, such an approach to weighting is sensitive to the choice of assets for the index calculation. The result is a lack of comparability over time and across countries (Abreu and Johnson 2013; Gwatkin and others 2007; McKenzie 2005). Weights matter because different countries often hold assets that are different in type or quality. They have a strong bearing on whether the index shows a close correlation with consumption.

We explore some of these issues and examine the patterns of accumulation for five privately held assets (television, refrigerator, computer, motorbike, and car), without indexing them into an aggregate indicator. Following the approach of Harttgen, Klasen, and Vollmer (2013), we restrict the focus to near-poor households (households with consumption within 5 percent above or below the poverty line).

Table 2.2 shows the results of regressions of asset ownership on consumption, the time-fixed effect, and the country typology using 32 household surveys for 16 countries with two comparable surveys. As consumption rises among the set of near-poor households, they are more likely to own each asset. The country typologies do not indicate a clear

pattern with respect to asset ownership conditional on household consumption level; but the statistically significant correlations indicate that, conditional on consumption, context partly drives asset ownership. This finding speaks to the concern about identifying a set of assets across countries that is consistently associated with monetary poverty. As indicated by the coefficient on the time indicator, asset ownership of each of the five assets increased from the earlier to later survey, conditional on household consumption, suggesting asset drift.

For this set of countries as a whole, there is evidence of asset drift, but there is variation across countries. The share of countries displaying asset drift is about 50 percent for television ownership, 36 percent for motorbikes, 33 percent for computers, 20 percent for refrigerators, and 10 percent for cars. This evidence is consistent with the size and significance of the time indicator in pooled country results in table 2.2.

Data on assets may be useful in specific ways as a proxy for consumption, such as ranking households within a survey. But given the methodological concerns and the limited empirical evidence, these data do not seem to offer a robust alternative to consumption data for measuring poverty and its trends.

Profiling the Poor

This section provides a brief description of the profiles of the poor. It begins with

TABLE 2.2   **Many country-level factors affect asset ownership of the near-poor**

Item	Television	Refrigerator	Computer	Motorbike	Car
Consumption	0.378***	0.335***	0.004	0.164	−0.062
Middle income	0.202***	0.123***	0.003	0.082***	0.011**
Resource rich	−0.015**	−0.081***	−0.003*	0.070***	0.027***
Landlocked	−0.014	−0.067***	−0.007	0.001***	−0.008**
Fragile	0.108***	−0.048***	−0.008**	−0.019***	−0.012***
Later survey	0.113***	0.014***	0.007***	0.068***	0.019***
Number of observations	16,884	16,847	12,269	15,678	11,859

Source: World Bank Africa Poverty database for recent surveys of Botswana, Cameroon, the Democratic Republic of Congo, Côte d'Ivoire, Ethiopia, Ghana, Madagascar, Malawi, Mozambique, Nigeria, Rwanda, Senegal, Sierra Leone, South Africa, Tanzania, and Uganda.
Note: Sample is households with consumption within 5 percent above or below the poverty line. Consumption is the log of consumption per capita (PPP 2011). Other variables are indicators taking a value of 0 or 1.
Statistical significance: * = 10 percent, ** = 5 percent, *** = 1 percent.

identification of the location of the poor using broad country classifications. Then it looks at urban and rural patterns within countries, and concludes with a discussion of poverty of female-headed households.

Differences in Poverty Reduction by Country Typologies

What distinguishes countries that have succeeded in reducing poverty from countries that have not? To answer this question, this section uses corrected data for all African countries and a classification of countries along four dimensions: fragility, resource richness, landlockedness, and low national income. It first examines simple changes in poverty rates between 1996 and 2012 for each country type. It then examines the relationship between country type and changes in poverty conditional on the other classifications, using a simple regression specification.

Fragility. The results show that poverty fell even in fragile states, albeit by less than in nonfragile states. Between 1996 and 2012, the poverty rate in fragile countries declined from 65 percent to 53 percent (a 12 percentage point change). This decline was much more modest than the 24 percentage point drop in nonfragile economies (from 56 percent to 32 percent). Some fragile countries are resource rich, landlocked, or both. Therefore, a simple binary comparison between fragile and nonfragile countries is unlikely to capture the contribution to poverty reduction of fragility alone. Conditional on the three other traits (resource richness, landlockedness, and income), poverty reduction for fragile countries was lower than for nonfragile countries by 15 percentage points, and the difference was statistically significant (figure 2.6).

Resource richness. Resource-rich countries experience more poverty reduction than non-resource-rich countries: the poverty rate fell 26 percentage points (from 62 percent to 36 percent), compared with 18 percentage points (from 55 percent to 37 percent) in non-resource-rich economies. Conditional on the other characteristics,

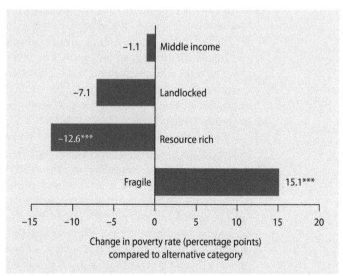

FIGURE 2.6 **Fragility is associated with significantly slower poverty reduction**

Change in poverty rate (percentage points) compared to alternative category

Source: World Bank Africa Poverty database.
Note: Figure shows results of a regression of the change in the poverty rate on country characteristics. Based on estimated poverty rates for 43 countries (1996–2012) using comparable and good-quality surveys.
*** Statistically significant at the 1% level.

on average resource-rich countries reduced poverty by about 13 percentage points more than non-resource-rich countries. However, a number of surveys were dropped from the set of resource-rich countries because of lack of comparability and quality, increasing reliance on GDP for imputations. To the extent that GDP tracks with consumption surveys less well in resource-rich countries, the rate of poverty reduction will be overestimated.

Empirical evidence on the latter is mixed. For Zambia imputations relying on GDP indicate more rapid poverty reduction, whereas S2S imputations show an increase in poverty. In Nigeria both methods predict roughly the same magnitude of poverty reduction. The main driver of the difference in poverty reduction between resource-rich and resource-poor countries is corrections to the Nigeria data. Nigeria's population share among resource-rich countries (44 percent) is even larger than for the region as a whole (18 percent). Before corrections for comparability and quality, Nigeria's surveys showed slow poverty reduction, despite relatively high GDP growth for more than a decade.

Poverty levels were higher in Nigeria than in many countries at much lower income levels in Africa and the rest of the world. This stagnant poverty rate has been considered an artifact of poor-quality data (World Bank 2014c). With the corrected data, Nigeria's poverty rates are much lower (and closer to countries in its income group) and the decline in poverty steeper, changing the performance of resource-rich countries (see box 2.1).

Landlockeness. Some researchers have posited that landlocked countries perform worse than coastal countries because transport costs impede trade and lower competitiveness (Bloom and Sachs 1998; Luke, Sachs, and Mellinger 1999). The results presented here provide no support for this hypothesis. Landlocked countries reduced poverty by 24 percentage points (from 65 percent to 41 percent)—3 percentage points more than coastal countries, where poverty fell from 56 percent to 35 percent. When resource richness, fragility, and income status are controlled for, the difference in favor of landlocked countries widens to 7 percentage points, but this difference remains statistically insignificant.

Low-income status. Middle-income countries reduced poverty by 26 percentage points—7 percentage points more than low-income countries. Conditional on other traits, however, they did not perform better than low-income countries (1 percentage point difference).

Differences in Poverty Reduction by Setting and Gender

Although Africa is urbanizing heavily, its population remains predominantly rural: in the majority of countries, 65–70 percent of the population resides in rural areas (World Bank 2015a). Rural residents have higher poverty rates across countries (figure 2.7).

The corrected data for all countries reveal that both urban and rural populations experienced declines in poverty between 1996 and 2012. Urban poverty rates dropped 16 percentage points (a 48 percent decline), and rural poverty rates fell 23 percentage points (a 33 percent decline). The gap in the poverty rate between urban and rural areas also declined (from 35 percentage points to 28 percentage points).

Among the four geographic regions, three of four (East, Southern, and West) have halved (or almost halved) poverty. No rural areas halved poverty. Rural populations in West and Southern Africa experienced declines in poverty of about 40 percent.

Africa is distinguished by the large share of female-headed households (26 percent of all households and 20 percent of all people). Among these households, 62 percent contain no adult men (15 or older).

These statistics hide large variations across countries and regions in Africa (Milazzo and van de Walle 2015). Southern Africa has the highest rate of female-headed households (43 percent). West Africa exhibits the lowest incidence: one household in five is headed by a woman, and female-headed households account for 15 percent of the population. The relatively low rate in West Africa reflects both polygamy and high remarriage rates among widows. Except in Southern Africa,

FIGURE 2.7   Urban poverty in Southern and West Africa fell by almost half between 1996 and 2012

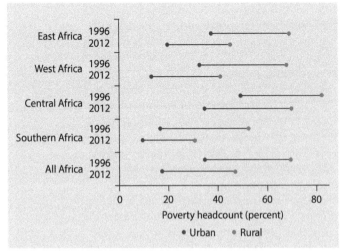

Source: World Bank Africa Poverty database. Estimates based on data corrected for comparability and quality.
Note: Data are population weighted.

female-headed households are more common in urban areas. Their prevalence is positively correlated with country income status but exhibits no relationship with state fragility or resource wealth.

Both the share of the population living in female-headed households and the share of households headed by women have been rising, across regions and with age (figure 2.8). According to Milazzo and van de Walle (2015), two recent developments across Africa explain this finding.[22] First, although economic growth is found to be associated with lower rates of female headship, presumably partly explained by lower work-related migration by men associated with growing local economies, there was an Africa-wide annual trend increase of 0.4 percent in the share of the population living in female-headed households (evaluated at the mean share over the entire sample) during the period of growth from the 1990s to 2013. Second, this seeming paradox is resolved by the fact that other things such as demographic and population characteristics, social norms, education, and the nature

FIGURE 2.8   Across Africa, more and more households are headed by women

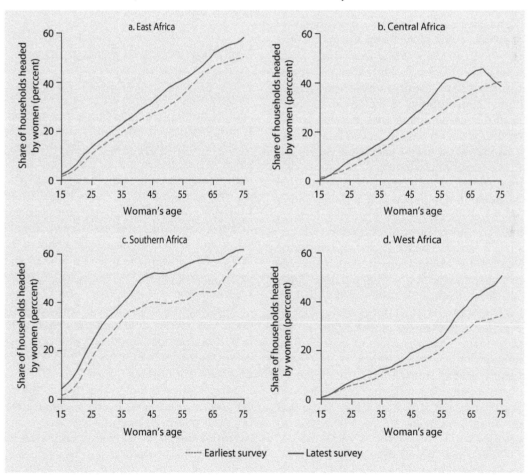

Source: Milazzo and van de Walle 2015.
Note: Estimates are from several rounds of Demographic and Health Surveys. Earliest refers to first survey, latest to last survey. East Africa includes Comoros, Ethiopia, Kenya, Madagascar, Malawi, Mozambique, Rwanda, Tanzania, Uganda, and Zambia. Central Africa includes Cameroon, Chad, the Republic of Congo, and Gabon. Southern Africa includes Lesotho, Namibia, and Zimbabwe. West Africa includes Benin, Burkina Faso, Côte d'Ivoire, Ghana, Guinea, Mali, Niger, Nigeria, and Senegal. Zimbabwe is classified here as Southern (instead of East) Africa in order to create large enough country samples for each subregion.

of the family are changing across Africa and encouraging female headship.

Should this steady rise in the incidence of female-headed households cause concern? Do female-headed households tend to be poorer and more vulnerable than others? Female heads are a diverse group that includes widows, divorced women, separated women, abandoned women, married women with nonresident husbands (polygamous or migrant), and single women. Households headed by certain categories of women—widows, divorced or separated women, and single women—frequently appear to be disadvantaged. Widow-headed households are significantly poorer than other households in Madagascar, Mali, Uganda, and Zimbabwe (Appleton 1996; Horrell and Krishnan 2007; van de Walle 2013; World Bank 2014a). But female-headed households that receive transfers from male members have consistently higher consumption or income than male-headed households and are substantially better off than other female-headed households.

Female- and male-headed households differ in terms of demographics in ways that potentially disadvantage female-headed households. On average, female heads are older (reflecting the many widowed heads) and have fewer years of education (4.1 versus 5.1 years). Their households tend to be smaller (3.9 people compared with 5.1 people in households headed by men) but have higher dependency ratios (1.2 compared with 1.0). Female heads are many times more likely to be living in households in which they are the only adult. Three-quarters of male-headed households, compared to just 44 percent of female-headed households, are composed of two adults and children. Female-headed households are also more likely to be single-adult households (16 percent versus 10 percent).

Poverty rates based on household per capita consumption are higher among people living in male-headed households (48 percent) than female-headed households (40 percent). But there are differences across region. By this metric, poverty in Southern Africa is higher among female-headed households;

in East Africa poverty rates are similar in female- and male-headed households.

The smaller household size of female-headed households means that using per capita household consumption as the welfare indicator will tend to overestimate the poverty of male-headed households relative to female-headed households if larger households enjoy economies of scale (Lanjouw and Ravallion 1995). Differences in poverty according to the gender of the head thus depend on the consumption indicator used to measure poverty. As the share of female heads continues to grow, this sensitivity to per capita or alternate adjustments for demographic composition may grow with it.

The Movement of People into and out of Poverty

To this point, this chapter provides a snapshot of poverty at different points in time. It does not describe dynamics—movements into and out of poverty. Many investigations of poverty dynamics rely on panel data, which track households and individuals over time. This analysis is complicated by a host of issues, such as the impact of attrition, measurement error, and sample selection bias (Christiaensen and Shorrocks 2012). In addition, few of the earlier and long-running panels in Africa are nationally representative.[23]

Two main messages emerge from the estimation of poverty dynamics from panel data in Africa. First, perhaps unsurprisingly, there is huge variation in estimates of both chronic and transient poverty (figure 2.9). Chronic poverty estimates range from 6 percent to 70 percent. Chronic poverty estimates for the same country—and in some cases using the same datasets—can also vary widely, depending on the method and the number of spells used.

Second, movement into and out of poverty is substantial: in 20 of 26 studies, transient poverty rates are higher than chronic poverty rates. The median transient poverty rate is about 32 percent while the median chronic

FIGURE 2.9   **Estimates of movements into and out of poverty vary widely across Africa**

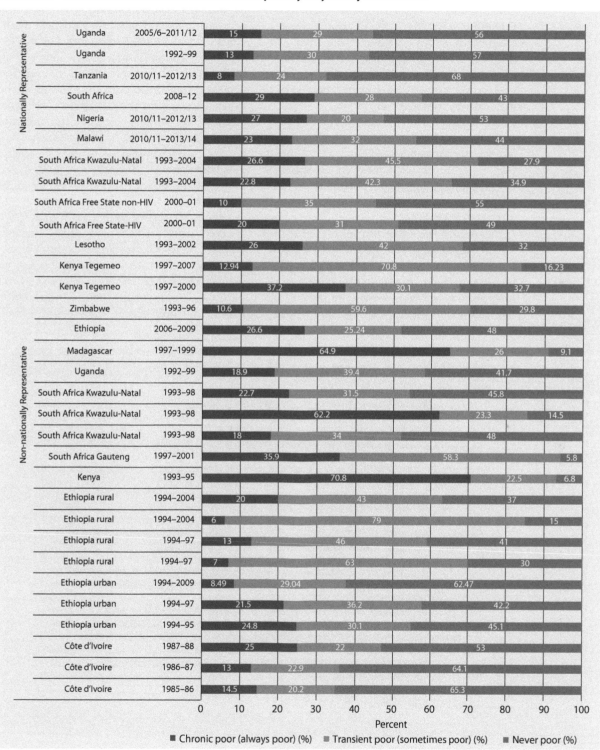

Sources: Baulch 2011; Duponchel, McKay, and Ssewanyana 2014 (Uganda 2005/06–2011/12); Finn and Leibbrandt 2013 (South Africa, National Income Dynamics Study); World Bank poverty assessments.
Note: Estimates for South Africa are based on Finn and Leibbrandt transition matrixes and a poverty rate of 45 percent using a national poverty line of R 620 a month in 2011.

poverty rate is 21 percent, implying that a household or individual is more likely to be sometimes poor than always poor (compare the median of chronic poverty [blue bars] to the median of transient poverty [orange bars] in figure 2.9). Health, labor market, conflict, and weather shocks have been identified as major drivers of these transitions.

How much of transitory poverty is real and how much reflects measurement error is a matter of debate. According to some researchers, measurement error of income or consumption may explain as much as half of transitory poverty (Dercon and Krishnan 2000; Glewwe 2012).

Revisiting the same household or individual over several years has its advantages, but doing so is costly—the main reason why large, nationally representative panels over long periods are rare. Given the paucity of nationally representative household panel surveys in the region, an alternative approach to obtaining evidence on the movement into and out of poverty is to use statistical methods to construct synthetic panels from available cross-sections (Dang and Lanjouw 2013, 2014; Dang and others 2014). In addition to generating more data on dynamics, the synthetic panel approach applies the same methodology and uses the same standard and welfare measure for all countries, which is not the case in most panel studies. Synthetic panel data may also be more representative of the population than panel data, which suffer from attrition.

In constructing synthetic panels, we selected countries with comparable surveys. Figure 2.10 decomposed each country's poverty over time into components: chronic poverty (households that were poor in both periods), downwardly mobile (households that fell into poverty in the second period),

FIGURE 2.10 The share of poor people in Africa who fall into poverty is about the same as the share of poor people who move out of poverty

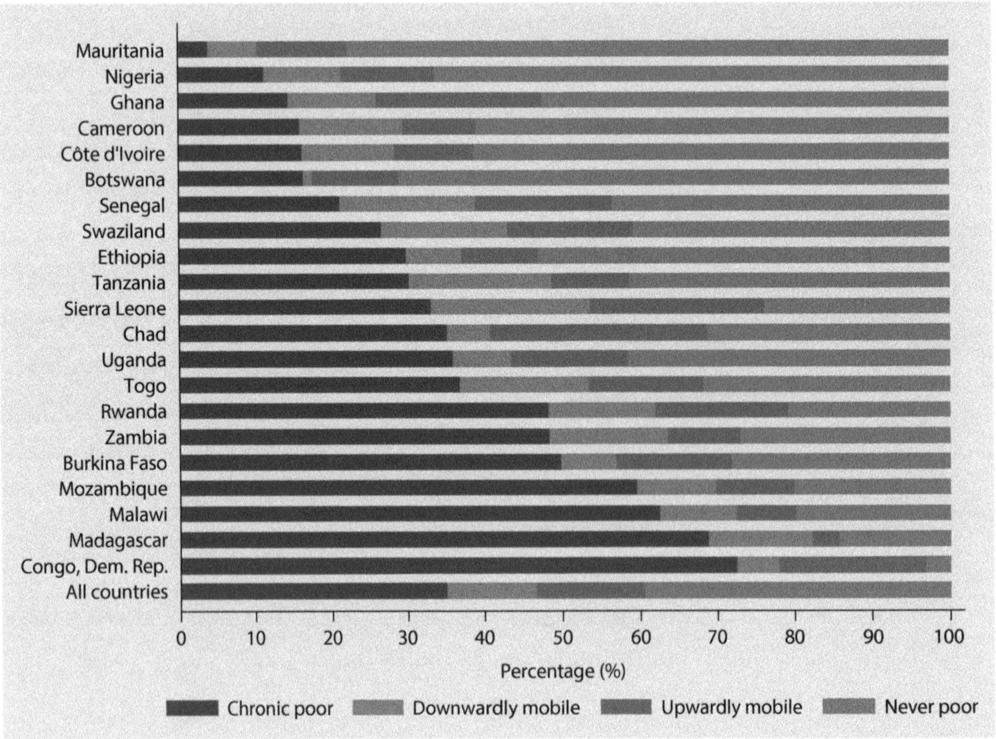

Source: Dang and Dabalen 2015.

and nonpoor. Rates of chronic poverty vary across countries and do not appear to be linked to overall poverty rates.[24] The non-poor are further decomposed into two components: households that were upwardly mobile (poor in the first period but not poor in the second period) and households that were never poor (nonpoor in both periods).

Figure 2.10 reveals three aspects of poverty dynamics in Africa. First, on average about 35 percent of the population of a country is chronically poor. These people account for 58 percent of the poor. About 26 percent of the nonpoor population emerged from poverty (that is, were poor in the first period but not the second).[24] This group could be considered vulnerable to falling back into poverty. Second, countries that are similar in terms of poverty rates may be dissimilar in terms of poverty dynamics. For instance, Ethiopia and Senegal both show similar average poverty rates, but the share of chronically poor people is larger in Ethiopia. Third, in some countries with low poverty rates, a large share of the poor are chronically poor. Botswana, for example, has poverty rates that are among the lowest in the sample, but almost all of its poor are chronically so (Dang and Dabalen 2015).

The review of the literature on poverty dynamics and the synthetic panel results depict a situation in which vulnerability is high, as evident from the prevalence of transient poverty. Because Africa's poor appear to be clustered around the poverty line, a small positive shock to incomes could lift many out of poverty, but a small negative shock could drive as many into poverty.

How large is the clustering around the poverty line? Raising the poverty line by $0.30–$0.50 (equivalent to a 16–26 percent negative shock to incomes) increases the poverty rate by 5 to 12 percentage points (figure 2.11). Raising the poverty line by $0.30 in 1990 increases the poverty rate from 55 percent to 60 percent. Raising the poverty line from $1.90 to $2.40 (that is by $0.50—or 26 percent) in 2012 increases the poverty

FIGURE 2.11 **Africa's poor are clustered around the poverty line**

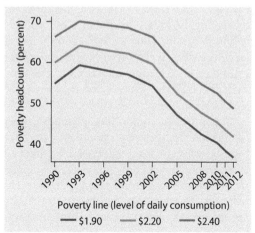

Poverty line (level of daily consumption)

— $1.90   — $2.20   — $2.40

Source: World Bank Africa Poverty database. The estimates use data corrected for comparability and quality.

rate by 12 percentage points. Poverty rates have declined, but the level of vulnerability remains very high.

Concluding Remarks

How much poverty reduction has been achieved since Africa's economic recovery began 15 years ago? The answer has been contentious, partly because the poverty data have not been properly scrutinized for comparability and quality.

Assessment of the data leads to three important conclusions. First, once known data problems are corrected, current poverty rates are lower and poverty reduction at least as large as international poverty estimates suggest. The most comprehensive source of household consumption survey data that provides country and regional estimates of poverty is the World Bank PovcalNet database. According to the surveys available on the database, Africa's poverty rate—defined in this report as people living on less than $1.90 per person per day (PPP 2011)—was 43 percent in 2012, a 14 percentage point decline since 1990. Accounting for the comparability and quality of data suggests that the decline may have been larger. The adjusted data imply that the poverty rate could be as much as 6 percentage points lower (37 percent instead of 43 percent) in 2012. Important drivers of the larger decline are corrections to the Nigeria data (which account for a large fraction of the difference between the estimates of the adjusted data and the PovcalNet data) and greater reliance on GDP simulations.

A number of robustness checks support the notion that poverty reduction may have been larger than assumed. Based on spells of comparable surveys only and excluding Nigeria, the implied annual change in poverty using GDP imputation is similar to the one recorded in the data correcting for comparability and quality. The results derived from survey-to-survey imputation methods suggest that the decline was larger than previously thought. This also applies to the S2S results for Nigeria, which supports the notion that poverty in Nigeria declined faster than current official estimates suggest. In addition, results from Engel curve estimation imply that CPIs may overestimate changes in the cost of living and hence underestimate poverty reduction.

Second, although this is good news, the challenge remains substantial; the region did not meet the MDG target of halving poverty by 2015 and many more people are poor in 2012 than in 1990 (even under the most optimistic scenario of poverty reduction). If the pace of poverty reduction does not pick up, it will take the region another decade to reach this target.

A major drag on reaching the goal is fragility. Among the four types of countries assessed—fragile, resource rich, landlocked, and low-income—fragile countries had the slowest rate of poverty reduction. Between 1996 and 2012, this group of countries reduced poverty by 12 percentage points—13 percentage points less than nonfragile countries. Controlling for other characteristics (resource richness, landlockedness, and low-income status) increases the difference in poverty reduction to 15 percentage points.

Third, about 58 percent of the poor in Africa may be chronically poor, although the lack of panel surveys with national coverage over long periods makes it difficult to establish this fact with certainty. The share of the transient poor (the sum of the upwardly and downwardly mobile), at roughly 25 percent of the population, also suggests a significant share of vulnerable population.

Notes

1. The term *poverty* is used here to refer to people with consumption levels below the international poverty line. The MDGs use the term *extreme poverty* to describe these people.
2. Some scholars argue, for example, that the African poverty rate has been falling much more quickly than internationally accepted conventional wisdom suggests (Pinkovskiy and Sala-i-Martín 2014; Young 2012).
3. This report does not address the problem of comparability across countries.
4. South Sudan—for which there are no purchasing power parity (PPP) exchange rates and, until recently, no consumer price index (CPI) data—was not included in the regional poverty estimate. No survey data were available for four countries (Equatorial Guinea, Eritrea, Somalia, and Zimbabwe). For these countries, the average regional poverty rate was assigned. Together these countries are home to about 5 percent of the population of Africa.
5. Where there are multiple surveys that are not comparable, only the survey that included the most comprehensive consumption data was used.
6. These poverty trends are robust to changes in country composition. The same imputation methods were applied to two subsamples: the 23 most populous countries and the 27 countries with at least two comparable surveys. For the 23 largest countries, which account for more than 88 percent of the total and the poor population, poverty declined from 55 percent to 36 percent (19 percentage points) based on the comparable and good-quality data and from 57 percent to 43 percent (14 percentage points) based on the full sample of surveys (PovcalNet). Among the 27 countries for which there are at least two comparable surveys, which represent about 76 percent of the population

and almost 80 percent of the poor, poverty dropped from 57 percent to 38 percent (19 percentage points) based on the comparable and good-quality data. As with the pattern among all countries, poverty measures peaked in the mid-1990s and declined more sharply after 2002 when comparable and good-quality data are used.

7. For Burundi, Gambia, and Seychelles, only one of the comparable consumption aggregates is available for use at the time of this report.

8. One of these countries is Zambia, where the finding is based on poor-quality data.

9. One of these countries is Nigeria, where the finding is based on poor-quality data.

10. Because the richness of survey data within and across countries varied widely over time, attempts were made to maintain the same model across time within but not across countries. Overall, for each model four clusters of variables were analyzed: demographics, education of the household head, housing and assets, and rural and urban location.

11. More specifically, if a survey and an estimate for a country were available in the period immediately before or after the period without a survey, the nearest available estimate was used for the period without a survey. For example, Ethiopia conducted a survey in 1994/1995. Assigning the poverty rate from 1994/95 to 1995–99 leaves the 1990–94 period without a poverty estimate for Ethiopia, as there were no surveys during this period. Therefore, we used the estimate from 1994/95 for both 1990–94 and 1995–99, keeping Ethiopia's poverty rate for that period unchanged. The main goal of the exercise is to avoid using GDP imputations to fill in missing data points and to avoid creating a series that would seem implausible. For instance, there are no surveys for the Democratic Republic of Congo before 2005. In 2005 the extreme poverty rate estimated from survey data was 91 percent. If we assign a regional poverty rate for the period without surveys, the poverty rate in the Democratic Republic of Congo would be half what the actual survey says and would make the country one of the least poor countries in Africa before 2005. To avoid such a series break, for all periods before 2005–09, we were compelled to hold the poverty rate

for the Democratic Republic of Congo at the 2005–09 rate.

12. For the period 1990–94, there was no survey coverage or surveys in the immediately following period for 4 of the 23 countries, so regional averages computed from the rest of the 19 countries were used. Similarly, regional averages were used for 3 countries for 1995–99, 2 countries for 2000–04, 1 country for 2005–09, and 1 country for 2010–12.

13. In general, only data that were subject to rigorous vetting (in terms of completeness of the sample and consumption aggregate, proper documentation, and consistency with consumption measures used by countries in their monitoring and analysis) are used in PovcalNet estimates. What is referred to as PovcalNet results here are estimates obtained by applying the methods used in PovcalNet (described in World Bank 2015b) to the vetted data for these 23 countries. We were able to closely replicate the official PovcalNet estimates for the period 1990–2012, in some cases differing only by a decimal point.

14. This discussion focuses on the role of the CPI in adjusting consumption in a given survey year to the benchmark year. Prices also matter for the profile of poverty within a country. For instance, urban-rural poverty gaps may be overestimated if price differences between urban and rural areas are underestimated. Cross-country comparisons—and therefore regional poverty levels and trends—will also be sensitive to changes and adjustments to PPP exchange rates. This section does not address these issues.

15. Engel Law is the observation that, as income rises, the share of income devoted to food falls, even if actual expenditure on food may be rising.

16. Where there are more than two comparable surveys per country, the CPI bias is estimated separately for each subperiod. The estimation is further restricted to countries for which monthly CPI data (food, nonfood, and all-item CPIs) from the national statistical agency are available, as these data are needed to control for relative price changes. The method only partially accounts for the quality change bias and does not capture the consumer surplus arising from the introduction of new commodities (Gibson, Stillman,

and Le 2008). Plutocratic bias (whereby the CPI gives more weight to the consumption of richer households) is addressed because the results are democratically weighted estimates (that is, use household sample weights that are more representative of their share in the population) among the subsample of urban households and do not weight households according to their total expenditures. Studies on the Russian Federation (Gibson, Stillman, and Le 2008) and Brazil and Mexico (de Carvalho Filho and Chamon 2012) use income as an instrumental variable for consumption to address endogeneity arising from the fact that total consumption enters both sides of the regression equation (that is, when computing budget shares and when controlling for consumption levels). The results suggest that ordinary least square estimates, such as the ones presented here, may suffer from some degree of bias because of correlated measurement error but are unlikely to show a different direction of bias than the instrumental variable estimates. Because many of the household surveys used in this report do not contain income aggregates, endogeneity concerns could not be addressed in the same manner.

17. For Nigeria and Rwanda, urban and rural CPI series were used. For Ethiopia, regional CPI (but collected from urban areas) were used. Finally in Mauritius, urban CPI was applied to rural and urban households during the Engel curve estimation because the household survey does not have urban and rural identifiers.

18. This finding contrasts with the view of Sandefur (2013), who argues that CPI inflation understates true inflation and hence provides too optimistic a view of poverty reduction in Africa. His analysis is based on a database of national poverty lines that tend to increase (in nominal terms) at a more rapid rate than official CPI inflation. Under certain conditions (related to how these national poverty lines are constructed), the poverty lines he proposes can reveal changes in the cost of living among the poor. However, the vast majority of the poverty lines Sandefur uses do not meet the necessary conditions (see Gaddis 2015) and are therefore inappropriate for inferring price changes between surveys.

19. Dropping outliers (differences of more than 3 percentage points in absolute value) does not change this result substantially (–1.1 becomes –0.8).

20. Nakamura, Steinsson, and Liu (2014) show that if inflation rates at different points in the income distribution are similar, the fact that the Engel curve deflator is for one unknown household and the CPI is for another household should not matter: one can attribute most of the gap between the two to genuine CPI bias. And in a recent analysis Hobijn and Lagakos (2005) suggest that, over long periods of time, the CPI inflation rate accurately represents changes in the cost of living for households at different parts of the income distribution.

21. See Ainsworth and Filmer (2006); Bicego, Rutstein, and Johnson (2003); Bollen, Glanville, and Stecklov (2002); Case, Paxon, and Ableidinger (2004); Filmer and Pritchett (1999, 2001); Gwatkin and others (2000); McKenzie (2005); Rao and Ibanez (2005); Sahn and Stifel (2000); Schellenberg and others (2003); and Stifel and Christiaensen (2007).

22. This trend is estimated from a regression (the log of the odds ratio) of the share of the population living in female-headed households using 98 country-year DHS surveys covering the last 25 years. Milazzo and van de Walle (2015) report that the trend is explained largely by rising age at marriage and higher education levels.

23. Since the introduction of the Living Standards Measurement Study–Integrated Surveys on Agriculture, surveys have been nationally representative.

24. In principle, poverty mobility is likely to be greater over longer intervals (see, for example, Dang and Lanjouw 2014). For these data, however, the Pearson correlation between chronic poverty and the length of time between the two cross-sections is weak (0.35 and not statistically significant).

25. Notice that the average upward mobility in these countries is about 14 percent and the nonpoor population is around 54 percent (40 percent never poor plus 14 percent upwardly mobile). Therefore, the fraction of the upwardly mobile among the nonpoor is 14/54, which is roughly 26 percent. Similarly, on average about 35 percent of

the poor were poor in both periods. The fraction of the population that was poor at least once in both periods includes the chronic poor (35 percent), the downwardly mobile (11 percent) and the upwardly mobile (14 percent). Therefore, the fraction of the chronic poor among the poor is about 58 percent (35/60).

References

Abreu, A., and D. Johnston. 2013. "Asset Indices as a Proxy for Poverty Measurement in African Countries: Reassessment." Paper presented at the Conference African Economic Development: Measuring Success and Failure. Vancouver: British Columbia, Canada. April 18-20, 2013.

Ainsworth, Martha, and Deon Filmer. 2006. "Inequality in Children's Schooling: AIDS, Orphanhood, Poverty, and Gender." *World Development* 34 (6): 1099–128.

Alfani, Fedrica, Carlo Azzarri, Marco d'Errico, and Vasco Molini. 2012. "Poverty in Mozambique: New Evidence from Recent Household Surveys." Policy Research Working Paper 6217, World Bank, Washington, DC.

Appleton, S. 1996. "Women-Headed Households and Household Welfare: An Empirical Deconstruction for Uganda." *World Development* 24 (12): 1811–27.

Baulch, Bob. 2011. *Why Poverty Persists: Poverty Dynamics in Asia and Africa*. Northampton, MA: Edward Elgar Publishing.

Bicego, George, Shea Rutstein, and Kiersten Johnson. 2003. "Dimensions of the Emerging Orphan Crisis in Sub-Saharan Africa." *Social Science & Medicine* 56 (6): 1235–47.

Bloom, David, and Jeffrey Sachs. 1998. "Geography, Demography, and Economic Growth in Africa." *Brookings Papers on Economic Activity* 2: 207–95.

Bollen, Kenneth, Jennifer Glanville, and Guy Stecklov. 2002. "Economic Status Proxies in Studies of Fertility." *Population Studies* 56 (1): 81–96.

Boskin, Michael J., Ellen R. Dulberger, Robert J. Gordon, Zvi Griliches, and Dale W. Jorgenson. 1996. "Toward a More Accurate Measure of the Cost of Living: Final Report to the Senate Finance Committee from the Advisory Commission to Study the Consumer Price Index."

Case, Anne, Christina Paxson, and Joseph Able-idinger. 2004. "Orphans in Africa: Parental Death, Poverty, and School Enrollment." *Demography* 41 (3): 483–508.

Christiaensen, Luc, Peter Lanjouw, Jill Luoto, and David Stifel. 2012. "Small Area Estimation-Based Prediction Methods to Track Poverty: Validation and Applications." *Journal of Economic Inequality* 10 (2): 267–97.

Christiaensen, Luc, and Anthony Shorrocks. 2012. "Measuring Poverty over Time." *Journal of Economic Inequality* 10 (2): 137–143.

Corral, Paul, Vasco Molini, and Gbemisola Oseni. 2015. "No Condition Is Permanent: Middle Class in Nigeria in the Last Decade." Policy Research Working Paper 7214, World Bank, Washington, DC.

Costa, Dora L. 2001. "Estimating Real Income in the United States from 1888 to 1994: Correcting CPI Bias Using Engel Curves." *Journal of Political Economy* 109 (6): 1288–310.

Dabalen, Andrew, Isis Gaddis, and Nga Thi Viet Nguyen. 2015. "CPI Bias and Its Implication for Poverty in Sub-Saharan African Countries." Background paper prepared for the *Poverty in a Rising Africa* report, World Bank, Washington, DC.

Dang, Hai-Anh, and Andrew Dabalen. 2015. "How Large Is Chronic Poverty in Africa: Poverty Dynamics using Synthetic Panels." Background paper prepared for the *Poverty in a Rising Africa* report, World Bank, Washington, DC.

Dang, Hai-Anh, and Peter Lanjouw. 2013. "Measuring Poverty Dynamics with Synthetic Panels Based on Cross-Sections." Policy Research Working Paper 6504, World Bank, Washington, DC.

———. 2014. "Welfare Dynamic Measurement: Two Definitions of a Vulnerability Line." Policy Research Working Paper 6944, World Bank, Washington, DC.

Dang, Hai-Anh, Peter Lanjouw, Jill Luoto, and David McKenzie. 2014. "Using Repeated Cross-Sections to Explore Movements in and out of Poverty." *Journal of Development Economics* 107: 112–28.

Dang, Hai-Anh, and Minh Nguyen. 2014. "povimp: Stata Module to Impute Poverty in the Absence of Consumption Data." World Bank, Development Research Group, Poverty and Inequality Unit and Global Poverty Practice.

Deaton, Angus. 2005. "Measuring Poverty in a Growing World (or Measuring Growth in a Poor World)." *The Review of Economics and Statistics* LXXXVII (1): 1–19.

de Carvalho Filho, Irineu, and Marcos Chamon. 2012. "The Myth of Post-Reform Income Stagnation: Evidence from Brazil and Mexico." *Journal of Development Economics* 97 (2): 368–86.

Dercon, Stefan, and Pramila Krishnan. 2000. "Vulnerability, Seasonality and Poverty in Ethiopia." *Journal of Development Studies* 36 (6): 25–53.

Diewert, W. Erwin. 1998. "Index Number Issues in the Consumer Price Index." *Journal of Economic Perspectives* 12 (1): 47–58.

Douidich, Mohamed, Abdeljaouad Ezzrari, Roy Van der Weide, and Paolo Verme. 2013. "Estimating Quarterly Poverty Rates Using Labor Force Surveys: A Primer." Policy Research Working Paper 6466, World Bank, Washington, DC.

Duponchel, Marguerite, Andy McKay, and Sarah Ssewanyana. 2014. "The Dynamics of Poverty in Uganda, 2005/6 to 2011/12: Has the Progress Stalled?" Working Paper, Centre for the Study of African Economies (CSAE), Oxford, United Kingdom.

Filmer, Deon, and Lant Pritchett. 1999. "The Effect of Household Wealth on Educational Attainment: Evidence from 35 Countries." *Population and Development Review* 25 (1): 85–120.

———. 2001. "Estimating Wealth Effects without Expenditure Data or Tears: An Application to Educational Enrollments in States of India." *Demography* 38 (1): 115–32.

Filmer, Deon, and Kinnon Scott. 2012. "Assessing Asset Indices." *Demography* 49 (1): 359–92.

Finn, Arden, and Murray Leibbrandt. 2013. "The Dynamics of Poverty in the First Three Waves of NIDS." NIDS Discussion Paper 2013/1, National Income Dynamics Study, Southern Africa Labour and Development Research Unit (SALDRU), University of Cape Town, Rondebosch, South Africa.

Gaddis, Isis. 2015. "Prices for Poverty Analysis in Africa." Background paper prepared for the *Poverty in a Rising Africa* report, World Bank, Washington, DC.

Gibson, John, Trinh Le, and Bonggeun Kim. 2014. "Prices, Engel Curves and Time-Space Deflation: Impacts on Poverty and Inequality in Vietnam." University of Waikato, New Zealand.

Gibson, John, Steven Stillman, and Trinh Le. 2008. "CPI Bias and Real Living Standards in Russia during the Transition." *Journal of Development Economics* 87 (1): 140–61.

Glewwe, Paul. 2012. "How Much of Observed Economic Mobility Is Measurement Error? IV Methods to Reduce Measurement Error Bias, with an Application to Vietnam." *World Bank Economic Review* 26 (2): 236–64.

Gwatkin, Davidson R., Shea Rutstein, Kiersten Johnson, Rohini Pande, and Adam Wagstaff. 2000. "Socio-Economic Differences in Health, Nutrition, and Population." World Bank, HNP/Poverty Thematic Group, Washington, DC.

Gwatkin, Davidson, Shea Rutstein, Kiersten Johnson, Eldaw Suliman, Adam Wagstaff, and Agbessi Amouzou. 2007. *Socio-Economic Differences in Health, Nutrition, and Population*. Washington, DC: World Bank.

Hamilton, Bruce W. 2001. "Using Engel's Law to Estimate CPI Bias." *American Economic Review* 91 (3): 619–30.

Harttgen, Kenneth, Stephan Klasen, and Sebastian Vollmer. 2013. "An African Growth Miracle? Or: What Do Asset Indices Tell Us about Trends in Economic Performance?" *Review of Income and Wealth* 59 (S1): S37–S61.

Hausman, Jerry. 2003. "Sources of Bias and Solutions to Bias in the CPI." *Journal of Economic Perspectives* 17 (1): 23–44.

Hobijn, Bart and David Lagakos. 2005. "Inflation Inequality in the United States," *Review of Income and Wealth*, 2005, 51 (4), 581–606.

Horrell, S., and Krishnan P. 2007. "Poverty and Productivity in Female-Headed Households in Zimbabwe." *Journal of Development Studies* 43 (8): 1351–80.

Howe, Laura, James R. Jargreaves, Sabrine Gabrysch, and Sharon Huttly. 2009. "Is the Wealth Index a Proxy for Consumption Expenditure? A Systematic Review." *Journal of Epidemiology and Community Health* 63 (11): 871–80.

Jerven, Morten. 2013. *Poor Numbers: How We Are Misled by African Development Statistics and What to Do about It*. Ithaca, NY: Cornell University Press.

Lanjouw, Peter, and Martin Ravallion. 1995. "Poverty and Household Size." *Economic Journal* 105 (433): 1415–34.

Luke, Gallup, Jeffrey D. Sachs, and Andrew Mellinger. 1999. "Geography and Economic Development." In *Annual Conference on Development Economics 1998*, edited by Boris Pleskovic and Joseph E. Stiglitz, 127–78. Washington, DC: World Bank.

McKenzie, David. 2005. "Measuring Inequality with Asset Indicators." *Journal of Population Economics* 18 (1): 229–60.

Milazzo, Annamaria, and Dominique van de Walle. 2015. "Women Left Behind? Poverty and Headship in Africa." Policy Research Working Paper 7331, World Bank, Washington, DC.

Nakamura, Emi, Jon Steinsson, and Miao Liu. 2014. "Are Chinese Growth and Inflation Too Smooth? Evidence from Engel Curves." NBER Working Paper No. 19893. Issued in February 2014.

Pinkovskiy, Maxim, and Xavier Sala-i-Martín. 2014. "Africa Is on Time." *Journal of Economic Growth* 19 (3): 311–38.

Rao, Vijayendra, and Ana Maria Ibanez. 2005. "The Social Impact of Social Funds in Jamaica: A 'Participatory Econometric' Analysis of Targeting, Collective Action, and Participation in Community-Driven Development." *Journal of Development Studies* 41 (5): 788–838.

Rutstein, Shea, and Kiersten Johnson. 2004. *The DHS Wealth Index*. DHS Methodological Report 6, ICF International, Rockville, MD.

Rutstein, Shea, and Sarah Staveteig. 2014. *Making the Demographic and Health Surveys Wealth Index Comparable*. DHS Methodological Report 9, ICF International, Rockville, MD.

Sahn, David, and David Stifel. 2000. "Poverty Comparisons over Time and across Countries in Africa." *World Development* 28 (12): 2123–55.

Sandefur, Justin. 2013. "Africa Rising? Using Micro Surveys to Correct Macro Time Series." Center for Global Development, Washington, DC.

Schellenberg, Joanna, Cesar Victora, Adiel Mushi, Don de Savigny, David Schellenberg, Hassan Mshinda, and Jennifer Bryce. 2003. "Inequalities among the Very Poor: Health Care for Children in Rural Southern Tanzania." *Lancet* 361 (9357): 561–66.

Smits Jeroen, and Roel Steendijk. 2015. "The International Wealth Index (IWI)." *Social Indicators Research* 122 (1): 65–85.

Stifel, David, and Luc Christiaensen. 2007. "Tracking Poverty over Time in the Absence of Comparable Consumption Data." *World Bank Economic Review* 21 (2): 317–41.

van de Walle, Dominique. 2013. "Lasting Welfare Effects of Widowhood in Mali." *World Development* 51: 1–19.

World Bank. 2012. *Zambia Poverty Assessment: Stagnant Poverty and Inequality in a Natural Resource-Based Economy*. Washington, DC: World Bank.

———. 2013. *Burkina Faso. A Policy Note: Poverty Trends and Profile for 2003–2009*. Washington, DC: World Bank.

———. 2014a. *Face of Poverty in Madagascar: Poverty, Gender, and Inequality Assessment*. Report 78131-MG, Washington, DC: World Bank.

———. 2014b. *Nigeria Economic Report*, No. 2, July. Washington, DC: World Bank.

———. 2014c. "Nigeria: Where Has All the Growth Gone?" Policy Note 78908, World Bank, Washington, DC.

———. 2015a. *Africa's Demographic Transition: Dividend or Disaster?* edited by David Canning, Sangeeta Raja, and Abdo S. Yazbeck. Washington, DC: World Bank.

———. 2015b. *A Measured Approach to Ending Poverty and Boosting Shared Prosperity: Concept, Data and the Twin Goals*. Policy Research Report. Washington, DC: World Bank.

———. 2015c. *United Republic of Tanzania: Tanzania Mainland Poverty Assessment*. Report AUS6819. Washington, DC: World Bank.

Young, Alwyn. 2012. "The African Growth Miracle." *Journal of Political Economy* 120 (4): 696–739.

Poverty from a Nonmonetary Perspective | 3

Chapter 2 considers poverty in monetary terms. Using income or the monetary value of consumption as a basis for defining the poor is appealing on several grounds. It allows for different preferences in purchases, the definition of a poverty threshold in "objective" ways (such as the cost of a minimum-calorie diet), and aggregation across domains (the value of food and nonfood consumed).

Yet, income fails to provide a complete picture of well-being for several reasons. First, many aspects of well-being are not just difficult to price but valuable in ways that cannot be monetized (Sandel 2012; Sen 1985). For example, commoditizing the right to vote by allowing people to sell it would yield a market value of voting rights that would not capture the full meaning and value of the right as an expression of citizenship and political participation. The list of difficult-to-monetize aspects of well-being is long, including the ability to read and write, longevity and good health, security, political freedoms, social acceptance and status, and the ability to move and connect.

Second, the benefit of income can be limited when it interacts with other conditions. The benefits of a bicycle as a means of transport, for example, are quite different for an able-bodied and a handicapped person. Such resources are instrumentally valuable; they have no intrinsic value. Relying on their monetary valuation as a measure of well-being can therefore be misleading.

Third, income measures are at the household level, which assumes the equal distribution of income across household members. Yet intrahousehold inequalities in the distribution of household income across household members can be substantial (Chiappori and Meghir 2015; see box 4.3 in chapter 4). Direct information on individuals avoids this strong assumption.

This chapter briefly reviews how the capability approach motivates a nonmonetary multidimensional perspective on poverty. It then assesses Africa's progress in literacy and education, life expectancy and health, freedom from violence, and self-determination (freedom to decide). It devotes special attention to displaced and disabled people, two vulnerable groups that are rarely covered in standard poverty reports (because of data limitations). Finally, it considers the four dimensions of well-being jointly, in order to

---

This chapter was written with Umberto Cattaneo, Camila Galindo-Pardo, and Agnes Said.

identify countries and individuals that are deprived in multiple dimensions.

The Capability Approach

Sen (1980, 1985, 1999) proposes the capability approach as an alternative to monetary measures of poverty. This approach focuses on what people effectively do and are (their functionings) and on the capacity of people to freely choose and achieve these functionings (that is, their capability) rather than on the commodities bought or consumed. There is broad consensus that functionings such as the ability to read and write and being well nourished, healthy, and free from violence and oppression are vital for human development. They are ontological needs (stemming from the condition of being human) that apply to every person regardless of geographic location or time (Max-Neef, Elizalde, and Hopenhayn 1991). Focusing on individual achievements in these areas thus provides a good basis to begin assessing poverty from a nonmonetary perspective.

Education, health, and security also expand the choices people can make and the range of things they can do and be (that is, their capabilities). But they are not sufficient. Social and political institutions often impede self-realization. Basic personal and political freedoms are equally essential. To appreciate the importance of opportunity and choice for assessing well-being, consider two people, both teachers. One chooses teaching from among a range of occupational options. The other becomes a teacher because other, preferred options are excluded because of cultural constraints (engineering is closed to women) or location (engineering jobs are not available in remote villages) or because someone else chose the profession for her (Foster 2011). Can they be considered equally well off? Clearly, personal autonomy and self-determination matter for well-being. The study of outcomes should not be indifferent to the process by which the choice was made.

The capability approach provides the philosophical underpinnings for the nonmonetary perspective on poverty examined in this chapter. Sen's vision of capabilities and functionings also underlies the rich and vibrant literature on multidimensional poverty (Alkire 2008; Bourguignon and Chakravarty 2003; Robeyns 2005; Sen 1999).

Using the capability approach to measure well-being is challenging. There are some common approaches to measuring certain basic functionings, such as the ability to read and write, adequate nourishment, and good health, even though measurement issues remain here as well (de Walque and Filmer 2012; UNESCO 2015). There is much less experience in measuring other functionings (including mobility, social integration, and even the capacity to aspire) and in measuring capability. An added complexity is determining thresholds below which a person is considered poor, as these cutoffs arguably depend on the individual's choices and preferences. Finally, there is the challenge of aggregation. For example, how much poorer should a person be considered when deprived in several functionings compared to when deprived in only one?

The human development index (HDI) and the multidimensional poverty index (MPI) (Alkire and Santos 2014) are applications of the capability approach to assessing progress in societies.[1] Both indexes focus on achievements in education, longevity/health, and living standards (through income and assets). The approach pursued in this chapter is in this tradition, though with a different emphasis in three areas.

First, to provide a more comprehensive view of people's basic capabilities, the chapter considers two additional dimensions: freedom from violence and the opportunity for self-determination (freedom to decide). Poverty analyses have largely ignored these dimensions.

Second, the degree of joint deprivation is explored by estimating the share of people deprived in one, two, and more dimensions. This approach achieves a middle ground between a single index of poverty (which requires weighting achievements in the various dimensions) and a dashboard approach (which simply lists achievements dimension by dimension, ignoring jointness in deprivation) (Ferreira and Lugo 2013).

Third, the focus is on outcomes measured at the individual (not the household) level. Where data on outcomes are not available, information on inputs (such as use of bednets and vaccination rates in lieu of disease prevalence measures) and proximate measures (such as governance indicators for freedom to decide) are used.

Data on nonmonetary dimensions of poverty are now much more widely and more regularly available than they once were, including at the individual level. This follows the rapid expansion and public availability of the Demographic and Health Surveys (DHS), as well as the Africa-wide and globally comparable national opinion surveys, such as the Afrobarometer, the Gallup World Poll, and the World Value Surveys. These data enable the much wider dimensional and more individualistic scope of this chapter. Some of the concerns regarding data availability, comparability, and quality highlighted in the context of the expenditure surveys apply here as well, however. Their implications are discussed throughout the chapter where relevant.

There has also been an upsurge in the availability and use of subjective measures of well-being and poverty, such as measures based on ordinal questions about happiness or life satisfaction (box 3.1). Given the lack of a common frame of reference, which makes it difficult to compare across people and time, these measures are not used here to assess poverty.

BOX 3.1   How useful are subjective data in monitoring poverty?

Subjective measures of well-being reflect utility as a mental state (happiness) or as a cognitive reflection of the condition of one's life. Unlike income measures of poverty, they do not rely on prices or monetary valuations, although they include both monetary and nonmonetary dimensions of well-being. These measures are based on the personal evaluation of individuals themselves, reflecting the value attached to individual sovereignty. Being one-dimensional, they facilitate complete orderings.

Answers to subjective well-being questions, such as questions based on ordinal questions about happiness, economic welfare, or life satisfaction, are intuitive and not time consuming to collect. They confirm that many dimensions beyond income and material consumption—health, job market status, the quality of relations and social interactions, and even political rights and freedom of speech (Frey and Stutzer 2002)—matter and that happiness and life satisfaction increase with income at a declining pace (or not at all beyond a certain level of income, according to the Easterlin paradox (Easterlin 1974), though the existence of this paradox remains debated [Stevenson and Wolfers 2008]).

One challenge with subjective well-being is the lack of a common frame of reference. As individuals adapt their tastes and aspirations to their circumstances, intrapersonal comparisons over time and interpersonal comparisons become difficult. Adaptation of happiness standards and aspirations—lowering them when conditions go awry and raising them when conditions improve—are pervasive worldwide. Countries with higher rates of HIV prevalence, for example, do not systematically report lower life satisfaction (Deaton 2008); people who lose limbs still record good well-being scores (Loewenstein and Ubel 2008; Oswald and Powdthavee 2008).

The subjective well-being approach also does not adjust for individual tastes or aspirations. This could lead to paradoxical policy actions, such as redistribution from poor happy subsistence farmers to unhappy millionaires. Subjective well-being data may therefore not yet be appropriate to monitor living standards. They do, however, contain important complementary information about people's preferences that could help inform policy makers about how to value public goods or weight nonmonetary dimensions of well-being (Decanq, Fleurbaey, and Schokkaert 2015) or set the poverty line (Ravallion 2012). As the capability approach emphasizes, personal preferences and choices cannot be ignored in assessing an individual's level of poverty and well-being. How to use questions about subjective well-being to learn about those aspects of people's preferences that policymakers want to take on board is an important research agenda.

Levels of and Trends in Well-Being

Education and Literacy

Education can expand people's capabilities. It helps people access and digest information and knowledge. Doing so requires at a minimum being literate. The focus here is mainly on adult literacy rates: the percentage of adults who can, with understanding, read and write a short, simple statement about their everyday lives.

Adult literacy rates evolve slowly in the absence of effective large-scale adult education programs, because their evolution is influenced mainly by the literacy levels of younger cohorts. Current school enrollment rates and test scores are therefore also considered, to assess how adult literacy is likely to evolve.

Africa's literacy rate stood at 58 percent in 2012: more than two in five Africans cannot read or write a sentence (figure 3.1 and box 3.2). There has been progress, but it has been slow. Between 1995 and 2012, the literacy level in the region increased by 4 percentage

points, despite a rapid increase in primary enrollment rates since 2000. This change compares unfavorably with the 17 percentage point increase in South Asia and in the Middle East and North Africa and the 10 percentage point increase in East Asia and Pacific, where the literacy rate is approaching 93 percent.

This low average for Africa masks substantial variation within the region. More than half the population is illiterate in seven countries, almost all of them in West Africa (figure 3.2). Niger (with an adult literacy rate of only 15 percent) and Guinea (where the rate is just 25 percent) have the lowest literacy levels in Africa. At the other extreme, literacy levels exceed 90 percent in Equatorial Guinea and South Africa, and they exceed 70 percent in some poor and fragile countries as well, such as Eritrea and Zimbabwe.

The gender literacy gap remains high, averaging about 25 percentage points, although gender parity in education is one of the Millennium Development Goals on which Africa has performed best. Gender parity in literacy is especially low in West Africa (figure 3.3).

FIGURE 3.1   **Africa's literacy rate is the lowest in the world**

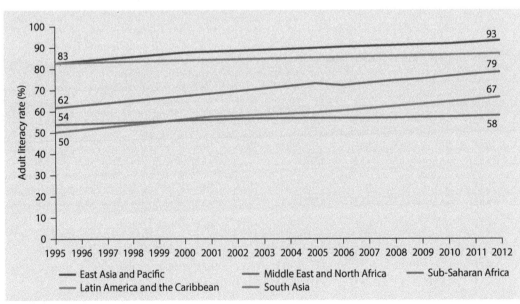

Source: EDSTAT data.
Note: The adult literacy rate is the percent of the population 15 and older that can, with understanding, read and write a short, simple statement about their everyday lives. Missing years were inter- or extrapolated.

BOX 3.2 Tracking adult literacy with data remains challenging

Following the launch of the Education for All initiative in 2000, much effort has been devoted to monitoring adult literacy. Nonetheless, data on adult literacy are still collected relatively infrequently, and both the definitions and methods of measurement keep changing, raising validity and comparability issues similar to the ones encountered in compiling expenditure data for poverty tracking (see chapter 1). On the upside, the UNESCO Institute for Statistics provides detailed and publicly accessible metadata of the data sources, definitions, and actual measures used (UNESCO 2015).

For the period 1995–2012, 109 annual literacy estimates are available—13 percent of the total possible number of 828 (18 years * 46 countries [no literacy data are available for Somalia and South Sudan]). Although the figure seems low, annual changes in literacy rates are small, meaning that the small number of estimates is less important than it would otherwise be. A more relevant metric is the number of countries with two or more surveys or censuses to estimate literacy rates and the proximity of the data sources to the beginning and end points of the study period (1995 and 2012).

On this count the picture is better. Only four countries, which together represent 6.4 percent of the 2013 African population, have only one estimate; the remaining 42 have two or more records. For these countries, linear interpolation and extrapolation are used to fill in the missing years. For countries with only one observation, the average African trend was applied to extrapolate. The average population-weighted literacy estimate in each country is 4.5 years removed from 1995 and 3.3 years from 2012. Given the small annual change in

literacy rates, the trends reported here are thus reasonably well supported by actual data, despite the small number of observations.

How comparable are these data? Until the mid-2000s, estimates of African literacy were based on self- or proxy declarations on whether a person could read or write, with countries sometimes assuming literacy among people who had completed primary school. Estimates were obtained from census or survey data. Since 2006, where self- or proxy declaration–based estimates are not available, literacy scores have increasingly been derived from direct assessments, in which respondents are asked to read a sentence from a card (this technique is used in the DHS and Multiple Indicator Cluster Surveys [MICS]). Twenty of the 56 literacy estimates recorded in Africa during 2006–12 were test based.

Literacy rates obtained through direct assessments were 8 percentage points lower on average across a sample of 20 countries (UNESCO 2015). Their increased use may partly explain why Africa's recorded progress on adult literacy has not been more rapid.

The measure of literacy as the self- or proxy-declared ability to read and write only a short simple statement about everyday life is rudimentary. Literacy today is seen as a "continuum of skills, such as the ability to identify, understand, interpret, create, communicate, and compute using printed and written materials associated with varied contexts, that enables individuals to achieve their goals in work and life and participate fully in society" (UNESCO 2015, 137). This shift toward a more demanding notion of literacy mirrors the notion of rising poverty lines as countries develop.

This gap partly accounts for the low levels of overall adult literacy there. Gender parity is much higher in Southern Africa. The ratio of literate women to literate men is only 0.32 in Guinea and 0.38 in Niger. In contrast, women are more likely to be literate than men in Lesotho (1.34) and Namibia (1.08).

What traits of households and countries explain the gender gap in literacy? Overall, female illiteracy rates are substantially higher in low-income countries than in

higher-income countries (by about 32 percentage points in upper-middle-income and high-income countries and about 14 percentage points in low-middle-income countries) (figure 3.4). In resource-rich countries, however, illiteracy rates are about 3 percentage points higher than in resource-poor countries (irrespective of the country's income level, landlockedness, or fragility), indicating that governance factors matter. Women in poor rural households are 36 percent more likely

FIGURE 3.2 **Literacy rates are lowest in West Africa**

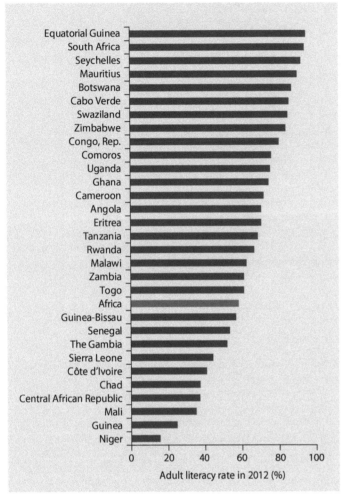

Adult literacy rate in 2012 (%)

Source: EDSTAT data.
Note: Figures cover only countries for which a survey was conducted in 2010–12. Missing years were inter- or extrapolated. Africa average is population-weighted.

countries could not read for meaning (figure 3.5). Even in Kenya 20 percent of sixth graders could not read for meaning. Among francophone countries in the region, 55 percent of fifth graders did not reach the minimum performance threshold, and half of them performed at or below the level expected from random guessing. Scores for numeracy skills and mathematics are equally poor.

Life Expectancy, Health, and Nutrition

A widely used measure of the ability to live a long and healthy life is life expectancy at birth. It provides a comprehensive reflection of the various factors that affect health and mortality. A more refined measure is healthy life expectancy, the number of years a newborn can expect to live in full health. Life expectancy and mortality indicators are estimated for a population (usually at the country level). In contrast, nutrition (and disability) indicators provide individual views of health status.

Life expectancy. Over the past decade, Africa experienced a massive increase in life expectancy: babies born in 2013 are expected to live 6.2 years longer than babies born in 2000 (figure 3.6). The change makes the region one of the strongest recent performers in the world, above South Asia, where life expectancy increased by 6.0 years since 1995. This progress follows directly from the rapid decline in under-five mortality rates in the region.

Even so, at 57 years, life expectancy in the region remains well below the average rate for the world (70.9 years). At the current annual rate of increase, it will take about two decades to reach the levels in South Asia (almost 67 in 2013), which lags other regions by several years.

Healthy life expectancy in Africa was 49 years in 2012, 8 years less than total life expectancy (WHO 2015). The gender gap favors women: in 2012 African women could expect to live 1.6 years longer in good health than men.[4] As with literacy, the differences in healthy life expectancy across countries are significant, ranging from 39 to

to be illiterate than their urban counterparts in richer households. Literacy is positively correlated with being divorced, widowed, or single (20 percent less likely to be illiterate). Illiteracy is much lower among younger people, holding hope for gender parity and overall literacy levels.

Progress has been slow despite the rapid increase in gross primary school enrollment, which rose from 75 percent in 1995 to 106 percent in 2012.[2,3] Despite gross primary school enrollment rates of 124 percent in Malawi and 119 in Zambia in 2007, a staggering 73 percent of sixth graders in the two

FIGURE 3.3   **The gender gap in literacy varies widely across Africa**

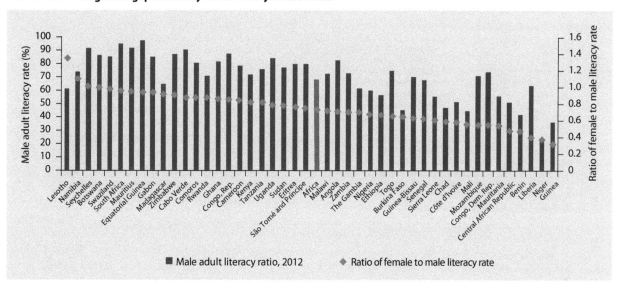

Source: EDSTAT data. Africa average is population-weighted.

FIGURE 3.4   **Illiteracy is higher among poorer people, older people, rural dwellers, and people in resource-rich and landlocked countries**

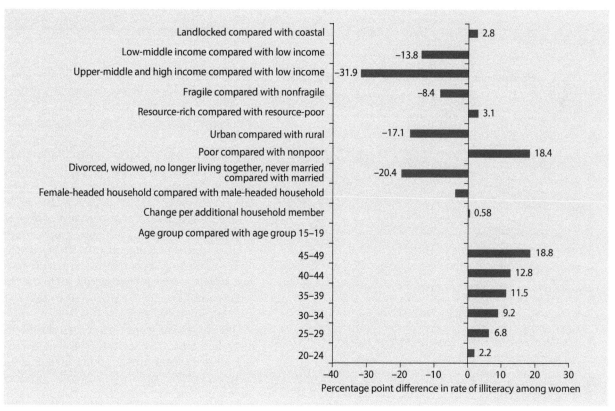

Source: Data from Demographic and Health Surveys 2005–13.
Note: Results are from ordinary least square regression. All estimated coefficients are statistically significant.

FIGURE 3.5   Many sixth graders in Africa lack basic reading skills

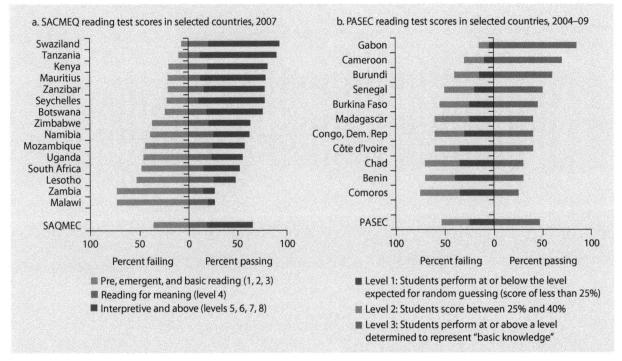

a. SACMEQ reading test scores in selected countries, 2007

b. PASEC reading test scores in selected countries, 2004–09

■ Pre, emergent, and basic reading (1, 2, 3)
■ Reading for meaning (level 4)
■ Interpretive and above (levels 5, 6, 7, 8)

■ Level 1: Students perform at or below the level expected for random guessing (score of less than 25%)
■ Level 2: Students score between 25% and 40%
■ Level 3: Students perform at or above a level determined to represent "basic knowledge"

Sources: Hungi and others 2010; World Bank estimates based on PASEC data.
Note: SACMEQ = Southern Africa Consortium for Measuring Educational Quality. PASEC = Programme d'Analyse des Systèmes Educatifs de la CONFEMEN. SAQMEC and PASEC statistic are the country averages.

FIGURE 3.6   Life expectancy in Africa is rising, but it remains the lowest in the world

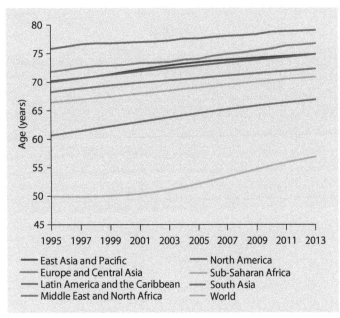

— East Asia and Pacific
— Europe and Central Asia
— Latin America and the Caribbean
— Middle East and North Africa
— North America
— Sub-Saharan Africa
— South Asia
— World

Source: World Development Indicators.

67 years (figure 3.7). Many of the countries in which healthy life expectancy is shortest are fragile or conflict-affected states. Healthy life expectancy is also low in some of Africa's oil giants, such as Angola and Nigeria. Among the top performers in 2012 are the island economies (Cabo Verde, Mauritius, and the Seychelles), which recorded healthy life expectancies of more than 60 years. Some countries saw very little change in healthy life expectancy between 2000 and 2012 (South Africa saw no change at all). Other countries—including some that were in conflict in the 1990s, such as Eritrea and Rwanda (15 years) and Ethiopia (11 years)—recorded significant improvements.

Healthy life expectancy is related to four key variables: country income, natural resources, fragility, and landlockedness. There are clear signs of a resource curse in terms of longevity (literacy is also inversely correlated with natural resource endowment) (figure 3.8): on average people born

FIGURE 3.7   Healthy life expectancy at birth ranges widely

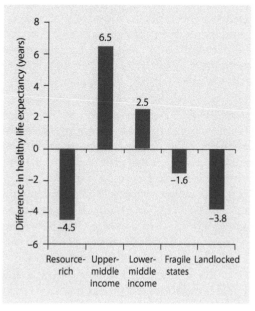

■ Healthy life expectancy at birth, 2012
■ Change in healthy life expectancy, 2000–12

Source: WHO 2015. Africa average is population-weighted.

in resource-rich countries have life spans that are 4.5 years shorter than people born in non-resource-rich countries (a difference of about 10 percent), after controlling for income level, fragility, and landlockedness. People in upper-middle-income and high-income countries can expect to live in good health 6.5 years longer than people in low-income countries, after controlling for the other country traits. People in coastal countries also have higher healthy life expectancy.

Under-five mortality and HIV prevalence. Two mortality indicators are significant drivers of changes in life expectancy in Africa: under-five mortality rates and HIV prevalence rates. For every 10 additional children per 1,000 live births surviving to the age of five, life expectancy increased by 0.7 years; for every percentage point increase in HIV prevalence, life expectancy decreased by 1 year. These two factors alone explain more than three-quarters of the variation in life expectancy in the region (under-five mortality explains 50 percentage points and HIV

FIGURE 3.8   Healthy life expectancy is lower in resource-rich countries

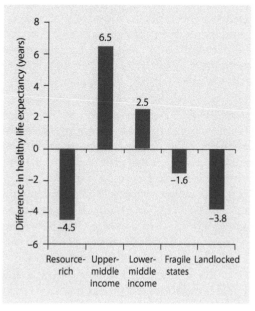

Source: Data from WHO 2015.
Note: Results are from ordinary least squares regression of data for 2000–12 including these four country traits.

FIGURE 3.9 **Vaccination rates rose and child mortality from malaria fell**

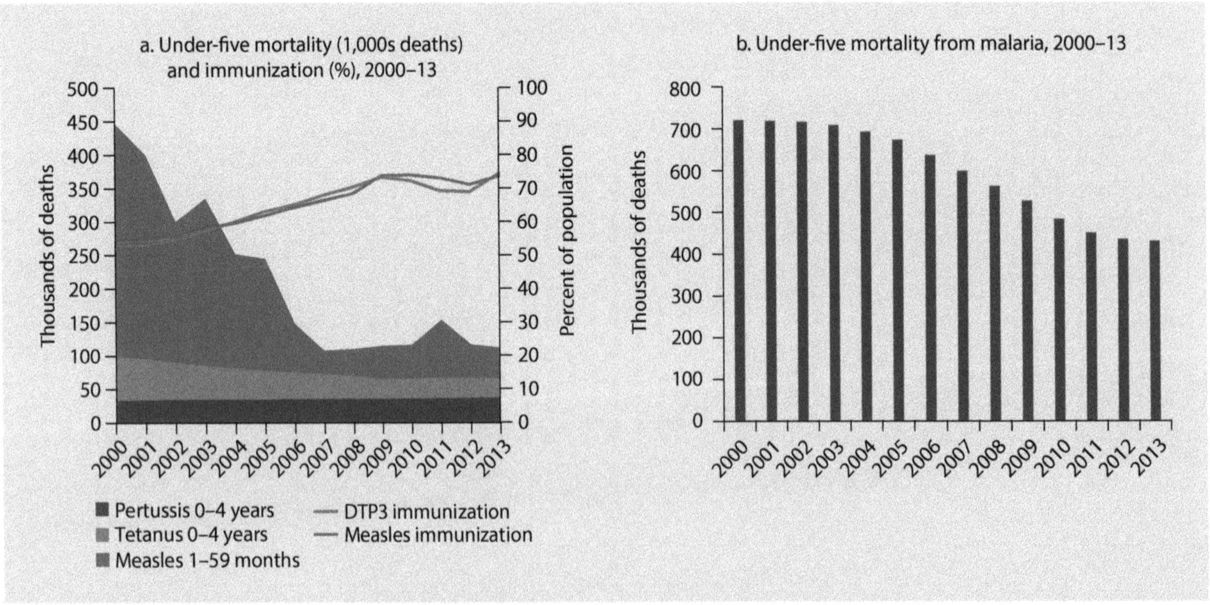

Sources: Panel a: Data from Health Nutrition and Population Statistics and WHO 2014a. Panel b: Data from WHO 2014b.
Note: Immunization measles age group is 12–23 months. Immunization DTP3 age group is 12–23 months. Measles age group is 1–59 months. Pertussis age group is 0–4 years. Tetanus age group is 0–4 years. DTP = diphtheria, tetanus, and pertussis.

prevalence explains 28 percentage points). Country gross domestic product (GDP) levels and the number of deaths from conflict in previous years do not have important effects on life expectancy beyond their effects on child mortality or HIV prevalence.[5]

The decline in the under-five mortality rate—from 173 in 1995 to 92 in 2013—went hand-in-hand with the increase in immunization rates and the decline in the incidence of malaria-related deaths (figure 3.9). Room for further decline through expansion of immunization remains—the immunization rate against measles is still only about 60 percent in some of the region's most populous (Ethiopia) and resource-rich (the Democratic Republic of Congo, Nigeria, South Africa) countries. In Equatorial Guinea, where GDP per capita is more than $15,000 a year, only about one child in two is vaccinated against measles.

In 2000 less than $100 million was disbursed to malaria-endemic countries to fight malaria; in 2013 the figure was $1.97 billion. As a consequence, the number of children dying from malaria fell dramatically,

partly as a result of the expanded use of insecticide-treated bednets.[6] Many more children still die annually from malaria than from measles, tetanus, and pertussis together, however (figure 3.9). The risk of a child under five dying from malaria is low in Southern Africa (excluding Malawi and Zambia), partly because of climatic conditions. It exceeds 20 deaths per 1,000 live births in Angola (21), Nigeria (24), Guinea and Sierra Leone (27), Chad (28), and the Central African Republic (35).

The second-most important disease holding back Africa's life expectancy is HIV/AIDS. In 2012, 1.1 million people in the region died of AIDS—almost four times as many as in the rest of world combined (about 300,000). The continent's HIV prevalence rate peaked at 5.8 percent in 2002, declining to 4.5 percent in 2013 (World Development Indicators).

Southern Africa has been especially hard hit by HIV/AIDS. At least 10 percent of 15- to 49-year-olds there are HIV-positive (10.3 percent in Malawi, 10.8 in Mozambique,

19.1 in South Africa, 21.9 percent in Botswana, 22.9 percent in Lesotho, and 27.4 percent in Swaziland). Prevalence rates of 5–7 percent are observed in East Africa (Kenya, Tanzania, and Uganda) (map 3.1). Despite substantial progress and the increased availability of better treatment options, HIV/AIDs will continue to hold back life expectancy in a number of countries, especially in Southern but also in East Africa.

Nutrition. A healthy life is also reflected in good nutritional status, commonly measured by assessing height and weight. For adults the body mass index (BMI)—the ratio of weight to height—is often used. Very low BMIs are indicative of undernourishment; high BMI is how obesity is often defined. Systematic BMI measures are not available for men. Among women in Africa, 13 percent are underweight and 5 percent are obese (population-weighted averages from Demographic and Health Surveys 2006–12).

Underweight is less common in middle-income countries and more prevalent in

MAP 3.1 HIV prevalence remains very high in Southern Africa

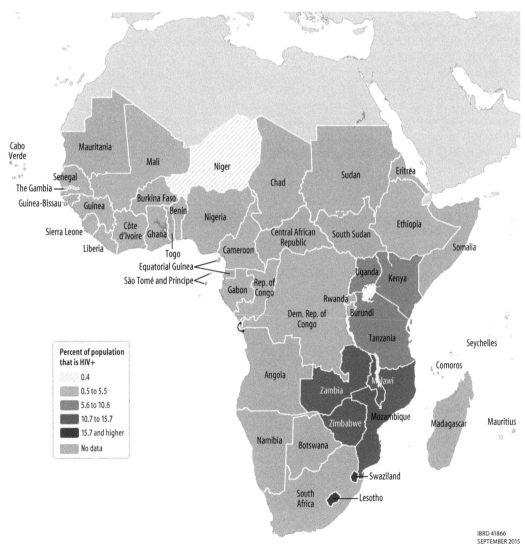

IBRD 41866
SEPTEMBER 2015

Source: DHS Statcompiler from latest Demographic and Health Surveys.

fragile states and, especially, resource-rich countries (where it is 3.7 percentage points higher than for non-resource-rich countries) (figure 3.10). This finding holds even after controlling for other country and household features, suggesting that policy choices underpin this poor health outcome in resource-rich countries. Malnutrition is more prevalent among poor households (by 3.2 percentage points) and in rural areas (by 1.6 percentage points). It declines with education. Widows, divorcées, and single women are at significantly greater risk than married women of being undernourished (by 2.7 percentage points). The role of marital status in women's health capabilities is an underappreciated aspect of well-being in Africa and highlights the importance of indicators of individual well-being (van de Walle and Milazzo 2015).

Trends in obesity suggest that poor nutritional habits are accompanying rising incomes. The condition is most prevalent among highly-educated women, women in urban settings, and women in middle-income countries. Based on an extrapolation of the data shown in figure 3.10, the total number of obese adults in Africa (both men and women) is estimated at 26.7 million. The figure is likely to reach epidemic proportions in the near future, presenting Africa with a new health challenge (Popkin 2001; Ziraba, Fotso, and Ochako 2009).

The long-run nutritional status of young children, often measured by low height-for-age (stunting) provides an important additional indicator of a population's capability of living a long and healthy life as well as an outlook on the future.[7] Chronically malnourished children face a higher risk of mortality and disease. Early growth retardation also impedes cognitive development and schooling achievements (Dercon and Portner 2014).

The prevalence of stunting has been declining across Africa. It fell from 44.6 percent in 1995 to 38.6 percent in 2012 (DHS 2015). Unlike in Asia, where there is a strong cultural preference for boys, who are therefore better fed, in Africa boys under five are

more malnourished than girls (39.5 percent compared with 35.2 percent). This difference largely reflects biological differences in health and survival between boys and girls (Kraemer 2000; Waldron 1983). If this biological disadvantage is not offset by cultural preferences for boys (as in Asia), higher malnutrition rates among boys result (Wamani and others 2007).

The prevalence of stunting is high in Burundi (57 percent), Madagascar (50 percent), and Africa's most populous countries—Nigeria (37 percent), Ethiopia (44 percent), and the Democratic Republic of Congo (42 percent). Only two countries (Gabon and Senegal) register rates under 20 percent. The overall level of development of a country matters for child nutrition, though other factors are likely even more important (Harttgen, Klasen, and Vollmer 2013). Children born to educated women enjoy chances of proper growth development that are 9.9 percentage points higher (for secondary education) and 19.8 percentage points higher (for higher education). Children in poor, rural households with undernourished mothers are 20 percent more likely to be stunted. Everything else equal, being born in a fragile or resource-rich country also reduces one's chances of proper early childhood growth. A continued focus on increasing education among women will have dramatic and long-lasting effects on Africa's human capabilities.

Physical impairment and disability also deprive people of opportunities (capabilities) and the ability to do and be what they value (their functionings) (Mitra 2006). As a group, the disabled are typically either undersampled or poorly identified in representative surveys and as a result often understudied. From a sample of seven countries across Africa on which comparable data are available, it appears that almost 1 working-age adult in 10 in Africa suffers from a disability, defined as reporting severe difficulties in moving about, concentrating, remembering, seeing or recognizing people across the road (while wearing glasses), or taking care of themselves (figure 3.11). The prevalence of disability ranges from 5.3 percent in Kenya

FIGURE 3.10   **Many factors contribute to underweight and obesity in African women**

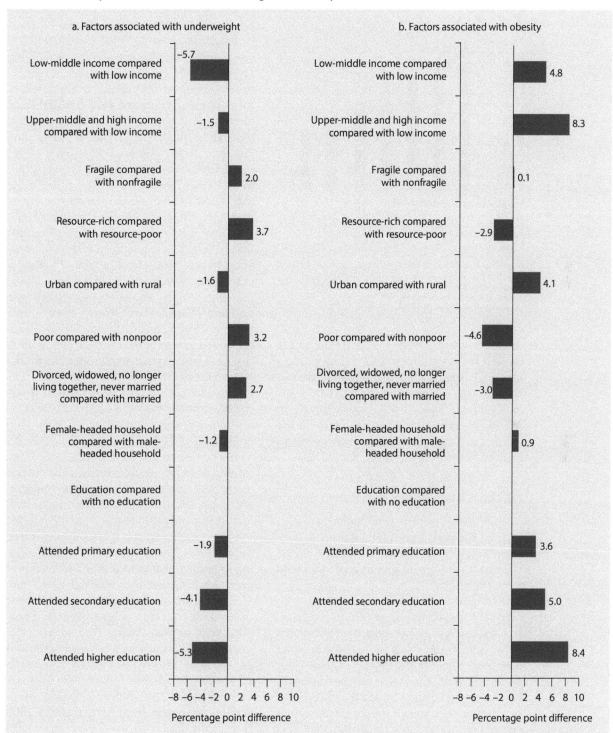

a. Factors associated with underweight

Low-middle income compared with low income	−5.7
Upper-middle and high income compared with low income	−1.5
Fragile compared with nonfragile	2.0
Resource-rich compared with resource-poor	3.7
Urban compared with rural	−1.6
Poor compared with nonpoor	3.2
Divorced, widowed, no longer living together, never married compared with married	2.7
Female-headed household compared with male-headed household	−1.2
Education compared with no education	
Attended primary education	−1.9
Attended secondary education	−4.1
Attended higher education	−5.3

Percentage point difference

b. Factors associated with obesity

Low-middle income compared with low income	4.8
Upper-middle and high income compared with low income	8.3
Fragile compared with nonfragile	0.1
Resource-rich compared with resource-poor	−2.9
Urban compared with rural	4.1
Poor compared with nonpoor	−4.6
Divorced, widowed, no longer living together, never married compared with married	−3.0
Female-headed household compared with male-headed household	0.9
Education compared with no education	
Attended primary education	3.6
Attended secondary education	5.0
Attended higher education	8.4

Percentage point difference

Source: Data from Demographic and Health Surveys 2005–13.
Note: Results are from ordinary least squares regression of an indicator variable of an adult woman being underweight (1 if the body mass index is less than 18.5, 0 otherwise) or overweight (1 if the body mass index is more than 30, 0 otherwise). Sample includes nonpregnant women who did not give birth in the three months before the interview. All estimated coefficients (except on Fragile) are statistically significant.

FIGURE 3.11   **About 1 in 10 Africans suffers from a disability**

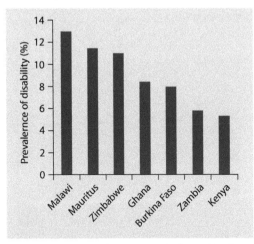

Source: Mitra, Posärac, and Vick 2013, based on data from World Health Surveys.
Note: Disability is defined as having severe difficulty moving about, concentrating, remembering, seeing or recognizing people across the road (while wearing glasses), or taking care of oneself.

to 13.0 percent in Malawi. The numbers are higher among women (10.6 percent) than men (7.3 percent). They are also higher in rural areas (9.9 percent) than urban areas (6.9 percent). Disability prevalence rates in Africa are similar to the average rates in the Asian and Latin American countries examined by Mitra, Posärac, and Vick (2013).

Freedom from Violence

The ability to live free from violence affects people's survival, dignity, and daily life. Insecurity significantly reduces the choices a person can make regarding what to do and who to be (capabilities).

Afrobarometer data from 2010–12 indicate that insecurity is pervasive in Africa. In these surveys, 12 percent of respondents indicate that either they or a family member had been physically attacked at least once during the past year. Fifty-three percent indicated that they feared political intimidation or violence at least once during election campaigns; 40 percent indicated that they or a family member had felt unsafe at least once while walking in the neighborhood during

the past year; and 33 percent report that they or a family member had feared crime in their home at least once in the past year.

Freedom from political violence. After years of multiple large-scale conflicts in the 1990s, Africa enjoyed a period of relative peace during the first decade of the 21st century (map 3.2). Between 1997 and 2014, the number of violent events against civilians more than quadrupled, reaching more than 4,000 in 2014. The number of victims per event declined (from 20 during the late 1990s to 4 in 2014), however, reflecting the changing nature of the events. The more conventional conflicts and civil wars of the 1990s (in Angola, Liberia, Mozambique, Rwanda, and Sierra Leone) have receded in scale and intensity, but election-related violence, extremism, terror attacks, drug trafficking, maritime piracy, and criminality have been growing. Wars are increasingly being fought by armed insurgents on the periphery of factionalized and militarily weak states, such as the Arab and Tuareg uprisings in Mali and Boko Haram in Nigeria. West Africa has emerged as a key transit point in the trafficking of narcotics between Latin America and Europe, and piracy has expanded in the Gulf of Guinea.

In addition to undermining the basic functioning of being secure, conflict also affects many of the other functionings and opportunities that are critical to self-determination. It affects not only the people directly affected but also the broader population inside and outside the country (by, for example, creating internally displaced persons and refugees [box 3.3]). Countries suffering more than 100 casualties in a year experience a decline in economic growth of 2.3 percent. These effects can be long-lasting. Annual economic growth in Burundi has hovered around 4 percent since the civil war ended in the early 2000s. But panel data indicate that the share of households that reported being (monetarily) poor rose from 21 percent in 1993 (before the civil war) to 46 percent in 1998 (during civil war) and 64 percent in 2007 (several years after the end of the civil war)

MAP 3.2 **The number of violent events against civilians is increasing, especially in Central Africa and the Horn**

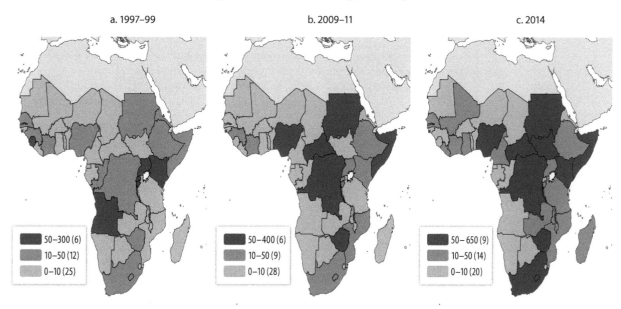

a. 1997–99   b. 2009–11   c. 2014

Source: Armed Conflict Location and Events Dataset (ACLED); Raleigh and others 2010.
Note: Maps indicate annual number of violent events against civilians; numbers in parentheses indicate number of countries. No data are available for Cabo Verde, Comoros, Mauritius, São Tomé and Príncipe, and Seychelles.

(Institute of Statistics and Economic Studies 2009). Conflict has also held back progress toward reducing under-five mortality and increasing life expectancy (figure 3.12).

Freedom from domestic violence. Physical and sexual violence (and the threat of such violence) at home are negatively associated with health outcomes, empowerment, employment trajectories, and the ability to engage in productive activities (Campbell 2002; Coker, Smith, and Fadden 2005; Duflo 2012; MacQuarrie, Winter, and Kishor 2013; Nyamayemombe and others 2010; Stöckl, Heise, and Watts 2012; Vyas 2013; Wayack, Gnoumou, and Kaboré 2013). The effects also extend well beyond the direct victims. Children's health and educational achievements are impeded, and social norms that condone violence perpetuate it (Rico and others 2011). A child whose mother experienced domestic violence is more likely to become a victim or a perpetrator of such violence later in life (Kishor and Johnson 2004). The incidence of and attitudes toward

domestic violence may also reflect broader social norms toward violence and gender roles.

Domestic violence affects more than 700 million women across the world. Africa and South Asia have the largest shares of women in partnerships who have been victims of domestic violence—an astounding 40 percent in Africa and 43 percent in South Asia (World Bank 2014). North America has the lowest share (21 percent).

Acceptance of domestic violence is measured by attitudes reported by women toward domestic violence. Women are considered accepting of domestic violence if they respond that husbands are justified in beating their wives if the wives do any of the following: go out without telling the husband, neglect the children, argue with the husband, refuse to have sex, or overcook food. Between 2000–06 and 2007–13, acceptance of domestic violence by women in Africa declined by almost 10 percentage points (figure 3.13); the incidence of domestic violence, which is

BOX 3.3   What happens to Africans who flee their homes?

Africa's refugee population peaked at about 6.5 million people in 1994 following the Rwandan genocide. It declined to 3.5 million in the late 1990s and 2.8 million in 2008, following the end of the genocide and the decline in large-scale conflicts in Southern and West Africa. The number of refugees increased again in 2010–13, to 3.7 million. Adding the estimated 12.5 million internally displaced persons (IDPs) brings the total number of African people displaced by conflict to about 16.2 million at the end of 2013, or about 2 percent of the total population. (Estimates of the number of refugees are from the United Nations High Commissioner for Refugees; estimates of the number of IDPs are from the International Displacement Monitoring Centre [see Maystadt and Verwimp 2015 for a discussion].)

The Greater Horn of Africa and Central Africa (especially the Democratic Republic of Congo) have been major sources of refugees. In some countries (Somalia, South Sudan, and Sudan), refugees have fled in the wake of extreme weather shocks and not only due to conflict (Calderone, Headey, and Maystadt 2014; Gambino 2011; Maystadt and Ecker 2014; O'Loughlin and others 2012).

Most African refugees remain in Africa. Since 2005 the region has also been receiving a large inflow of refugees from North Africa and, since 2013, Iraq, Syria, and Yemen, bringing the total number of refugees in Africa to 5.6 million.

Socioeconomic data on refugees and IDPs during or immediately after conflicts are scant. A recent study tracking the welfare of people displaced during the 2012 crisis in northern Mali sheds some light on the consequences (Etang-Ndip, Hoogeveen, and Lendorfer 2015). Welfare losses were substantial: the value of durable assets fell by 20–60 percent, and the value of livestock declined by 75–90 percent. But loss of welfare and wealth is only part of the story. In June 2014, 52 percent of the IDPs in Bamako felt insecure on the street at night, and 30 percent felt insecure during the day. The share rose to 85 percent among returnees in Gao and Kidal.

Fourteen percent of IDPs, 4 percent of returnees, and 1 percent of refugees reported that they had experienced death or physical violence within their household. Overall, better-educated and wealthier households managed to flee the conflict area; poorer people had to stay behind. Among people who returned by 2014, mainly IDPs, escape seemed to have helped them mitigate the effects of violence. They suffered less than the average population of northern Mali. But many people also responded to the crisis by leaving the country, and refugee situations often become protracted, extending the suffering (Kreibaum 2014).

Over the past decade there has been an expansion of microhousehold studies examining the evolution of well-being among refugees, host communities, and returnees. These studies show refugees also as economically active people who often engage in entrepreneurship; they are not always worse off than nonrefugees or the hosting communities, partly because of the support received. Singh and others (2005) find, for example, no difference in under-five mortality rates between refugee and nonrefugee households in western Uganda and South Sudan. In contrast, Verwimp and Van Bavel (2005) find higher under-five mortality rates and fertility among (former) Rwandan refugees in the Democratic Republic of Congo. Verwimp and Van Bavel (2013) report a reduction in schooling among Burundi children associated with displacement that is distinct from the effects of exposure to violence.

Insights from three country case studies (of Kenya, Tanzania, and Uganda) suggest that the local economy often benefits from the influx of refugees, through increased demand for local goods and services and better connectivity following investment in new roads and transport services to reach the camps (Maystadt and Verwimp 2015). But not everyone benefits. The landless and agricultural workers, whom refugees may compete with on the labor market, and net food buyers suffer, at least in the short run.

correlated with acceptance, also fell. Acceptance of domestic violence in the region is still exceptionally high, however (30 percent), more than twice the average in the rest of the developing world (14 percent) (figure 3.14).

Both the levels of and changes in acceptance of violence vary widely across countries. Women's acceptance of domestic violence is deeply engrained in some countries (77 percent acceptance rates in Mali and Uganda); in

FIGURE 3.12   **Conflict slows progress in reducing under-five mortality and increasing life expectancy in Africa**

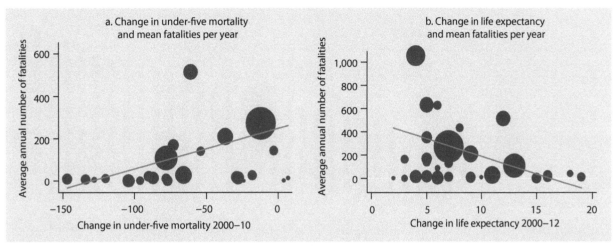

Source: Data from the Armed Conflict Location and Events Dataset (ACLED) and World Development Indicators.
Note: Results are population weighted (the size of each dot represents the population). Fatalities are measured for 2000–10. Under-five mortality is taken from the last Demographic and Health Survey (DHS) in the 20th century in a country (up to 2004 if no earlier survey available) and the last DHS survey in the first decade of the 21st century (up to 2013 if no earlier survey available).

FIGURE 3.13   **The incidence and acceptance of domestic violence in Africa has declined**

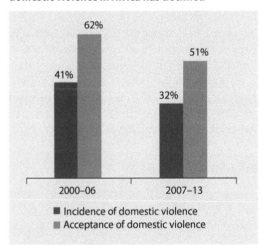

Sources: Demographic and Health Surveys 2000–13; World Development Indicators.
Note: Figures are population-weighted averages of ever-partnered women in 20 African countries.

FIGURE 3.14   **Acceptance of domestic violence is twice as high in Africa as in other developing countries**

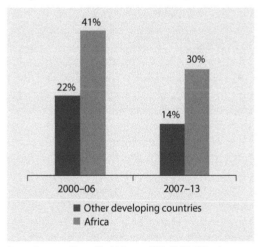

Sources: Demographic and Health Surveys 2000–13; World Development Indicators.
Note: Figures are population-weighted averages of 32 African and 28 non-African developing countries.

others, only small minorities accept domestic violence (13 percent in Malawi, 16 percent in Benin) (figure 3.15). Declining acceptance does not always translate into declining incidence, however. In Malawi, for example, while acceptance decreased 13 percentage points, incidence rose almost 1 percentage point. In Mali incidence increased 8 percent, but there was no change in acceptance rates.

Acceptance of domestic violence is much greater among women in resource-rich (16 percent) and fragile (9 percent) countries (controlling for other country traits) (figure 3.16). Surprisingly, tolerance of violence

FIGURE 3.15   **Women's acceptance of domestic violence varies widely across countries in Africa**

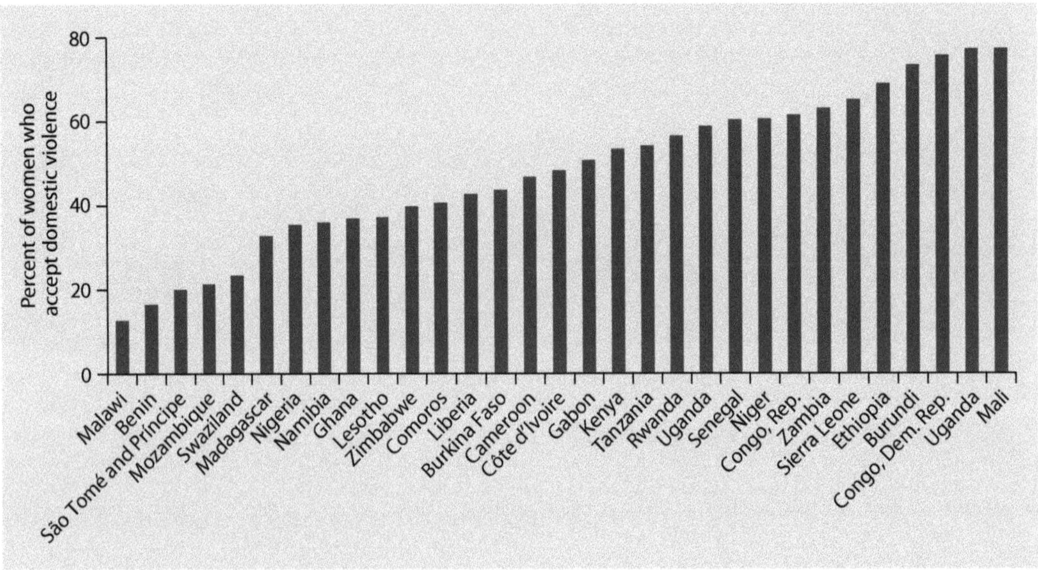

Source: Data from Demographic and Health Surveys 2007–13.

is also greater among younger women; it declines with age, possibly because its incidence rises (domestic violence is more common in the 20–35 age group than among the 15–19 age group). Tolerance of violence fell by 1.7 percent a year between 2000 and 2013 and the incidence of violence fell by 0.6 percent, but no broad generational shift in mindset has yet occurred.

A main distinguishing factor in acceptance is education. Better-educated women are 31 percent less likely to be tolerant of domestic violence than women with no education, and women with secondary education are 16 percent less likely to be tolerant. Education is not associated with a lower incidence of domestic violence, however. In fact, women with primary and secondary education are more than 10 percent more likely to have experienced domestic violence than uneducated women, among whom incidence rates are similar to rates among women with higher education.

Income reduces tolerance of domestic violence, especially in upper-middle-income and high-income countries and the richest segments within countries. Women in the richest quintile are 7.1 percent less likely than women in the poorest quintile to be tolerant of domestic violence. The incidence of domestic violence is just 3.9 percent lower, however. Africa's upper-middle-income and high-income countries have higher rates of domestic violence (despite lower acceptance rates) than poorer countries. After controlling for age, educational attainment, and income, there is no discernable difference between rural and urban areas.

Freedom to Decide

The second critical dimension of the capability approach is the ability to shape one's life—that is, to determine what one values. This dimension concerns opportunities. A woman who cannot leave her house without her husband's permission or who has no say about her own health is not free to determine her choices in life. Homosexuals who are afraid of revealing their sexual orientation for fear of persecution are constrained in their life choices.

People gain access to a broader set of opportunities if they can participate in the processes that affect their lives and are allowed to make their own choices. These choices are often politically and socially constrained.

FIGURE 3.16 **Acceptance and incidence of domestic violence are greater among younger women and women in resource-rich and fragile states; acceptance is also higher among uneducated women, but not incidence**

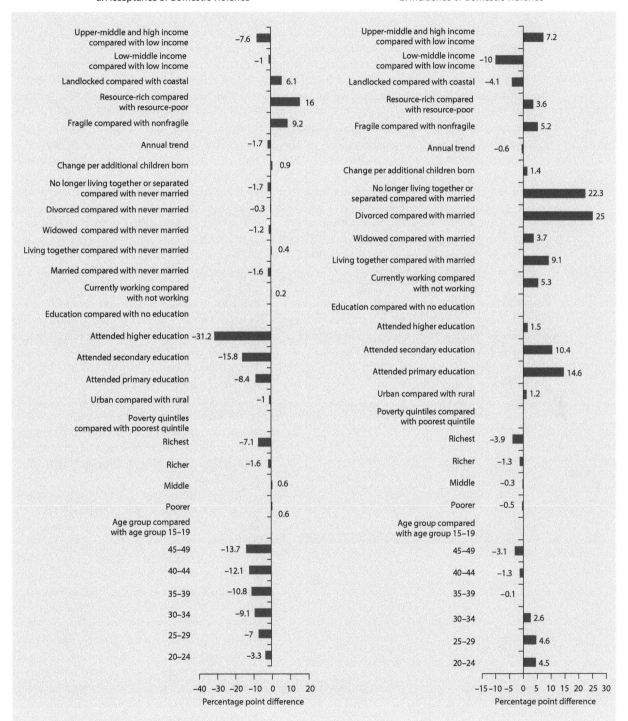

a. Acceptance of domestic violence

Upper-middle and high income compared with low income	−7.6
Low-middle income compared with low income	−1
Landlocked compared with coastal	6.1
Resource-rich compared with resource-poor	16
Fragile compared with nonfragile	9.2
Annual trend	−1.7
Change per additional children born	0.9
No longer living together or separated compared with never married	−1.7
Divorced compared with never married	−0.3
Widowed compared with never married	−1.2
Living together compared with never married	0.4
Married compared with never married	−1.6
Currently working compared with not working	0.2
Education compared with no education	
Attended higher education	−31.2
Attended secondary education	−15.8
Attended primary education	−8.4
Urban compared with rural	−1
Poverty quintiles compared with poorest quintile	
Richest	−7.1
Richer	−1.6
Middle	0.6
Poorer	0.6
Age group compared with age group 15–19	
45–49	−13.7
40–44	−12.1
35–39	−10.8
30–34	−9.1
25–29	−7
20–24	−3.3

Percentage point difference (−40 −30 −20 −10 0 10 20)

b. Incidence of domestic violence

Upper-middle and high income compared with low income	7.2
Low-middle income compared with low income	−10
Landlocked compared with coastal	−4.1
Resource-rich compared with resource-poor	3.6
Fragile compared with nonfragile	5.2
Annual trend	−0.6
Change per additional children born	1.4
No longer living together or separated compared with married	22.3
Divorced compared with married	25
Widowed compared with married	3.7
Living together compared with married	9.1
Currently working compared with not working	5.3
Education compared with no education	
Attended higher education	1.5
Attended secondary education	10.4
Attended primary education	14.6
Urban compared with rural	1.2
Poverty quintiles compared with poorest quintile	
Richest	−3.9
Richer	−1.3
Middle	−0.3
Poorer	−0.5
Age group compared with age group 15–19	
45–49	−3.1
40–44	−1.3
35–39	−0.1
30–34	2.6
25–29	4.6
20–24	4.5

Percentage point difference (−15 −10 −5 0 5 10 15 20 25 30)

Source: Data from Demographic and Health Surveys 2000–13.
Note: Results are from ordinary least squares regressions. All estimated coefficients are statistically significant except coefficients on divorced in acceptance of domestic violence and age 35–39 and poorer and middle-income quintiles in incidence of domestic violence.

This dimension is not so much about democracy per se but about the degree to which political systems give people voice and participation in the processes that affect their lives at all levels of society. It is about not only political freedom and participation but also social norms and the freedom to decide about routine matters in life, including within the household. Constraints can be based on gender, religion, ethnicity, sexual orientation, or other reasons.

Indicators that measure freedom to decide are often not available, particularly at the individual level. We draw on three measures: a country-level measure of voice and accountability, as a broad indicator of enabling the expression of voice; exposure to mass media, as an indicator of access to information to inform decisions; and the extent to which women have control over decision making in various domains of living.

The Worldwide Governance Indicators (WGI) project scores countries in terms of voice and accountability. It captures perceptions of the extent to which a country's population is able to participate in selecting the government and enjoy freedom of expression, freedom of association, and a free media.

WGI scores range from –2.5 to 2.5 units in a normal standard distribution.

The WGI data indicate that perceptions of political constraints have not changed much worldwide in the past few years, although there was a slight improvement in Africa, albeit from low levels (figure 3.17). The region is doing better than the Middle East and North Africa and East Asia and Pacific.

Improvements have been especially noteworthy in West Africa (Burkina Faso, Ghana, Liberia, Niger, and Nigeria) (figure 3.18). Countries that experienced a large decline in their voice and accountability scores include the Central African Republic, Eritrea, Gabon, and Madagascar. The results for country groupings are consistent with the findings about education, health, and violence. Countries that are resource rich or fragile are less well off than countries that are not (by –0.5 units each), and upper-middle-income and high-income countries score 0.6 points higher than low-income countries, controlling for other country traits. The WGI findings are highly correlated with the findings of the Afrobarometer.[8] There is no systematic difference in perceptions of political freedoms by gender and area of residence (rural or urban).

The second measure of freedom to decide reflects the ability to make informed decisions. Access to media provides an important source of information, and educational attainment helps people digest the information and act on it.

Almost 40 percent of Africans do not regularly listen to the radio, watch television, or read a newspaper at least once a week (figure 3.19). Exposure to the media is lower in Africa than in the rest of the developing world (excluding China), where only 25 percent of the population lacks regular media exposure. African countries with high media exposure (more than 80 percent of the population exposed) include Gabon, Ghana, and Kenya. Media exposure is typically lower around the Sahel, in many of the coastal countries of West Africa, and in Africa's populous countries (the Democratic Republic of Congo and Ethiopia), where only about 40 percent of the population have regular access to the media. There is also an important gender gap. On

FIGURE 3.17 **Voice and accountability levels remain low in Africa**

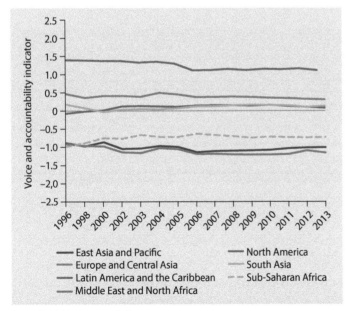

Source: Worldwide Governance Indicators.

FIGURE 3.18 **Voice and accountability are stronger in middle-income countries, and often lower in resource-rich economies**

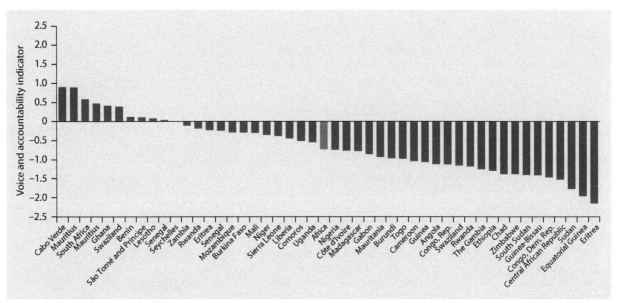

Source: Worldwide Governance Indicators 2013. Africa average is population-weighted.

FIGURE 3.19 **Less than half of Africa's population has regular access to mass media**

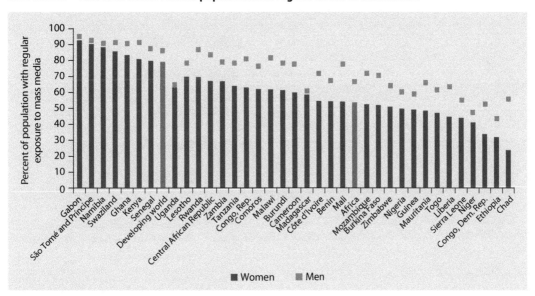

Source: Latest available Demographic and Health Surveys 1994–2013.
Note: Exposure to mass media means a person listened to the radio, watched TV, or read the newspaper at least once a week. Developing world excludes Africa and is population-weighted. Africa average is population-weighted.

average media access is 15 percentage points lower among women than men (54 percent versus 69 percent). Poverty, rural residence, and lack of education are key differentiators. Media access is also 6 percent lower in resource-rich countries and 5 percent lower

in fragile states. Increased use of cellphones can partly substitute for traditional media (Aker and Mbiti 2010).

The third set of indicators of freedom to decide are measures of decision making in the lives of women from household surveys.

FIGURE 3.20 **Women's participation in their own health care decisions is lower among younger women, women in poor and rural households, and women in resource-rich and landlocked countries**

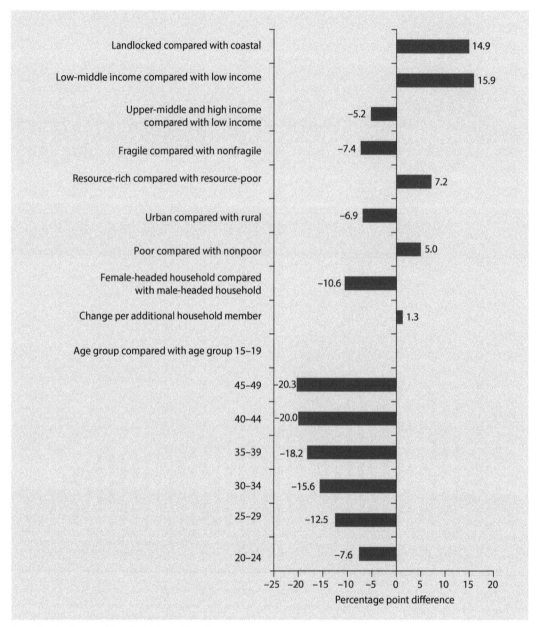

Source: Data from Demographic and Health Surveys 2005–13.
Note: Results are from ordinary least squares regression. All estimated coefficients are statistically significant.

The share of husbands who have the final say in decisions regarding their wives' health care is 21 percent in the Middle East and North Africa, 39 percent in South Asia, and 46 percent in Africa. Women's participation in their own health care decisions tends to be lower among younger women, women in poor and rural households, and women in resource-rich and landlocked countries (figure 3.20). It is greater in fragile states. That such participation increases with age is consistent with the trends in women's attitudes toward domestic violence.

The final decision on whether a married woman can visit friends or family lies with the husband alone in 40 percent of African households, compared with 33 percent in the rest of the developing world. Control over a women's earnings lies fully with someone else in only 10 percent of households. Overall, the general trend in Africa is toward greater participation of women in household decision-making processes.

Multiple Deprivation

Thus far this chapter has examined the region's well-being by assessing progress on each functioning and capability separately. Using a dashboard approach (listing achievements by dimension) instead of aggregating the measures into an index avoids having to assign weights to different dimensions.[9] It also allows researchers to draw on different datasets. It does not require a measure of several dimensions of poverty (for the same individual or household) simultaneously. From a practical perspective, policies typically aim to address shortcomings in a particular dimension (education, health care, the incidence of violence). The gains from combining scores across dimensions to obtain a complete ranking may be limited.

These advantages come at the expense of being able to assess the extent to which people suffer multiple deprivations. People suffering in different dimensions are arguably worse off than people suffering in one dimension. Omission of valuable dimensions underestimates their poverty, especially when dimensions are poorly correlated (that is, when they are poor substitutes or poor complements).[10] In addition, the deprivation associated with simultaneous deprivation in two dimensions may well be worse than twice the deprivation associated with each of them. As a result, country rankings may differ when simultaneity in deprivations is considered. Consider, for example, two countries with 20 people.

In Country A, 10 people are illiterate and the other 10 are in poor health. In Country B, 10 people are both illiterate and in poor health and the other 10 are literate and healthy. Under the dashboard approach, which considers poverty dimension by dimension, both countries are equally poor (10 people are deprived in each dimension). But because the deprivation associated with simultaneous deprivation in two dimensions may be worse than the sum of the deprivations associated with each of them, the case could be made that B is poorer. The dashboard approach ignores jointness in deprivation.

Important insights regarding the degree of interdependency can be obtained by counting the number of dimensions in which an individual is deprived and calculating the shares of the population deprived in a given number of dimensions (Ferreira and Lugo 2013). This counting approach does not require that weights be imposed on dimensions or that the degree to which deprivations are substitutable be determined (Atkinson 2003). This approach is akin to the MPI proposed by Alkire and Foster (2011), but it does not impose a number of deprivations to qualify as poor. By capturing the essence of the interest in multidimensional poverty, it provides a middle ground between the dashboard approach (Ravallion 2011), which ignores jointness in deprivation, and the scalar MPI, which assigns a minimum number of deprivations for a person to qualify as poor (Alkire and Foster 2011; Decancq and Lugo 2013).

Measuring multidimensional deprivation requires information on each dimension for the same individual. To look at Africa wide patterns, such information is available only for women of reproductive age from 25 countries covered in the DHS. Proxy indicators for the four dimensions are used (box 3.4). Considering each dimension separately (as in the dashboard approach), about one adult woman in two is illiterate (56 percent), exposed to violence (54 percent), or insufficiently empowered (51 percent), and about one in seven (14 percent) is undernourished. For the four dimensions considered here, the

BOX 3.4   Demographic and Health Surveys make it possible to measure multidimensional poverty

To measure deprivation in multiple dimensions, we use data from the Demographic and Health Surveys (DHS) on 25 countries, covering 72 percent of the population of Africa. We focus on the four areas of deprivation discussed earlier. Illiteracy is defined as being unable to read a full sentence, being blind, or having no reading card for the required language. More than half (56 percent) of women in the sample countries are illiterate.

Women are classified as deprived in health if they are undernourished (BMI below 18.5). There is no direct information on life expectancy. The correlation coefficient between country life expectancy and the proportion of undernourished women is 0.3.

Women's attitudes toward domestic violence are used as an indicator of physical security. Across countries, social norms toward domestic violence and the incidence of casualties from political violence are correlated (the correlation coefficient is 0.4).

Freedom to decide is measured by an indicator capturing lack of frequent media exposure (not using at least one media channel [newspaper, television, radio] at least once a week) or not being involved in decisions regarding own health care, family visits, or spending. Both indicators are correlated with the Worldwide Governance Indicator of voice and accountability (correlation coefficient is 0.4).

For comparison, we augment these dimensions by adding a fifth aspect: asset poverty. We use the DHS asset index to classify women as asset poor or nonpoor (Christiaensen and Stifel 2007; Filmer and Scott 2012; Sahn and Stifel 2000 establish correlations with consumption). Country cutoffs are defined based on the share of the population living below $1.90 for the corresponding survey year. The correlation of this indicator with the other dimensions is 0.33, underscoring the fact that asset wealth does not capture deprivation in many basic functionings and capabilities.

average woman suffers 1.75 deprivations (56 + 54 + 51 + 14 = 175/100).

Does everyone suffer equally, or is deprivation concentrated among a subset of the population? Under a perfectly equal distribution of deprivations, everyone would be deprived in 1.75 dimensions. Under perfect concentration (or full inequality), all deprivations would be concentrated within a single group: 43.7 percent (175/4) of the population would suffer in each of these four dimensions, while the remaining 56.3 percent would be deprivation free. The larger the share of people suffering in three or more dimensions, the more concentrated is the deprivation.

Deprivation among African women is widespread: more than four women in five (86 percent) are deprived in at least one dimension; only 14 percent are free of deprivation (figure 3.21). Multiple deprivation characterizes a sizable group of women: almost one woman in three is poor in three or four dimensions; 55 percent suffer in one or two dimensions. Deprivation is widespread, but for a sizable group it is also highly concentrated: about one-third of women realize only one functioning or none at all.

Multiple deprivations and the concentration of deprivation are more common among women with less wealth: 42 percent of asset-poor women versus 18 percent of non-asset-poor women are deprived in at least three

FIGURE 3.21   **A large share of African women suffers from multiple deprivations**

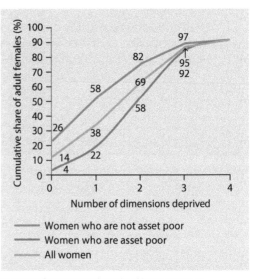

Source: Data from Demographic and Health Surveys 2005–13.

dimensions. But three out of four non-asset-poor women suffer at least one deprivation, confirming that income poverty provides only a partial picture of a population's well-being.

Multiple deprivation is more prevalent among younger women: women 35–49 experience on average half the deprivation of women 15–19 (figure 3.22). After controlling for education and illiteracy, tolerance for domestic violence and social control over one's actions tend to decline with age. This evidence suggests that there is a positive dynamic as life progresses, but it is also

FIGURE 3.22 **Multidimensional poverty is more prevalent among young women, divorced women, poor women, rural women, and women living in low-income, fragile, and resource-rich countries**

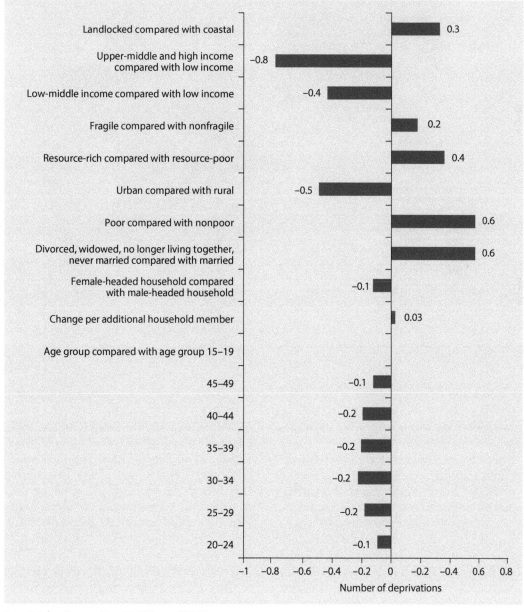

Source: Data from Demographic and Health Surveys 2005–13.
Note: Results are from ordinary least squares regression on the number of deprivations out of a total of four deprivations. All estimated coefficients except the annual trend are statistically significant.

MAP 3.3 **Multiple deprivation is substantial in the Western Sahel and Africa's populous countries**

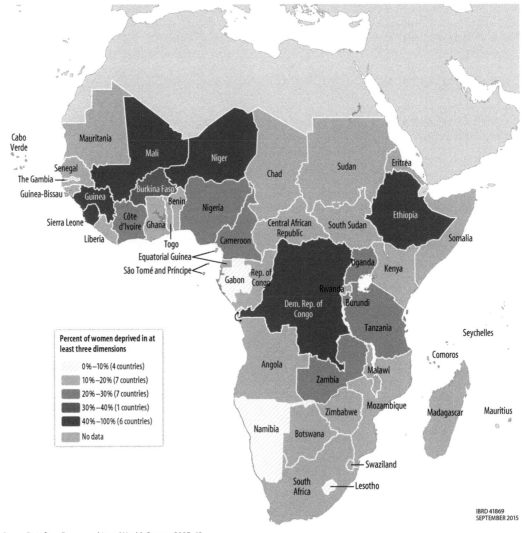

Source: Data from Demographic and Health Surveys 2005–13.

indicative of the strong persistence of cultural habits across generations.

Poor women experience 0.6 more deprivations than rich women, and rural women suffer 0.5 more deprivations than urban women, holding other factors constant. As these women also have lower levels of education and poverty is more prevalent in rural areas, the unadjusted gaps are much larger. Multiple deprivations are also more common in low-income, fragile, and resource-rich states. Multiple deprivation is 10 percent higher in resource-rich countries. Countries

in West Africa and the Sahel (Guinea, Mali, Niger) display high levels of multiple deprivation, as do Africa's most populous countries (map 3.3): the share of women suffering three or more deprivations is 68 percent in Ethiopia, 40 percent in the Democratic Republic of Congo, and 22 percent in Nigeria. High rates of multiple deprivation in these populous countries partly explain the large share of multidimensional poverty in Africa, where 31 percent of women in the 25 countries studied are deprived in three dimensions or more.

BOX 3.5   What is the multidimensional poverty index (MPI)?

Considering the share of women deprived in one, two, three, ... k dimensions (with k the total number of dimensions considered) is similar to one of the family of multidimensional poverty measures proposed by Alkire and Foster (2011). They use two thresholds to determine whether a person is multidimensionally poor: a dimension-specific cutoff to determine whether he or she is deprived in each dimension and a dimension threshold (k) that is the number of dimensions in which a person needs to be deprived to be considered multidimensionally poor. Relative rather than equal weighting of the dimensions can be applied. The second cutoff is then a proportion (not the number) of weighted deprivations.

The multidimensional poverty rate (H) is the share of the population that is poor in at least k dimensions.

Alkire and Foster also consider the intensity of deprivations (A), the average number of dimensions in which the multidimensionally poor are deprived. Adjusting the multidimensional poverty rate (H) for deprivation intensity (A) helps differentiate countries with an equal share of multidimensionally poor. A country in which 30 percent of women have three deprivations and none has four would rank higher than a country in which 30 percent of women are multidimensionally poor but half of them suffer four deprivations. The MPI can then be written as $M = H \times A$.

The approach adopted here is similar to the MPI approach proposed by Alkire and Foster (2011) (box 3.5). To illustrate this similarity, figure 3.23 displays the share of the population in each country that is deprived in one, two, three, and four dimensions. Countries are ranked by the share of the population deprived in three or more dimensions.

In Alkire/Foster notation, figure 3.23 ranks countries based on a multidimensional poverty rate based on k of 3, with no adjustment for intensity of deprivation (A). Using the MPI, that is adjusting the results in figure 3.23 for A, does not change the ranking.

Mitra, Posärac, and Vick (2013) use this approach to compare poverty among abled

FIGURE 3.23   Country ranking changes only slightly when the dimension threshold changes

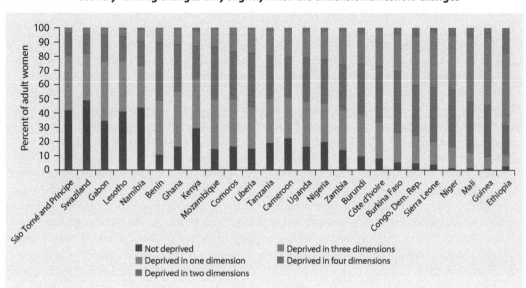

Source: Data from Demographic and Health Surveys 2005–13.
Note: Countries are ranked by the share of the female adult population deprived in at least three out of four dimensions.

and disabled populations. They include 10 dimensions capturing both monetary and nonmonetary aspects of poverty among individuals (primary school completion, employment) and households (nonhealth expenditures, the ratio of health expenditures to total expenditures, and six indicators of assets, amenities, and housing conditions). People are considered poor if the weighted sum of their deprivations in each of these dimensions exceeds 40 percent. In the seven countries in their sample, the MPI is on average 7.2 percent larger for people with disabilities. The difference is largest in Kenya (12 percent) and smallest in Malawi (5 percent).

Concluding Remarks

This chapter reviews Africa's progress since the mid-1990s in a number of nonmonetary dimensions of poverty. The dimensions include education and health, two focus areas of the Millennium Development Goals, as well as freedom from violence and freedom to decide. Wider data availability makes this possible, though some measurement issues remain, even when tracking traditional indicators, such as adult literacy. Progress has been achieved in all four domains, albeit with wide variation across countries and population groups.

Between 1996 and 2012, Africa's adult literacy rates rose 4 percentage points, the gender gap shrank, and gross primary enrollment rates increased dramatically. Life expectancy at birth rose 6.2 years, and the prevalence of chronic malnutrition among under-five-year-olds fell 6 percentage points (to 38.6 percent). The number of deaths from politically motivated violence declined, and tolerance and the incidence of gender-based domestic violence dropped 10 percentage points each. Scores on the voice and accountability indicators rose slightly, and women's participation in household decision-making processes increased.

This progress notwithstanding, levels of deprivation remain high in all domains and the rate of progress has leveled off. Despite substantial increases in school enrollments, more than two out of five adults in Africa cannot read or write, and the quality of schooling is poor. Improving Africa's primary educational outcomes is urgent. Health outcomes mirror the results for literacy. Progress is happening, but outcomes are still the worst in the world. Increases in immunization and bednet coverage are slowing. Nearly two in five African children is malnourished, one in eight adult women is underweight, and obesity is emerging as a new health concern.

Africans enjoyed considerably more peace in the 2000s than before, but since 2010 the number of violent events has been four times what it was in the mid-1990s. Violence in Africa is experienced not only in terms of political unrest and large-scale civil conflicts but also in the form of domestic violence. At 30 percent, tolerance of domestic violence is twice as high as in the rest of the developing world and the incidence of domestic violence is more than 50 percent higher. Higher tolerance of domestic violence and less empowered decision making among younger (compared with older) women suggest that a generational shift in mindset is still to come. On voice and accountability, Africa remains among the bottom performers, albeit with slightly higher scores than countries in the Middle East and North Africa and East Asia and Pacific.

Around these region-wide trends is remarkable variation across countries and population groups. Rural populations and the income poor are worse off in all domains, though other factors, such as gender and female education, often matter as much or more and at times in unexpected ways. Women in Africa can, for example, expect to live in good health 1.6 years longer than men, and boys under five years are 5 percentage points more likely to be malnourished than girls. At the same time, the gender gap in literacy remains substantial, women suffer more than men from violence (especially domestic violence), and they are more curtailed in their access to information and decision making. Literacy is especially low in West Africa, where gender disparities are large. High HIV prevalence rates are holding life expectancy back in Southern Africa. Conflict events are concentrated in the greater Horn of Africa and the Democratic Republic of Congo. The low levels of Africa's capability achievements are driven partly by below-average performance in its three most populous countries (Nigeria, the Democratic Republic of Congo, and Ethiopia). Multiple deprivations characterize life for a sizable share of African women (data on men are unavailable).

Two important findings stand out. First, fragile and resource-rich countries tend to perform worse and middle-income countries better than other countries. This finding confirms the pernicious effects of conflict and is consistent with the widely observed association with overall economic development. People in resource-rich countries experience a resource penalty in their human development outcomes. They are less literate (by 3.1 percentage points), have shorter average life spans (by 4.5 years) and higher rates of malnutrition among women (by 3.7 percentage points) and children (by 2.1 percentage points), suffer more from domestic violence (by 9 percentage points), and have less voice and accountability than people in non-resource-rich countries.[11]

Women's education (secondary schooling and above) makes a decisive difference across dimensions (health, violence, and freedom in decision), among both adults and children. Improving women's education and socioeconomic opportunities can be game changing for Africa's capability achievement.

Notes

1. UNDP (1990, page 10) describes the HDI as follows: "Human development is a process of enlarging people's choices. In principle, these choices can be infinite and change over time. But at all levels of development, the three essential ones are for people to lead a long and healthy life, to acquire knowledge and to have access to resources needed for a decent standard of living. If these essential choices are not available, many other opportunities remain inaccessible."

2. UNESCO (2015) discusses reasons for limited progress in global adult literacy since the 2000s, including the underperformance of adult literacy programs. All progress has come from better literacy among younger cohorts.

3. The gross enrollment ratio can exceed 100 percent because of the inclusion of over-age and under-age students following early or late school entrance and grade repetition.

4. Higher life expectancy for women is possible even in an environment that is disadvantageous to them, given that women are genetically predisposed to live longer (Sen 2002; World Bank 2011).

5. The results are based on a country fixed-effect regression analysis of life expectancy in 2000–12 in 39 countries on the under-five mortality rate, the HIV prevalence rate, an indicator variable taking the value of 1 if the average annual number of deaths from conflict in the five years preceding the year of recorded life expectancy exceeded 100, and GDP (in constant 2005 U.S. dollars per capita) and its square. De Walque and Filmer (2013) also find no effect of GDP on adult mortality in Africa and relatively little effect of recent conflict, unless the conflicts escalated, as in the Rwandese genocide. Elsewhere in the world GDP is negatively correlated with adult mortality.

6. The increase in funding has slowed in recent years, causing both the increase in the use of treated bednets and the decline in child mortality from malaria to level off (WHO 2013, 2014b).

7. Children are considered stunted if their height-for-age is more than two standard deviations from the median height-for-age of the reference population.

8. There is a high correlation between the WGI's voice and accountability score and the responses from 35 African countries to the Afrobarometer's "freedom to say what you think" (0.67) and "freedom to join any political organization" (0.65) questions; the correlation with "the extent of democracy" is 0.58. Because the Afrobarometer does not measure free media but only exposure to mass media, the correlation with the WGI's voice and accountability score is slightly lower.

9. The debate about defining weights is lively (see Alkire and Foster 2011 and critiques by Ravallion 2011). Some of it concerns whether deprivations should be treated as substitutes or complements (Bourguignon and Chakravarty 2003). Appropriate weights should reflect ethically or empirically grounded trade-offs among the components of deprivation (see Decancq and Lugo 2013; Ferreira and Lugo 2013); they should not be set for the sake of convenience.

10. At the country level, there is limited correlation in the population shares of people deprived in the four dimensions. The correlation coefficient is 0.22 on average (in absolute value); it ranges from 0.12 (for the correlation between the voice and accountability indicator and the illiteracy indicator) to 0.39 (for the correlation between the voice and accountability indicator and the indicator of the number of fatalities from violence). This low correlation is consistent with lack of interchangeability across functionings and capabilities (as emphasized by the capability approach). The overlap is greatest in the prevalence of $1.25 income poverty (33 percent) for asset-poverty and each of the other four dimensions, which could be seen as providing support for the welfarist (monetary poverty) approach to measuring poverty (that asset poverty is an indicator of multiple deprivation). Yet, even though the overlap is highest, the correlation remains nonetheless rather low, underscoring that income poverty remains a rather incomplete proxy for well-being and that good scores on income poverty hide deprivation in many basic functionings and capabilities.

11. De la Brière and others (2015) discuss how resource-rich countries could harness their mineral wealth to build more human capital.

References

ACLED (Armed Conflict Location and Event Data) Project. n.d. http://www.acleddata.com/about-acled/.

Afrobarometer. 2010–12. http://www.afrobarometer.org.

Aker, Jenny C., and Isaac Mbiti M. 2010. "Mobile Phones and Economic Development in Africa." *Journal of Economic Perspectives* 24 (3): 207–32.

Alkire, Sabina. 2008. "Choosing Dimensions: The Capability Approach and Multidimensional Poverty." MPRA Paper 8862, Munich Personal RePEc Archive.

Alkire, Sabina, and James Foster. 2011. "Understandings and Misunderstandings of Multidimensional Poverty Measurement." *Journal of Economic Inequality* 9 (2): 289–314.

Alkire, Sabina, and Maria Emma Santos. 2014. "Measuring Acute Poverty in the Developing World: Robustness and Scope of the Multidimensional Poverty Index." *World Development* 59: 251–74.

Atkinson, Anthony B. 2003. "Multidimensional Deprivation: Contrasting Social Welfare and Counting Approaches." *Journal of Economic Inequality* 1 (1): 51–65.

Bourguignon, François, and Satya R. Chakravarty. 2003. "The Measurement of Multidimensional Poverty." *Journal of Economic Inequality* 1 (1): 25–49.

Calderone, Margherita, Derek Headey, and Jean-François Maystadt. 2014. *Enhancing Resilience to Climate-Induced Conflict in the Horn of Africa*, vol. 12. International Food Policy Research Institute, Washington, DC.

Campbell, Jacquelyn C. 2002. "Health Consequences of Intimate Partner Violence." *Lancet* 359 (9314): 1331–36.

Chiappori, Pierre-André, and Costas Meghir. 2015. "Intrahousehold Inequality." In *Handbook of Income Distribution*, vol. 2, edited by Anthony B. Atkinson and François Bourguignon, 1369–418, Amsterdam: Elsevier.

Christiaensen, Luc, and David Stifel. 2007. "Tracking Poverty over Time in the Absence of Comparable Consumption Data." *World Bank Economic Review* 21 (2): 317–41.

Coker, Ann L., Paige H. Smith, and Mary K. Fadden. 2005. "Intimate Partner Violence and Disabilities among Women Attending Family Practice Clinics." *Journal of Women's Health* 14 (9): 829–38.

Deaton, Angus. 2008. "Income, Health and Well-Being around the World: Evidence from the Gallup World Poll." *Journal of Economic Perspective* 22 (2): 53–72.

Decancq, Koen, Marc Fleurbaey, and Erik Schokkaert. 2015. "Inequality, Income and Well-Being." In *Handbook of Income Distribution*, vol. 2, edited by Anthony B. Atkinson and François Bourguignon, 67–140, Amsterdam: Elsevier.

Decancq, Koen, and María Ana Lugo. 2013. "Weights in Multidimensional Indices of Well-Being: An Overview." *Econometric Reviews* 32 (1): 7–34.

de la Brière, Benedicte, Deon Filmer, Dena Ringold, Dominic Rohner, Karelle Samuda, and Anastasiya Denisova. 2015. *From Mines to Minds: Turning Sub-Saharan's Mineral Wealth into Human Capital.* Washington, DC: World Bank.

Dercon, Stefan, and Catherine Portner. 2014. "Live Aid Revisited: Long-Term Impacts of the 1984 Ethiopian Famine on Children." *Journal of the European Economic Association* 12 (4): 927–48.

de Walque, Damien, and Deon Filmer. 2012. "The Socioeconomic Distribution of Adult Mortality during Conflicts in Africa." *Peace Economics, Peace Science, and Public Policy* 18 (3): 1–12.

———. 2013. "Trends and Socioeconomic Gradients in Adult Mortality around the Developing World." *Population and Development Review* 39 (1): 1–29.

DHS (Demographic and Health Surveys). Various years. ICF International, Calverton, MD.

Duflo, Esther. 2012. "Women's Empowerment and Development." *Journal of Economic Literature* 50 (4): 1051–79.

Easterlin, Richard. 1974. "Does Economic Growth Improve the Human Lot? Some Empirical Evidence." In *Nations and Households in Economic Growth: Essays in Honor of Moses Abramovitz*, edited by Paul A. David and Melvin W. Reder. New York: Academic Press.

EDSTAT. Education Statistics. World Bank, Washington, DC. http://datatopics.worldbank.org/education.

Etang-Ndip, Alvin, Johannes G. M. Hoogeveen, and Julia Lendorfer. 2015. "Socioeconomic Impact of the Crisis in North Mali on Displaced People." Policy Research Working Paper 7253, World Bank, Washington, DC.

Ferreira, Francisco H. G., and María Ana Lugo. 2013. "Multidimensional Poverty Analysis: Looking for a Middle Ground." *World Bank Research Observer* 28 (2): 220–35.

Filmer, Deon, and Kinnon Scott. 2012 "Assessing Asset Indices." *Demography* 49 (1): 359–92.

Foster, James E. 2011. "Freedom, Opportunity and Well-Being." In *Handbook of Social Choice and Welfare*, vol. 2, edited by Kenneth J. Arrow, Amartya Sen, and Kotaro Suzumura, 687–728. Amsterdam: Elsevier.

Frey, Bruno S., and Alois Stutzer. 2002. "What Can Economists Learn from Happiness Research?" *Journal of Economic Literature* 40 (2): 402–35.

Gambino, Tony. 2011. "Democratic Republic of the Congo." Background paper for the *World Development Report 2011*. World Bank, Washington, DC.

Harttgen, Kenneth, Stephan Klasen, and Sebastian Vollmer. 2013. "Economic Growth and Child Undernutrition in Sub-Saharan Africa." *Population and Development Review* 39 (3): 397–412.

Hungi, Njora, Demus Makuwa, Kenneth Ross, Mioko Saito, Stephanie Dolata, Frank van Cappelle, Laura Paviot, and Jocelyne Vellein. 2010. "SACMEQ III Project Results: Pupil Achievement Levels in Reading and Mathematics." Working Document 1, Southern Africa Consortium for Measuring Educational Quality (SACMEQ), Harare, Zimbabwe. http://www.sacmeq.org/sites/default/files/sacmeq/reports/sacmeq-iii/working-documents/wd01_sacmeq_iii_results_pupil_achievement.pdf.

Institute of Statistic and Economic Studies. 2009. *Welfare and Poverty in Rural Burundi: Results of the Priority Survey, Panel 2007.* Bujumbura, Burundi.

Kishor, Sunita, and Kiersten Johnson. 2004. *Profiling Domestic Violence: A Multi-Country Study.* Calverton, MD: ORC Macro.

Kraemer, Sebastian. 2000. "The Fragile Male." *British Medical Journal* 321 (7276): 1609–12.

Kreibaum, Merle. 2014 "Their Suffering, Our Burden? How Congolese Refugees Affect the Ugandan Population." Households in Conflict Network Working Paper 181, Institute of Development Studies, University of Sussex, Brighton, UK.

Loewenstein, George, and Peter A. Ubel. 2008. "Hedonic Adaptation and the Role of Decision and Experienced Utility in Public Policy." *Journal of Public Economics* 92 (8–9): 1795–810.

MacQuarrie, Kerry L., Rebecca Winter, and Sunita Kishor. 2013. *Spousal Violence and HIV: Exploring the Linkages in Five Sub-Saharan African Countries.* DHS Analytical Study 3. Calverton, MD: ICF International.

Max-Neef, Manfred A., Antonio Elizalde, and Martin Hopenhayn. 1991. *Human Scale*

Development: Conception, Application and Further Reflections. New York: Apex Press.

Maystadt, Jean-François, and Olivier Ecker. 2014. "Extreme Weather and Civil War: Does Drought Fuel Conflict in Somalia through Livestock Price Shocks?" *American Journal of Agricultural Economics* 96 (4): 1157–82.

Maystadt, Jean-François, and Philip Verwimp. 2015. "Forced Displacement and Refugees in Sub-Saharan Africa: An Economic Inquiry." Background paper prepared for this study. World Bank, Washington, DC.

Milazzo, Annamaria, and Dominique van de Walle. 2015. "Women Left Behind? Poverty and Headship in Africa." Policy Research Working Paper 7331, World Bank, Washington, DC.

Mitra, Sophie. 2006. "The Capability Approach and Disability." *Journal of Disability Policy Studies* 16 (4): 236–47.

Mitra, Sophie, Aleksandra Posärac, and Brandon Vick. 2013. "Disability and Poverty in Developing Countries: A Multidimensional Study." *World Development* 41: 1–18.

Nyamayemombe, Caroline, C. Benedict, V. Mishra, M. Gwazane, S. Rusakaniko, and P. Mukweza. 2010. "The Association between Violence against Women and HIV: Evidence from a National Population-Based Survey in Zimbabwe." Zimbabwe Working Paper 4, ICF Macro, Calverton, MD.

O'Loughlin, John, Frank D. W. Witmer, Andrew M. Linke, Arlene Laing, Andrew Gettelman, and Jimy Dudhia. 2012. "Climate Variability and Conflict Risk in East Africa, 1990–2009." *Proceedings of the National Academy of Sciences* 109 (45): 18344–49.

Oswald, Andrew J., and Nattavudh Powdthavee. 2008. "Death, Happiness, and the Calculation of Compensatory Damages." *Journal of Legal Studies* 37: S217–S251.

PASEC (Programme d'Analyse des Systèmes Educatifs de la CONFEMEN). http://www.confemen.org/le-pasec/.

Popkin, Barry M. 2001. "The Nutrition Transition and Obesity in the Developing World." *Journal of Nutrition* 131 (3): 871S–873S.

Raleigh, Clionadh, Andrew Linke, Håvard Hegre, and Joakim Karlsen. 2010. "Introducing ACLED: Armed Conflict Location and Event Data." *Journal of Peace Research* 47 (5): 651–60.

Ravallion, Martin. 2011. "On Multidimensional Indices of Poverty." *Journal of Economic Inequality* 9 (2): 235–48.

———. 2012. "Poor, or Just Feeling Poor? On Using Subjective Data in Measuring Poverty." Policy Research Working Paper 5968, World Bank, Washington, DC.

Rico, Emily, Bridget Fenn, Tanya Abramsky, and Charlotte Watts. 2011. "Associations between Maternal Experiences of Intimate Partner Violence and Child Nutrition and Mortality: Findings from Demographic and Health Surveys in Egypt, Honduras, Kenya, Malawi and Rwanda." *Journal of Epidemiology and Community Health* 65 (4): 360–67.

Robeyns, Ingrid. 2005. "The Capability Approach: a Theoretical Survey." *Journal of Human Development* 6 (1): 93–117.

SACMEQ (Southern and Eastern Africa Consortium for Monitoring Educational Quality). 2007. United Nations Educational, Scientific and Cultural Organization (UNESCO), International Institute for Educational Planning, Paris.

Sahn, David, and David Stifel. 2000. "Poverty Comparisons over Time and across Countries in Africa." *World Development* 28 (12): 2123–55.

Sandel, Michael J. 2012. *What Money Can't Buy: The Moral Limits of Markets.* New York: Farrar, Straus and Giroux.

Sen, Amartya. 1980. "Equality of What?" In *The Tanner Lectures on Human Values,* vol. 1, edited by MacMurrin, Sterling M., 195–220, Cambridge, UK: Cambridge University Press.

———. 1985. *Commodities and Capabilities.* Amsterdam: North-Holland.

———. 1999. *Development as Freedom.* New York: Anchor Books.

———. 2002. "Why Health Equity?" *Health Economics* 11 (8): 659–66.

Singh, Kavita, Unni Karunakara, Gilbert Burnham, and Kenneth Hill. 2005. "Forced Migration and Under-Five Mortality: A Comparison of Refugees and Hosts in Northwestern Uganda and Southern Sudan." *European Journal of Population/Revue Européenne de Démographie* 21 (2–3): 247–70.

Stevenson, Betsey, and Justin Wolfers. 2008. "Economic Growth and Subjective Well-Being: Reassessing the Easterlin Paradox." *Brookings Papers on Economic Activity,* 1–87.

Stöckl, Heidi, Lori Heise, and Charlotte Watts. 2012. "Moving beyond Single Issue Priority Setting: Associations between Gender Inequality and Violence and Both HIV Infection and Poor Maternal Health in Malawi." UNAIDS, Geneva.

UNDP (United Nations Development Programme). 1990. *Human Development Report 1990*. Oxford, UK: Oxford University Press.

UNESCO (United Nations Educational, Scientific and Cultural Organization). 2015. *Education for All 2000–2015: Achievements and Challenges*. EFA Global Monitoring Report 2015. Paris.

UNHCR (United Nations High Commissioner for Refugees). 2014. *UNHCR Global Trends 2013*. Geneva.

van de Walle, Dominique, and Annamaria Milazzo. 2015. "Are Female Headed Households Poorer? New Evidence for Africa." mimeo, World Bank, Washington, DC.

Verwimp, Philip, and Jan Van Bavel. 2005. "Child Survival and Fertility of Refugees in Rwanda." *European Journal of Population/Revue Européenne de Démographie* 21 (2–3): 271–90.

———. 2013 "Schooling, Violent Conflict, and Gender in Burundi." *World Bank Economic Review* 28 (2): 384–411.

Vyas, Seema. 2013. *Estimating the Association between Women's Earnings and Partner Violence: Evidence from the 2008–2009 Tanzania National Panel Survey*. Women's Voice, Agency, & Participation Research Series 2, World Bank, Washington, DC.

Waldron, Ingrid. 1983. "Sex Differences in Human Mortality: The Role of Genetic Factors." *Social Science & Medicine* 17 (6): 321–33.

Wamani, Henry, Anne N. Åstrøm, Stefan Peterson, James K. Tumwine, and Thorkild Tylleskär. 2007. "Boys Are More Stunted than Girls in Sub-Saharan Africa: A Meta-Analysis of 16 Demographic and Health Surveys." *BMC Pediatrics* 7 (17): 1–10.

Wayack Pambè, Madeleine, Bilampoa Gnoumou, and Idrissa Kaboré. 2013. "Relationship between Women's Socioeconomic Status and Empowerment in Burkina Faso: A Focus on Participation in Decision-Making and Experience of Domestic Violence." DHS Working Paper 99, Demographic and Health Surveys and USAID.

WHO (World Health Organization). 2013. *World Malaria Report 2013*. Geneva: WHO.

———. 2014a. *Global Health Observatory 2015*. Geneva: WHO.

———. 2014b. *World Malaria Report 2014*. Geneva: WHO.

———. 2015. Global Health Observatory 2015. Geneva: WHO.

World Bank. 2011. *World Development Report 2012: Gender and Development*. Washington, DC: World Bank.

———. 2014. *Voice and Agency Report: Empowering Women and Girls for Shared Prosperity*. Washington, DC: World Bank.

World Development Indicators (database). World Bank, Washington, DC. http://data.worldbank.org/data-catalog/world-development-indicators.

Ziraba, Abdhalah K., Jean C. Fotso, and Rhoune Ochako. 2009. "Overweight and Obesity in Urban Africa: A Problem of the Rich or the Poor?" *BMC Public Health* 9 (1): 465.

Inequality in Africa | 4

Inequality in Africa is complex. Of the 10 most unequal countries in the world, 7 are in Africa. But African countries other than these seven do not have higher inequality than developing countries elsewhere in the world. For the region as a whole, however, inequality is high, because of the wide variation in income across countries. As a complement to the description of poverty, freedoms, and capabilities in the previous two chapters, this chapter profiles inequality in Africa, describing it in terms of consumption inequality (including from the perspective of extreme wealth) as well as inequality of opportunity.

An important distinction is between inequality of outcomes (such as income, consumption, and wealth) and inequality of opportunity. In the case of the latter, in many settings, circumstances over which a person has little control—mother's education, father's occupation, birth in a rural area or into a particular ethnic group—may largely dictate one's future. Being born poor often means being the beneficiary of less investment in human development, which determines future living standards.

Being born poor can also influence one's aspirations. Hoff (2012) describes how aspirations can be affected if inequality is entrenched. The expectation of having no chance of obtaining wealth or the feeling that the cards are stacked against one can yield precisely these outcomes, for example. This lack of a level playing field—the structural or ex ante component of inequality—is usually perceived to be unfair. Cultures around the world value fairness—so much that in some cases people make seemingly irrational decisions (that is, decisions that do not serve their self-interest) to punish others who behave unfairly (World Bank 2005).

Inequality in outcomes—the gap between the poorest and the richest—depends not only on opportunities but also on effort and the degree to which individuals take risks. Rewarding people for effort or risk taking can incentivize and motivate them. From this perspective, not all aspects of inequality are necessarily bad, although high levels of inequality can impose large socioeconomic costs on society.

Inequality can influence the ability of communities to coordinate and provide social services and public goods.[1] It can also induce conflict, although the empirical evidence that substantial inequality leads to conflict or is the source of most conflict is mixed (Cramer 2005; Lichbach 1989).[2]

Inequality influences how economic growth translates into poverty reduction,

---

This chapter was written with Camila Galindo-Pardo.

and it may affect growth prospects. With respect to poverty reduction, when initial inequality is higher, a larger share of poor households will have incomes farther below the poverty line, so that growth (the increase in income) will result in less poverty reduction (Bourguignon 2004; Klasen 2004; Ravallion 2001). Tentative evidence also suggests that inequality leads to lower and less durable sustainable growth processes and thus less poverty reduction (Berg, Ostry, and Zettelmeyer 2012; OECD 2015) if, for example, wealth is used to engage in rent seeking and other distortionary economic behaviors (Stiglitz 2012). The pathway by which inequality evolves thus matters for growth. Marrero and Rodriguez (2013) find a robust negative relationship between growth and inequality of opportunity in the United States. Ferreira and others (2014) find suggestive evidence of a negative association between inequality and growth but conclude that the data do not show a robust negative association between inequality of opportunity and growth. Other studies conclude that as countries reach higher levels of development, greater emphasis should be given to reducing inequality over spurring growth to reduce poverty (Olinto, Lara Ibarra, and Saavedra-Chanduvi 2014). For high-inequality, low-income countries, then, there is tension between a focus on growth and an emphasis on addressing inequality

On the basis of the growing body of literature on the effects of initial and changing inequality on growth and poverty, some observers argue that reducing inequality should be an explicit development goal (Shepherd and others 2014). For the few African countries for which there is evidence, this notion seems to resonate with policy makers. In its survey of 15 developing countries (in Africa, this included Cameroon, Malawi, Nigeria, and South Africa), the United Nations Development Programme (UNDP 2014) finds that 77 percent of policy makers perceive the current level of inequality as a threat to long-term national development. Only 10 percent consider inequality conducive to long-term development.

Perceptions of Inequality

Several survey efforts capture the perceptions and attitudes of citizens toward inequality. The picture that emerges is not clear, in part because the survey questions differ.[3]

The World Values Survey asks respondents if more or less inequality is needed in their country. Its results reveal polarization: in some countries, more than 20 percent of respondents indicate that more inequality is needed and more than 20 percent indicate that less inequality is needed. Figure 4.1 shows the results for four countries; the results are similar for the seven other African countries covered by the World Values Survey, and the pattern does not change markedly between country survey rounds. These results are consistent with the point made in *World Development Report 2006: Equity and Development* (World Bank 2005) that, contrary to preconceived notions, citizens do not by and large view inequality negatively. The share of the population in the African countries that indicated that income should be more equal was just 21 percent—lower than the 28 percent for all countries included in the World Value Survey.

Afrobarometer surveys find that among a list of more than 30 possible responses, respondents rarely cite inequality as one of the most important problems facing their countries. In these surveys, poverty and employment are the primary concerns of respondents in most countries. In the majority of the 30 African countries surveyed in the Gallup Poll (2013), most respondents report that individuals can get ahead by working hard.

In contrast, in the Pew Global Attitudes Survey, 70–81 percent of respondents in the six African countries covered agreed that inequality is a major problem in their country (Pew Research Center 2013). Similarly, Afrobarometer surveys show that most Africans respond that their government is doing quite or very badly at narrowing the income gap between the rich and poor. These sentiments do not correlate with the level of inequality in the country (figure 4.2).

FIGURE 4.1   Views on inequality differ within and across countries

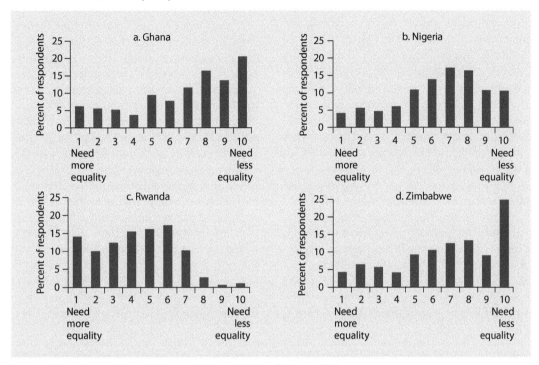

Source: World Values Surveys of Ghana (2012), Nigeria (2011), Rwanda (2012), and Zimbabwe (2012).
Note: 1 = "Incomes should be made more equal," 10 = "We need larger income differences as incentives for individual effort."

FIGURE 4.2   Survey respondents' perceptions of the adequacy of their government's efforts to narrow the income gap differ across countries

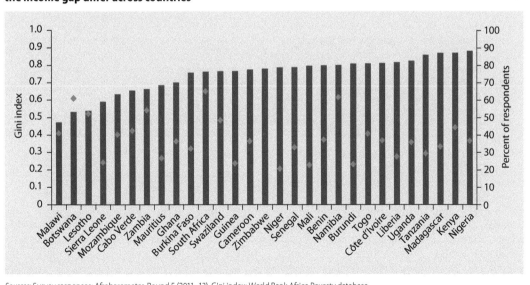

Sources: Survey responses: Afrobarometer, Round 5 (2011–13). Gini index: World Bank Africa Poverty database.
Note: Blue bars show the share of the population that perceives that the government is not doing enough to narrow the income gap (right axis). Orange diamonds are Gini indexes (left axis).

Measurement of Inequality

Like the poverty analysis in chapter 2, the analysis of inequality in this chapter is based on data on consumption from nationally representative household surveys. With few exceptions, the factors that make measuring poverty a challenge also complicate the measurement of inequality.[4] Changes in the questionnaire or the seasonal timing of fieldwork can distort apparent trends in inequality. To prevent this problem, the analysis presented in this chapter excludes surveys that are not comparable (as defined in chapter 1).[5]

Surveys in Africa measure inequality based on consumption. Cross-regional comparisons typically ignore the difference between income and consumption measures of inequality (as noted in the next section), but it is an important distinction because consumption inequality is typically lower than other monetary inequality measures.

This chapter focuses on inequality as measured by the Gini index (box 4.1) in consumption per capita, the same metric used to assess poverty in chapter 2. Consumption is generally regarded as easier to measure than income in low-income economies (Deaton and Zaidi 2002). Current consumption generally does not reveal the full extent of economic inequality, however, because consumption does not capture savings and wealth.

Income and wealth inequality are alternatives to consumption-based measures. In most economies, income-based measures of inequality are higher than consumption-based measures (Blundell, Pistaferri, and Preston 2008; Krueger and others 2010; Santaeulàlia-Llopis and Zheng 2015), and wealth inequality is typically higher than income inequality (Davies and others 2011;

BOX 4.1   A Primer on the Gini Index

The Gini index can be explained using the Lorenz curve, which plots the cumulative share of total consumption on the vertical axis against the cumulative proportion of the population on the horizontal axis, starting with the poorest individual or household (figure B4.1.1). If there is perfect equality, the bottom X percent of the population accounts for X percent of consumption (or earns X percent of income), and the Lorenz curve coincides with the diagonal. If there is some degree of inequality, the bottom X percent of the population accounts for less than X percent of consumption. The Lorenz curve bows outward; the farther it is from the diagonal line, the higher the degree of inequality. In the extreme case of perfect inequality, all consumption is concentrated in the hands of the richest individual, and the Lorenz curve coincides with the line from 0 to X to Y. The Gini index reflects the area between the line of perfect equality (the diagonal) and the Lorenz curve (A), relative to the maximum area that would be attained under perfect inequality (A + B).

An alternative measure of inequality is the mean log deviation (MLD), also called Theil's L index,

FIGURE B4.1.1   The Lorenz curve illustrates the Gini measure of inequality

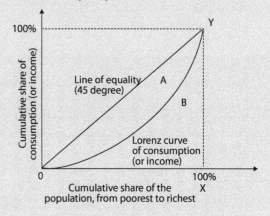

which is part of the generalized entropy class of inequality indexes (Cowell 2000). As in the Gini index, higher values of the MLD represent higher levels of inequality, but unlike the Gini index, the MLD is not bound by 1. The MLD shows the per-

(Box continues next page)

BOX 4.1   A Primer on the Gini Index *(continued)*

centage difference between the consumption of a randomly selected individual and the population's average consumption. One attractive feature of the MLD is that it is sensitive to inequality among the poor. Another is that, unlike the Gini index, the MLD is decomposable: the contribution of inequality across different groups and the contribution of the inequality within these groups can be calculated. Doing so helps unpack the nature of inequality, as done later in this chapter.

A third, more recent inequality measure is the Palma ratio, the ratio of the consumption share of the richest 10 percent of the population to the share of the poorest 40 percent of the distribution (Palma 2006, 2011). In its original formulation, the index was expressed in terms of gross national income. It is an intuitive measure of inequality that highlights the large gaps in consumption often found between the rich and the poor.

Each of these measures has different properties and can produce different results. But cross-country rankings of inequality in Africa are not strongly affected by the measure of inequality used. Figure B4.1.2 plots country inequality rankings according to the MLD (panel a) and Palma (panel b) against the ranking based on the Gini index. In most cases, countries line up on the diagonal, which means that their rank position is unaffected by the measure used. These findings are similar to the finding by Cobham and Sumner (2013).

FIGURE B4.1.2   **Different inequality measures reveal a similar story**

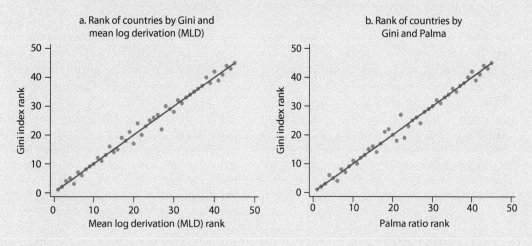

a. Rank of countries by Gini and mean log derivation (MLD)

b. Rank of countries by Gini and Palma

Diaz-Gimenez, Glover, and Rios-Rull 2011; Piketty 2014; Rama and others 2015; for Africa, see de Magalhães and Santaeulàlia-Llopis 2015). Consumption and income are flow measures that relate to a specific period (for example, one year); wealth is a stock measure that reflects assets accumulated over a lifetime (through savings) and across generations (through bequests).

Most household surveys in Africa lack detailed data on the value of household wealth. Taking advantage of the select few that include partial wealth data, de

Magalhães and Santaeulàlia-Llopis (2015) compare inequality in consumption, income, and wealth in Malawi, Tanzania, and Uganda. Their measure of wealth includes land, housing, livestock, agricultural equipment, and household durable goods, net of any debt (their data exclude housing in Tanzania and debt in Uganda). Because financial assets are not included, total wealth is understated, particularly among urban households.

Their results show the pattern observed in other regions. In Malawi wealth inequality is almost twice as large as consumption inequality. In rural areas, the wealth Gini is 0.60, compared with 0.54 for income and 0.39 for consumption. In urban areas, these estimates are 0.84 for wealth, 0.71 for income, and 0.44 for consumption. A similar picture emerges in Tanzania and Uganda.

A second concern with consumption inequality is that, in practice, consumption inequality measures will be biased downward if the set of goods in the consumption measure does not include items consumed by the rich (luxury goods such as vacations as well as irregularly purchased consumer durable purchases such as cars). These goods are sometimes not included in surveys or are excluded from the measure of consumption if they are.[6] Consumption surveys also struggle to include hard-to-survey populations, including both the extreme poor (who may live in remote areas or informal settlements) and the extreme rich (who may refuse to participate in surveys). Applying imputation methods for mismeasured income data and accounting for expatriates not included in surveys in Côte d'Ivoire and Madagascar significantly increase measured inequality, according to Guénard and Mesplé-Somps (2010). The net effect of missing these households is ambiguous in terms of the bias in inequality, contingent on which household groups are excluded from the survey. However, if top income earners or the very poor are systematically excluded, inequality measures will be understimated.

Methods have been proposed to address some of these problems (see Korinek, Mistiaen, and Ravallion 2006). One approach is to compare top incomes in household surveys with tax records (Atkinson, Piketty, and Saez 2011; Banerjee and Piketty 2005). Studies adopting this approach typically conclude that surveys underestimate top incomes. The evidence on South Africa is ambiguous, because most surveys provide estimates of top income shares that are close to the tax data (Morival 2011). Many developing countries lack administrative tax data with which to assess the level of underreporting in household surveys (see, for example, the discussion

on the Middle East in Alvaredo and Piketty 2015). One study that attempts to assess the extent of the underestimation (the study of Egypt by Hlasny and Verme 2013) shows, perhaps surprisingly, that it is not large.

Another approach for gauging underestimation at the top of the distribution is to compare consumption from household surveys with private consumption in national accounts. Although there are conceptual differences between these two measures of consumption, the growing gap between national accounts and survey consumption in countries such as China and India is often interpreted as an indicator that surveys miss out on a growing share of private expenditures (Deaton 2005). This problem appears to be less important in Africa, where household surveys and national accounts have not been observed to be diverging, as discussed in chapter 1.

To study inequality in the distribution of consumption, the Gini index across countries is compared. The Gini index is a widely used measure of inequality (box 4.1). It ranges between 0 (every individual enjoys the same level of consumption per capita, perfect equality) and 1 (a single individual accounts for all consumption). A Gini index of 0.4 means that the expected difference in consumption between any two people chosen from the population at random will be 80 percent (two times the Gini). This chapter focuses on Gini indexes as derived from household surveys, rather than efforts to impute a Gini from other sources (box 4.2)

Inequality Patterns and Trends

This section explores both national and regional aspects of inequality and then describes core household traits that explain inequality across groups in countries.

Inequality across African Countries

Gini indexes from the most recent household surveys in Africa range from 0.31 (Niger and São Tomé and Príncipe) to 0.63 (South Africa). Comparing these estimates with estimates from other countries (based on the

BOX 4.2   Can the Gini index be estimated without a survey?

Issues of comparability and data availability hamper studies of inequality in Africa. For the Gini results in this chapter, only nine countries have more than three data points, and seven countries have just a single data point.

Can this dearth of data be circumvented by estimating the Gini? The Standardized World Income Inequality Database (SWIID) takes this approach, seeking to maximize the comparability and coverage of Gini estimates worldwide (Solt forthcoming a). This effort works best in countries with better and more data, but it is still subject to critique (see Jenkins 2014 and the response to his critique in Solt forthcoming b).

Using a missing-data algorithm and drawing on information from proximate years within a country and various data collection efforts (such as the World Bank's PovcalNet, the UNU-WIDER database, and country statistical reports), SWIID produces Gini estimates for 45 countries in Africa. For 1991–2012, SWIID has 16 or more annual estimates of the Gini for more than half these countries. Because of the lack of survey data in developing countries, the

SWIID imputations show substantial variability in the region, as Solt (forthcoming a) notes (figure B4.2.1). Most of the estimates computed directly from the surveys are within the SWIID confidence interval, but that interval is wide.

The two sources are highly correlated (with a correlation of 0.83 between the survey estimate and the average SWIID estimate from 100 imputations). The correlation is higher (0.91) if the comparison is limited to surveys deemed comparable within the country. The correlation is low (only 0.15) among the nine countries in Central Africa.

The direction of the changes in the Gini in the SWIID does not match well with the trends revealed by the surveys (as in figure 4.4). In only 11 of 20 countries with a trend in both sources does the direction of change match. There is a high degree of uncertainty in the SWIID estimates. In only 1 of the 20 countries studied is the change in the Gini statistically significant. Until better and more surveys are conducted in the region, imputing inequality measures is fraught with serious concerns.

FIGURE B4.2.1   **Standardized World Income Inequality Database (SWIID) estimates of the Gini index show great variability**

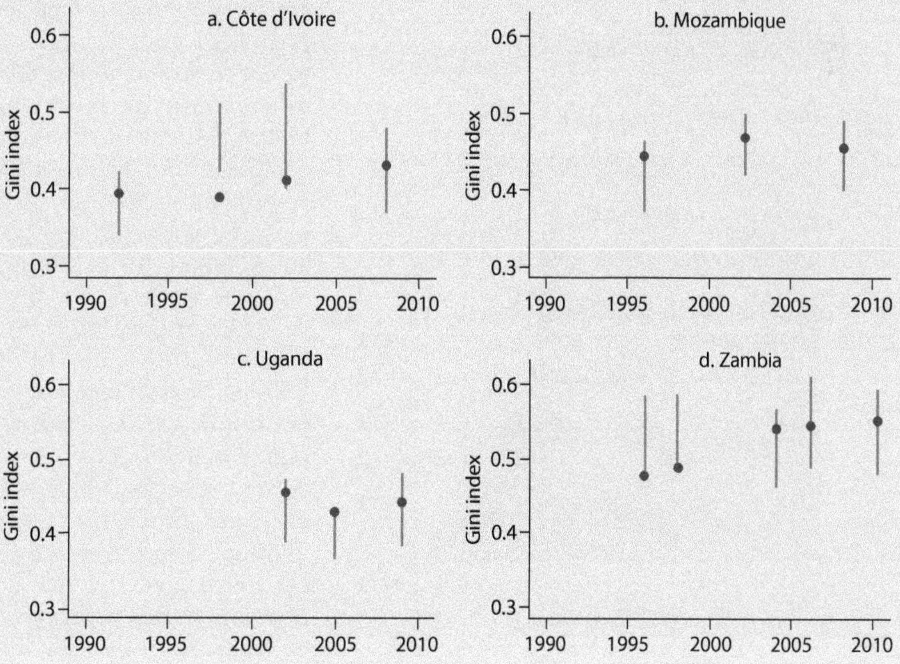

Source: World Bank Africa Poverty database and Solt forthcoming a.
Note: Orange lines show the 95 percent confidence intervals on the SWIID Gini imputations. Blue dots are the survey-based Gini estimates from the World Bank Africa Poverty database.

FIGURE 4.3 **The world's most unequal countries are in Africa**

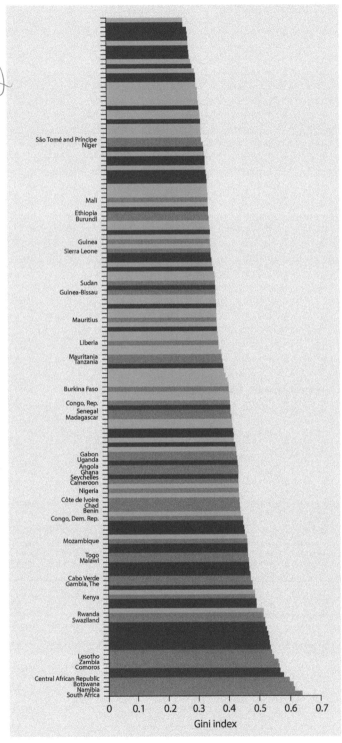

Source: PovcalNet for countries outside Africa; World Bank Africa Poverty database.
Note: Orange bars are African countries (based on consumption); light blue bars are other countries using consumption surveys; dark blue bars are other countries using income surveys.

PovcalNet database) reveals that 7 of the 10 most unequal countries in the world are in Africa (figure 4.3). All but two of the seven countries (South Africa and Zambia) have populations of less than 5 million.

The levels of inequality in Africa appear even more remarkable if one considers that many countries outside Africa—particularly advanced economies and countries in Latin America—use income rather than consumption per capita to measure inequality. Relative to consumption data, income data generally produce higher levels of inequality.

The heterogeneity in inequality across Africa is substantial and shows a geographical pattern (map 4.1). Inequality is higher in Southern Africa (Botswana, Lesotho, Namibia, South Africa, Swaziland, and Zambia), where Gini indexes are above 0.5, as well as in Central African Republic and the Comoros. West African countries exhibit lower levels of inequality, and countries in East Africa are mixed. These findings are robust to other measures of inequality (box 4.1).

Some researchers have argued that these patterns in inequality have historical roots. In particular, the high levels of inequality in Southern Africa are legacies of the land dispossession and racially discriminatory policies of the colonial period. There are notable differences in the history of communal land tenure systems in West and Central Africa compared with white settler economies (characterized by privately owned small family plots, large estates, and plantations) in East and Southern Africa (Cornia 2014).

There are few other discernable patterns in terms of country traits and inequality. Inequality levels do not differ statistically between coastal and landlocked, fragile and nonfragile, or resource-rich and resource-poor countries, controlling for the four subregions. Bhorat, Naidoo, and Pillay (2015) also conclude that the average level of inequality is not different between resource-rich and other economies, but they note that a number of resource-rich economies have high levels of inequality. If the eight most unequal countries in the region (South Africa, Zambia, and six small economies) are excluded and one

MAP 4.1   Inequality in Africa shows a geographical pattern

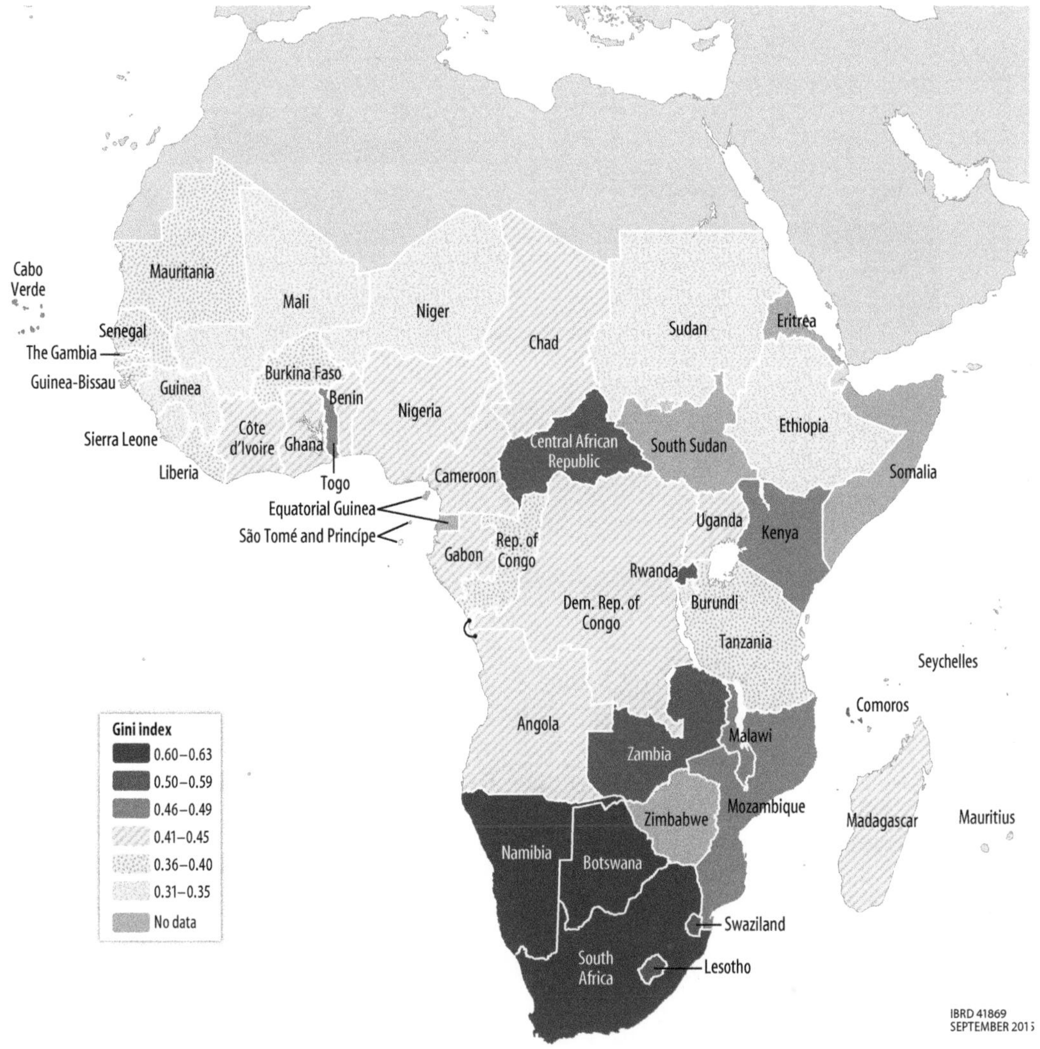

Gini index

- 0.60–0.63
- 0.50–0.59
- 0.46–0.49
- 0.41–0.45
- 0.36–0.40
- 0.31–0.35
- No data

IBRD 41869
SEPTEMBER 2015

Source: World Bank Africa Poverty database.

controls for country-level income, Africa has inequality levels comparable to developing countries in other parts of the world (Bhorat, Naidoo, and Pillay 2015 draw the same conclusion).

Are African countries becoming more unequal? Analysis of 23 countries for which there are two comparable surveys to measure inequality reveals that about half the countries experienced a decline in inequality while the other half saw an increase (figure 4.4).[7] No clear patterns based on resource status,

income status, or initial level of inequality in the first survey are evident.

The picture is the same if one looks at the longest available time period for which comparable data are available. Cornia (2014) describes this pattern as "inequality trend bifurcation."[8] Within-country trends in inequality in Africa differ from trends in both Asia, where inequality is on the rise, and Latin America, where inequality has been declining since the early 2000s (see Ferreira and others 2013 for Latin America;

FIGURE 4.4 **Inequality rose in about half of the countries and fell in the other half**

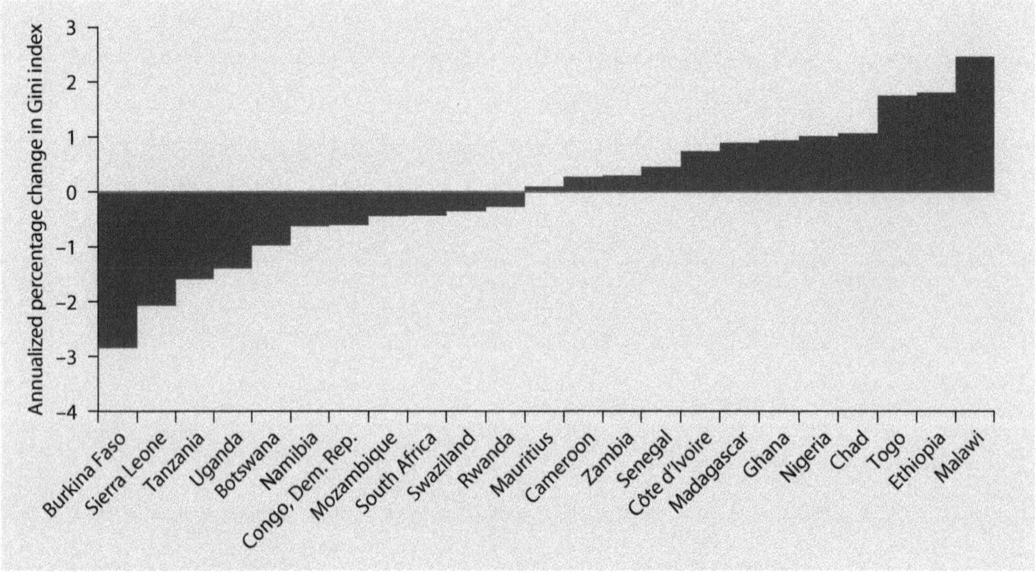

Source: World Bank Africa Poverty database.
Note: Annualized percentage change in the Gini index is based on the two most recent and comparable surveys available.

Asian Development Bank 2014 and Rama and others 2015 for Asia).

Should one expect a more systematic increase in inequality given Africa's double decade of growth? One of the long-standing debates in economics is about the trends in inequality during periods of economic growth. In the 1950s, Simon Kuznets formulated the hypothesis that inequality first increases and then declines as GDP per capita rises (Kuznets 1955). Because most countries in Africa still have low levels of GDP, the Kuznets hypothesis suggests that inequality should increase with rising GDP per capita.

Empirical studies have not produced robust support for the Kuznets hypothesis (Bruno, Ravallion, and Squire 1998; Deininger and Squire 1996; Milanovic 2011). The African data also fail to provide strong evidence for a Kuznets-type trajectory.

Panel a of figure 4.5 compares the level of inequality (measured by the Gini) with GDP per capita. Although there is a significant positive relationship between the level of GDP and inequality, it is driven almost entirely by the upper-middle-income countries in Southern Africa (Botswana, Namibia, and South Africa), which differ in many ways (in addition to GDP per capita) from the rest of Africa. A more appropriate test of the Kuznets hypothesis is to compare changes in inequality with changes in GDP per capita using multiple observations per country (panel b of figure 4.5). If the Kuznets hypothesis holds, the data should trace out an inverted U-pattern or at least—given that most of the countries in the sample are poor and hence likely to be shifting along the rising portion of the U—an upward slope to show inequality rising as GDP increases. This is not the case: inequality is not moving in a clear direction and does not appear to be systematically related to changes in GDP per capita. Other researchers have reached similar conclusions based on examination of recent data (Bhorat, Naidoo, and Pillay 2015) and growth spells in the 1990s (Fields 2000).

All else constant, a reduction in inequality is associated with a decline in poverty (Bourguignon 2004; Klasen 2004). Many countries in figure 4.6 are in quadrant 4, where both inequality and poverty declined.

FIGURE 4.5   There is no systematic relationship between growth and inequality in Africa

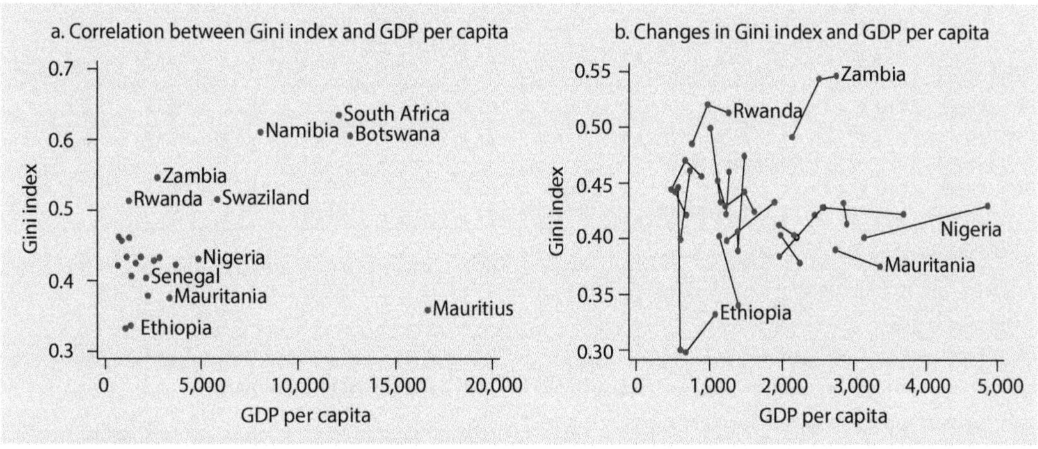

a. Correlation between Gini index and GDP per capita

b. Changes in Gini index and GDP per capita

Sources: World Bank Africa Poverty database (subset of countries with comparable surveys); World Development Indicators database.
Note: Panel a is based on the most recent survey. Panel b excludes the five highest-income countries in panel a.

However, in a number of countries poverty fell despite increasing inequality (quadrant 1 in figure 4.6). In these countries, the growth in mean consumption was large enough to offset the rise in inequality.

Inequality in Africa as a Whole

Combining survey data across countries enables the study of the Africa-wide distribution of consumption.[9] For this exercise, surveys are grouped into benchmark years (1993, 1998, 2003, and 2008).[10] The data cover 81 percent of regional GDP and 72 percent of the population, indicating that richer countries are more likely to be included.[11] Given this coverage, the results probably represent a lower bound on African inequality.

The African Gini index is 0.52–0.56 across the benchmark years, much higher than individual-country inequality measures (table 4.1). Only four countries (Botswana, the Central African Republic, Namibia, and South Africa) have Gini indexes that are higher than the African Gini in 2008. As discussed earlier, by and large, African countries have levels of inequality that are similar to other developing countries if measured in terms of average country inequality.

But Africa as a whole has the highest level of inequality of any region in the world.[12] The African Gini index rose by almost 9 percent between 1993 and 2008. By contrast, the average country Gini fell by almost 5 percent, and no change is observed if countries are weighted by their population.

FIGURE 4.6   Declining inequality is often associated with declining poverty

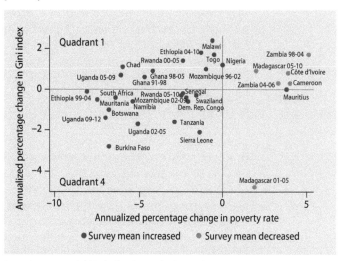

Source: Countries in World Bank Africa Poverty database with comparable surveys.
Note: Ethiopia 1995–99, an outlier, is excluded. Survey years are indicated for countries with more than one pair of comparable surveys.

TABLE 4.1   **Inequality in Africa, 1993–2008**

Indicator	Benchmark year				Percentage change
	1993	1998	2003	2008	1993–2008
Gini index for Africa	0.52	0.52	0.54	0.56	8.6
Average country Gini index	0.47	0.45	0.45	0.45	3.8
Average country Gini index, population weighted	0.44	0.44	0.43	0.44	−0.5
African mean log deviation	0.47	0.47	0.51	0.57	20.0
Within-country contribution to African mean log deviation (percent)	73.4	71.3	64.3	59.7	

Source: Jirasavetakul and Lakner 2015.

The level of inequality in Africa is largely driven by within-country inequality, which explains considerably more than half of the inequality measured by the mean log derivation (MLD). However, the increase in African inequality was driven by a widening between countries, as opposed to within-country changes in inequality. Over time, a greater share of African inequality is explained by gaps across countries. These results stand in sharp contrast to global inequality, where within-country inequality increased both in the level of inequality and as a share of total inequality (even though between-country differences remain the dominant source of global inequality).

Does country GDP explain African inequality? To some extent, it does. Figure 4.7 divides the African distribution of consumption in 2008 into 20 ventiles, from poor to rich, each representing 5 percent of the African population. For each ventile, the figure shows the share of the population in low-, lower-middle-, and upper-middle-/high-income countries. In 2008, 54 percent of the population in the top 5 percent of the African distribution were living in upper-middle-/high-income countries, 36 percent in lower-middle-income countries, and 10 percent in low-income countries. The share of the African population in upper-middle-/high-income countries rises as one moves up the distribution, while the share of the population in lower-income countries declines. However, there is much overlap across these country classifications, meaning there are very rich households in poor countries and vice versa.

FIGURE 4.7   **The richest households in Africa live mostly in the richer countries**

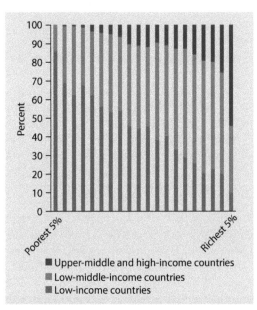

Source: Jirasavetakul and Lakner 2015.

Between-Group Inequality

This section explores the extent to which consumption levels differ across groups in an economy based on some socioeconomic or other household trait. Between-group (or horizontal) inequality is measured by decomposing overall inequality into two parts: inequality attributed to between-group (horizontal) differences and inequality within groups. Horizontal inequalities can come at a high cost to society. Between-group inequalities can perpetuate intergenerational persistence in poverty, and social exclusion and can limit socioeconomic mobility. They have been linked to violent conflict and social unrest and are therefore particularly detrimental for economic development and poverty reduction (Cramer 2005; Langer and Stewart 2015). In a similar vein, ethnic fractionalization has been associated with poor outcomes in the provision of local public goods (Miguel and Gugerty 2005) and lower levels of overall economic growth in Africa (Easterly and Levine 1997).

To explore between-group inequality in Africa, seven groups are defined based on the consensus in the literature and the availability of information in the household surveys to define groups.[13] Of the seven groups examined, geographical location, education, and demographics are the most important drivers of inequality (figure 4.8).[14]

Spatial inequalities are important for both the urban-rural group and the regional group

FIGURE 4.8   Location, education, and demographics are the most important drivers of inequality

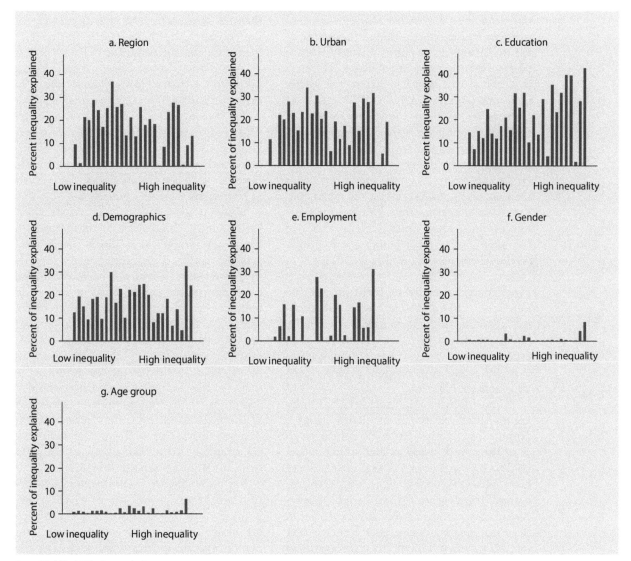

Source: World Bank Africa Poverty database.
Note: Figure shows the percent of total inequality explained by differences in mean consumption between the groups indicated for 26 countries in Africa. For employment, the number of countries included is 17 because of missing data on employment status or industry. Inequality is measured by the mean log deviation. Countries are sorted by the overall level of inequality, from low to high (left to right).

classifications.[15] In Senegal one-third of total inequality is attributed to gaps between households in urban and rural areas. On the lower end of the spectrum are some of the small island states (the Comoros, São Tomé and Príncipe), where urban-rural gaps are virtually nonexistent. A similar picture holds for inequality between regions (first-tier administration units). The two between-group components (urban-rural and regions) are correlated (0.73); countries with large urban-rural gaps in living standards also tend to have significant gaps across regions. Spatial inequalities may be even higher than captured by household consumption, because of the spatial aspects of public service provision (the fact that the value of public services, such as health services and schools, may be higher in urban areas).

Another way to view the extent of regional inequality is to compare mean consumption per capita across areas. The gap (as measured by the ratio between the richest and the poorest regions) often shows that the richest regions have twice the mean consumption of the poorest. The gap for first-tier administration units is 2.1 in Ethiopia (regions), 3.4 in the Democratic Republic of Congo (provinces), and more than 4.0 in Nigeria (states).[16] Inequality associated with geographical income segregation may be more politically destabilizing than inequality in which the poor and rich are equally dispersed geographically (Milanovic 2011), especially if geographical inequalities coincide with ethnicity or religion, as in northern and southern Nigeria.

In most household surveys, the samples are too small to estimate inequality for geographical areas smaller than regions. Such estimates can be made by combining household surveys with census data to yield poverty maps (also known as small area poverty estimates). The poverty map of Zambia shows that of the more than 1,400 constituencies in the country, about one in seven has a poverty rate of less than half the country mean (de la Fuente, Murr, and Rascón 2015). At the other extreme, 20 percent of constituencies have poverty rates that are more than 25 percent higher than the national average.

Educational attainment of the household head is an even more important driver of gaps in consumption across households. In three countries (Rwanda, South Africa, and Zambia), educational attainment explains about 40 percent of overall inequality. Higher inequality is associated with greater inequality between education categories, an association that is not observed among most of the other socioeconomic groupings. Education tends to explain a greater share of inequality than the broad economic activity category of the household head, an important driver of inequality in some countries.

The demographic composition of the household also explains a large share of inequality, up to 30 percent of overall inequality in Senegal and 32 percent in Botswana. This finding is consistent with the fact that larger households in Africa, especially households with many children, show significantly lower levels of consumption and higher levels of poverty than smaller households.

Some demographic characteristics—for example, the gender of the household head—do not explain a substantial share of total inequality. This finding is not surprising, given that in many African countries, consumption per capita levels of male- and female-headed households do not differ widely. A shortcoming of this method of decomposing inequality is that the decomposition reveals nothing about the direction of bias (that is, whether the disadvantage lies with female- or male-headed households). Moreover, because consumption is measured at the household level, the decomposition does not provide any information about how consumption is distributed between men and women within households (box 4.3).

For many countries, horizontal inequalities can be measured for more than one point in time. The main drivers of horizontal inequalities (geography, education, and demographics) did not change during the period for which survey data are available (from the early 1990s to the present).

BOX 4.3   Are resources within households shared equally? Evidence from Senegal

Little is known about interpersonal inequality in living standards *within* households, including between men and women, because consumption data are collected at the household level and standard measures of poverty and inequality are calculated assuming that resources are shared equally within the household (even if there is some normalization for size and demographic composition).

The idea that individuals within a household do not always have the same living standards and that income is not shared equally is not new (see Strauss, Beegle, and Mwabu 2000 and the ample evidence in World Bank 2011). Gender and age are arguably the most prominent individual attributes along which differentiation takes place within the household.

The household structure in Senegal (as well as in other West African countries) is unique in its complexity and offers opportunities to explore the extent of intrahousehold inequality. Households are structured like compounds. Within each household are "cells" made up of a head and unaccompanied dependent members, while married brothers and each wife of the head and her children form separate cells. Surveying and paying careful attention to the compound structure and consumption patterns among members reveals within-household consumption patterns (De Vreyer and others 2008). Food expenditures are compiled based on a detailed account of who shares which meal and how much money is used to prepare it. Individual consumption data are then collected at the cell level. Finally, expenditures that are shared by several cells are collected and attributed equally to all household members. A measure of consumption per capita is then constructed at the cell level.

The results clearly show that not everyone in the household gets the same resources. The ratio between the consumption of the richest and poorest cells within a household can be as high as 23 (and is still above 4 after trimming off the 5 percent of most unequal households). In general, food expenditures are equitably distributed, a critical insight that underscores basic solidarity. In contrast, nonfood expenditures are not divided equally. Overall inequality is higher for cell-level consumption (Gini = 0.567) than for a household-level measure that assumes equal consumption across household members (Gini = 0.548).

These unique consumption data also reveal a sizable gender gap. Cells headed by men have significantly higher consumption.

The poverty status of the household can hide poverty *within* the household. About 1 nonpoor household in 10 has a poor cell within it (De Vreyer and Lambert 2014). There are also nonpoor cells in poor households. Targeting poor households would miss 6–14 percent of poor children (depending on the poverty line), namely, children who reside in poor cells within nonpoor households.

Unequal Opportunities

Inequality across households is the product of many forces. The circumstances in which one is born—in a rural area, to uneducated parents—are one important force. Inequality of opportunity is the extent to which such circumstances dictate the outcomes of individuals in adulthood. In economics this concept has been articulated by Fleurbaey (2008) and Roemer (2000), among others. In the field of sociology, inequality of opportunity is the concept of achieved versus ascribed status (Linton 1936) and ascriptive inequality. It can exacerbate overall inequality and violate principles of fairness and equal opportunity.

A growing body of literature in the past 15 years tries to assess the degree of inequality of opportunity and evaluate the opportunity-equalizing effects of public policies (see the recent surveys by Ferreira and Peragine 2015 and Roemer and Trannoy 2015)—efforts that face a number of challenges (Kanbur and Wagstaff 2014). Building on the previous discussion of horizontal inequalities, which described the contribution of different individual characteristics to total inequality, this section presents evidence on inequality of economic opportunity and the intergenerational transmission of education and occupation.[17]

Inequality of Economic Opportunity

The approach to measuring inequality of economic opportunity entails unpacking how much of current consumption can be explained by a person's circumstances in childhood and how much is explained by individual responsibility, luck, or effort (obtained as the residual).[18] Such estimates of inequality of economic opportunity are available for many countries worldwide, but evidence for Africa has been limited to date.[19] Drawing on surveys from 10 countries (the Comoros, Ghana, Guinea, Madagascar, Malawi, Niger, Nigeria, Rwanda, Tanzania, and Uganda), this section presents more comprehensive evidence for countries in Africa.[20]

The circumstances used to measure inequality of economic opportunity include ethnicity, parental education and occupation, and region of birth.[21] The analysis focuses on individuals 15 years and older. Like other researchers in this field (see, for example, Ferreira and Gignoux 2011), inequality is measured using the MLD.[22]

The share of inequality that can be attributed to inequality of opportunity ranges from 8 percent (Madagascar) to 20 percent (Malawi) (figure 4.9). The ranking of countries changes considerably if one looks at inequality of opportunity rather than overall inequality (note that the countries in figure 4.9 are sorted by inequality): Countries with higher inequality in outcomes are not necessarily characterized by a larger share of the inequality attributed to inequality of opportunity. The Comoros, for instance, has the highest overall level of inequality, but its share of inequality of opportunity is among the lowest. Furthermore, the magnitude of inequality of opportunity is only partly correlated with the number of circumstances available in the data, suggesting that the differences observed across countries do not solely reflect differences in the availability of circumstance variables but say something meaningful about the structure of inequality (however, more circumstances are also typically expected to yield greater inequality of opportunity).

Estimates of inequality of opportunity calculated in this manner represent a lower bound, because many circumstance variables (family wealth, parenting time, the quality of education) are not observed in household surveys and hence cannot be considered in the estimation.[23] This issue also complicates comparisons across countries, because the surveys differ in the number and granularity of the circumstance variables.

FIGURE 4.9   Unequal opportunities account for up to 20 percent of inequality in Africa

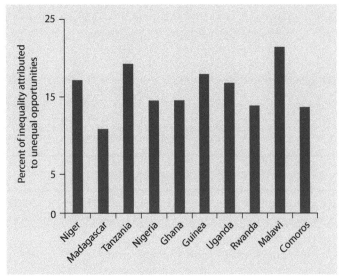

Source: Brunori, Palmisano, and Peragine 2015b.
Note: The figure shows the share of total mean log deviation (MLD) that is attributed to inequality of economic opportunity. Countries are ordered by their level of inequality measured by the MLD, with the least unequal countries on the left and the most unequal on the right.

Intergenerational Persistence in Education and Occupation

Does the educational attainment of parents matter less today to a child's schooling than it did 50 years ago? [24] Is the occupation of a farmer's son less affected by his father's occupation than it was a generation ago? Using data from several recent household surveys in Africa and drawing on a set of surveys with information on adult children and their fathers, the extent of intergenerational mobility in education and occupation is examined, as well as whether the extent of this mobility is changing among younger generations. [25]

To measure educational mobility from the perspective of intergenerational persistence, education is regressed on the educational attainment of one's parents. The coefficient from this simple regression, β, measures education persistence (see Black and Devereux 2011 for a recent overview of approaches to this measurement). Another measure of mobility is the correlation coefficient between the outcomes of parents and their children (ρ), which is the intergenerational gradient (β), multiplied by the ratio of the standard deviation across the two generations. [26] Three factors are explored—the intergenerational gradient, the correlation coefficient, and the ratio of standard deviations—for different cohorts to study intergenerational persistence in schooling across generations (figure 4.10).

The correlation coefficient on intergenerational mobility (the blue line in figure 4.10) slightly increased in most countries. Conversely, the intergenerational gradient, β, is falling in most countries (the orange line in figure 4.10). An additional year of schooling of one's parent has a lower association with one's own schooling than it used to. This reflects, however, that the ratio of the standard deviations (the red line in figure 4.10) is rising, which in turn is related to the low levels of schooling among parents in the oldest generation. For example, people born in 1949 in Rwanda have on average 1.5 years of schooling, while their parents have only 0.1 years. The Africa intergenerational mobility trends are broadly comparable to estimates in other developing

countries (Ferreira and others 2013; Hertz and others 2007). These changes may partly reflect the fact that since the 1990s, many countries have eliminated school fees at the primary level (Bhalotra, Harttgen, and Klasen 2015). In terms of level of mobility in general, Africa has greater intergenerational educational mobility than Latin America. However, mobility is lower than developed countries in Europe, the United States, and the former Eastern Bloc.

Like education, one's occupation may be determined largely by the occupations of one's parents. The limited literature on this issue in Africa focuses on intergenerational occupational persistence from farm to nonfarm occupations. Here this analysis is extended to look at three occupational classifications among men 20–65 (agriculture, services, and other occupations) and their fathers. The analysis is restricted to the occupation of fathers because fewer surveys have information on the occupation of mothers.

Intergenerational occupational persistence in farming has been falling rapidly in some countries (table 4.2). In the Comoros, the share of farmers' sons working in other sectors is more than twice as large for the youngest cohort as it is for older cohorts. Guinea is the most rigid economy in terms of occupational shifting. There is substantial intergenerational mobility in work among people with fathers in services and other sectors; generally less than half of the youngest cohort are performing the same services or other sector work as their fathers. This change in intergenerational occupational persistence is consistent with the overall shifts in occupational structure in each country, specifically the falling employment shares of agriculture (World Bank 2014a).

To separate out economy-wide shifts, the share of job mobility associated with expansion in nonagricultural sectors is netted out (following the approach of Bossuroy and Cogneau 2013). Net mobility shows

FIGURE 4.10   **Intergenerational persistence in schooling is weaker among younger Africans than older Africans**

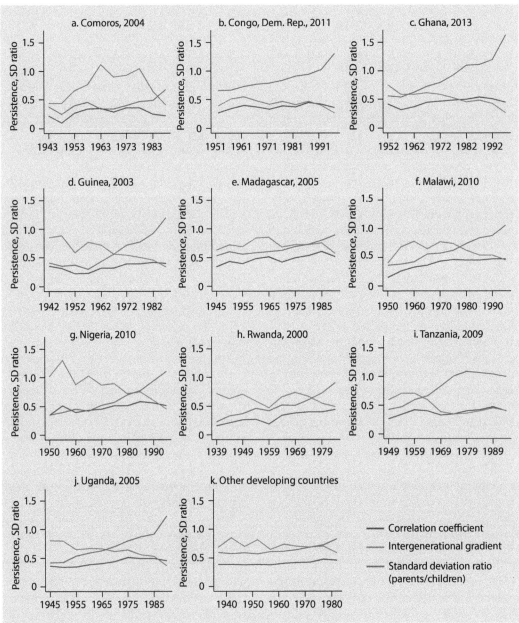

Source: Azomahou and Yitbarek 2015. Data for other developing countries from Hertz and others (2007).

that shifts in the structure of occupations in the economy (sometimes called structural change) are not the only factor driving changes in intergenerational occupational mobility (table 4.3). The Comoros, Rwanda, and Uganda exhibit the highest rates of intergenerational mobility that is not attributable to structural change.

TABLE 4.2   Likelihood of remaining in one's father's sector in selected African countries

Country	Sons of farmers stay in sector					Sons of service sector employees stay in sector					Sons of other sector employees stay in sector				
	1 Oldest	2	3	4	5 Youngest	1 Oldest	2	3	4	5 Youngest	1 Oldest	2	3	4	5 Youngest
Comoros	80	55	55	45	48	34	53	45	40	55	7	41	37	42	17
Ghana	76	65	64	59	71	47	50	51	60	52	21	22	32	25	32
Guinea	79	69	73	76	80	26	40	34	36	41	24	28	43	40	32
Rwanda	86	83	84	77	78	32	18	22	28	31	0	34	12	22	8
Uganda	78	72	66	60	72	33	39	40	37	27	32	28	34	43	33

Source: Azomahou and Yitbarek 2015.
Note: Table shows the percent of each cohort with the same occupation as their father. 1–5 are 10-year birth cohorts. The table should be read as follows: Among the youngest cohort (cohort 5) in the Comoros, the son of a farmer has a 48 percent likelihood of also being a farmer. Members of the oldest cohort of farmers' sons have a much higher chance of being farmers (80 percent).

TABLE 4.3   Gross and net occupational intergenerational mobility out of farming in selected African countries

Country	Gross mobility					Net mobility				
	1 Oldest	2	3	4	5 Youngest	1 Oldest	2	3	4	5 Youngest
Comoros	29	47	49	56	57	15	24	24	29	28
Ghana	31	42	43	45	36	12	13	7	7	7
Guinea	30	38	34	35	30	16	19	11	8	8
Rwanda	17	22	21	29	31	12	14	14	17	13
Uganda	29	35	40	45	40	14	17	21	21	12

Source: Azomahou and Yitbarek 2015.
Note: Table shows the percent of each cohort with the same occupation as their father. 1–5 are 10-year birth cohorts. The table should be read as follows: Among the youngest cohort (cohort 5) in the Comoros, for example, 57 percent of sons do not have the same occupations as their fathers. Net mobility is computed as gross mobility minus the share of mobility associated with structural change in employment.

Extreme Wealth and Billionnaires

Household surveys are not suited for capturing very high levels of income or wealth. Missing information on extreme wealth leads to underestimation of the extent of economic inequality in a broader sense. Wealthy households are often not surveyed and household surveys generally measure current consumption or income (a flow measure) rather than the stock of household assets. Surveys are also likely to fail to capture rare income events or income (and the wealth from it) that is obtained illegally (Africa Progress Panel 2013). Data on holders of extreme wealth are difficult to collect. The Forbes World's Billionaires list, the World Top Incomes Database (currently covering South Africa and ongoing in 15 other African countries), and the Global Wealth Databook have made inroads, but they still generally cover little of Africa compared with other regions.

South Africa was the first African country to be represented on Forbes' list, with two billionaires in the late 1990s, followed by Nigeria in 2008. By 2014 the region had 19 billionaires: 8 in South Africa, 7 in Nigeria, and 1 each in Angola, Kenya, Tanzania, and Uganda.[27] Countries such as India experienced a much sharper rise during a similar period. The number of billionaires there rose from 2 in the mid-1990s to 46 in 2012, according to Gandhi and Walton (2012).

Although there are fewer billionaires in Africa, their average aggregate net wealth in 2012 was higher ($5.2 billion per billionaire) than in India ($3.8 billion). Aggregate billionaire wealth as a percent of GDP increased steadily in Nigeria and South Africa from,

FIGURE 4.11 **Billionaire wealth in Africa is growing**

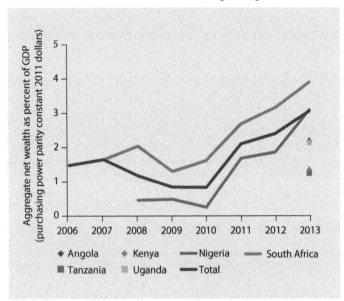

Sources: Aggregate net wealth: Forbes' "The World's Billionaires." GDP: World Development Indicators.

0.3 and 1.6 percent in 2010 to 3.2 and 3.9 percent in 2013 (figure 4.11). The increase is partly explained by the rise in the number of billionaires in both countries over the period. Nigeria's rapid climb also stems from the fact that, since 2011, it has been the home of the

FIGURE 4.12 **Extreme wealth increases with GDP in Africa and elsewhere**

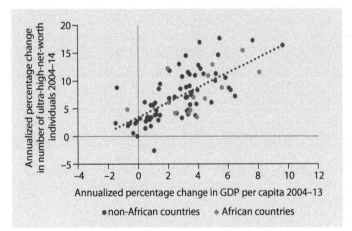

Sources: Data on number of ultra-high-net-worth individuals are adapted from World Bank 2014b, based on Knight Frank 2015. GDP data are from World Development Indicators.
Note: GDP is measure in purchasing power parity constant 2011 dollars. Black dotted line shows the global trend (African and non-African countries).

richest African (Aliko Dangote), whose fortune grew by a factor of 10 between 2010 and 2014.

The growth in extreme wealth in the region since 2010 can be decomposed into two components: the increase in the wealth of veteran billionaires and the addition of new billionaires. More than half of the growth in Nigeria's extreme wealth is explained by the growth in the wealth of the veterans. The weight of newcomers in the growth in extreme wealth in South Africa rose from 40 percent in 2011 to 54 percent in 2013. Across the set of six countries, the contribution of newcomers to the growth in extreme wealth jumped from 37 percent in 2011 to 61 percent in 2013.

With a focus on billionaires, the Forbes list captures only the very top of extreme wealth. In 2013 Forbes reported on 50 Africans worth at least $400 million. This list still leaves out lower levels of wealth that are high by any standard.

Knight Frank (2015) surveys private bankers and wealth advisors to collect data on ultra-high-net-worth individuals (individuals whose net worth exceeds $30 million) in 90 countries, of which 14 are in Africa. Across countries, the number of ultra-high-net-worth individuals increases with GDP per capita growth. The number tends to increase even where economies are in decline or stagnating (in Zimbabwe, for example, the number of ultra-high-net-worth individuals rose by 5.2 percent while GDP per capita declined by 0.12 percent). Africa's trend (not shown) is very similar to the global trend (the gray dotted line in figure 4.12).

What do these data reveal about inequality? Given the limited data on these extremely wealthy individuals, there is no straightforward answer. Credit Suisse (2014) presents estimates of the distribution of wealth using the Forbes list and imputations based on cross-country relationships and consumption surveys. Using these data, Lakner (2015) finds that the 10 richest people in Africa possess wealth equivalent to the wealth of the poorest half of the population. (His findings include North Africa, where 3 of the 10 richest people reside.) Oxfam International (2015) estimates that globally 80 individuals possess as much wealth as half the world's population (the regional and global results are not strictly comparable).[28] Few detailed studies explore the level of extreme wealth of nationals at the country level. One exception is the New World Wealth (2014) study of Kenya, which estimates that about 8,300 people own 62 percent of that country's wealth.

Does the source of this wealth matter? Particularly in sectors where rent-seeking behavior is more likely, the role of political connections in the wealth-generating process could have implications for development and growth. Gandhi and Walton (2012) find that in India in 2012, 60 percent of total net wealth was derived from "rent-thick" sectors, such as real estate, infrastructure, construction, mining, telecommunications, cement, and media, where the influence of political connections and the potential for rent extraction are important (Rama and others 2015). In Africa the share of extreme wealth derived from extractives has been declining. During 2011–14, about 20 percent of African billionaires derived their wealth mainly or partially from telecommunications, and the share of extreme wealth derived from services and the broad category of investment jumped from 1 percent to 13 percent.

Forbes classifies the majority of net wealth in Africa in 2014 as self-made as opposed to inherited. It estimates that self-made aggregate net wealth in the region represented 74 percent of total net wealth and that 81 percent of the billionaires in Africa reported being self-made. This classification of self-made does not necessarily imply returns to successful entrepreneurship and innovation (as opposed to accumulating extreme wealth through political influence or corrupt business practices). Bagchi and Svejnar (2015) assess wealth accumulation through political connections by looking at evidence in news sources that suggests whether billionaires would have become billionaires in the absence of political connections. Among total billionaire wealth

in their sample, the fraction of politically connected billionaires in 1987, 1992, 1996, and 2002 ranges from 4 percent to 13 percent. They conclude that politically connected wealth accumulation has a negative effect on economic growth worldwide. In resource-rich countries in Africa, there is concern that the elites gain wealth from resources through political connections (see the examples and broad discussion in Burgis 2015).

Concluding Remarks

The latest evidence on inequality in Africa paints a complicated picture. The most unequal countries in the world are in Africa, mostly in the southern part of the continent, but excluding the seven countries with extremely high inequality, inequality is not higher or lower than in other countries at similar income levels. In countries with comparable surveys over time, inequality is falling in half and rising in half, without a clear association with factors such as resource-richness, income level, or state fragility. A clearer pattern emerges for horizontal inequalities within countries, which continue to be dominated by unequal education levels and high urban-rural and regional income disparities.

From a regional perspective, inequality among Africans is rising and is high compared with other regions. This pattern reflects the range in national income levels across countries and the fact that most of the poor in Africa reside in the poorest countries. The income gap between African countries is growing.

Another aspect of inequality—extreme wealth—is missed altogether by household surveys. Africa has seen a rise in billionaire wealth, at least in countries for which data are available.

A portion of inequality in Africa can be attributed to inequality of opportunity, circumstances at birth that are major determinants of one's poverty status as an adult. Fortunately, at least in some countries, there has been a rise in intergenerational educational mobility, holding out hope that inequality of opportunity will decline. Nevertheless, intergenerational occupational persistence, at least as captured by three broad occupation categories, remains high in many countries.

Notes

1. According to Olson (1965), if a public good is of interest to the rich, inequality could facilitate collective action and allow the poor to free ride. In fact, the evidence shows, more often the opposite occurs. Wealthy households, which can afford private providers, opt out of financing public services such as schools and health care facilities and redirect resources to efforts that do not serve poor families. Mansuri and Rao (2013) present a range of evidence indicating that communities with high inequality have worse local development processes and outcomes. They find that highly unequal incomes amplify market failures.

2. Some studies find evidence that high inequality within ethnic groups rather than in the country as a whole is a driver of civil conflict (Huber and Mayoral 2014). Others find that it is inequality between ethnic groups that matters (Stewart 2008). Parallel with these efforts to explain civil conflict is the literature that explores how inequality, especially ascriptive and horizontal inequalities, explains crime rates (see, for example, Blau and Blau 1982).

3. Similar contradictions in perceptions can be found in views on inequality in the United States (Fitz 2015).

4. Purchasing power parity (PPP) adjustments to convert local currency units into U.S. dollars do not affect national inequality measures. National temporal price adjustments (to bring a survey from year 1 to year 2 prices) also do not typically affect national inequality measures. In contrast, within-survey spatial price adjustments change inequality measures. Both the World Bank Africa Poverty Database (used here) and PovcalNet compute Gini indexes based on nominal consumption measures. They do not adjust for the fact that the households interviewed pay different prices depending on where in a country they live or the time of year they

are interviewed. If prices differ spatially and temporally, deflated aggregates may produce different inequality measures and trends. For most of the surveys analyzed here, a deflated (real) consumption measure is available. The general findings on the levels and trends in inequality are not substantially different if Gini indexes are estimated using deflated (real) consumption. One exception is the findings on between- and within-inequality by region or urban location, which tends to decline using spatially deflated aggregates. Székely and Hilgert (2007) analyze some of these issues in Latin American countries.

5. Excluding these surveys has implications for how the results compare with the results of other studies. For example, excluding the first of the three most recent national household surveys in Malawi (on the grounds of incomparability in survey design), the inequality trend in Malawi is not decreasing, as Bhorat, Naidoo, and Pillay find (2015).

6. Expenditure on consumer durables is not always included in the consumption measure, because it represents highly irregular purchases (Deaton and Zaidi 2002). The recommended practice is to include durable goods "use values" in the consumption measure.

7. Bhorat, Naidoo, and Pillay (2015) use a different inequality measure but show similar results: of 34 countries in Sub-Saharan Africa, inequality rose in 18 and fell in 16. Cornia (2014) and Fosu (2014) draw similar conclusions. All three reports draw on the World Bank PovcalNet database. From a population perspective, the results lean toward increasing inequality; 57 percent of the population in these countries are residing in a country with increasing inequality.

8. Measuring polarization is another approach to looking at the consumption distribution, a concept related to but distinct from inequality. Polarization measures separation (distance) across clustered groups in a society. Clementi and others (forthcoming) show that Nigeria experienced both rising inequality and rising polarization between 2003/04 and 2012/13, which contributed to the eroding of the middle class. Keefer and Knack (2002) argue that, in practice, polarization measures are strongly positively correlated with inequality measures across countries.

9. For details on the calculations on African inequality, see Jirasavetakul and Lakner (2015). This idea has also been pursued globally, including in global inequality studies by Anand and Segal (2015), Atkinson and Brandolini (2010), and Milanovic (2005). The analysis here draws heavily on Lakner and Milanovic (2015), who analyze the global income distribution in 1988–2008.

10. Because of the limited availability of household surveys, the analysis cannot start before 1993, and there are not enough surveys for a benchmark year after 2008.

11. General coverage of Africa is good, but the coverage of fragile countries is low: on average, the surveys cover only 28 percent of the population in fragile countries between 1993 and 2003. The rate improves markedly in 2008 with the inclusion of the Democratic Republic of Congo and Sudan.

12. Inequality in Africa as a whole is higher than in Latin America (0.528); Asia other than China (0.450) and China (0.427); mature economies (0.419); the Russian Federation, Central Asia, and Southeast Europe (0.419); and India (0.331) (Lakner and Milanovic 2015). Estimates by Pinkovskiy and Sala-i-Martín (2014) for Africa are even higher but show a decrease. However, their estimates are not drawn solely from a set of recent surveys in Africa but rather from a combination of inequality measures from surveys, national accounts, mean and growth rates, and interpolations and extrapolations for missing inequality data (including imputations of inequality measures from other countries if no survey is available for a country).

13. There are several main approaches to decomposing inequality into within- and between-group inequality. The traditional version of the decomposition apportions total inequality into a component explained by differences in mean consumption between groups and a component that reflects inequality within each group. The between-group component measures the share of overall inequality that would be obtained if every individual had the average consumption level of his or her group. However, as Elbers and others (2008) note, in this approach between-group inequality reaches a maximum if each individual constitutes a separate group—the yardstick against which between-group gaps are evaluated. In addition, the between-group component mechanically increases with the number of categories used. Elbers and others propose an alternative decomposition that compares between-group differences with the maximum inequality that would be obtainable if the number and size of groups were fixed at their actual levels, while the ranking of the groups is preserved. For instance, urban-rural inequality would be evaluated against a benchmark in which all individuals living in rural areas appear at the lower end of the distribution and all individuals living in urban areas appear at the upper end of the distribution, with the urban and rural population shares fixed at their actual levels. The decomposition thereby takes into consideration the existing configuration of population groups. Only the traditional results are reported here but broadly similar patterns result from the Elbers and others (2008) method (even though the estimated between-group shares are generally higher in the latter variant). For the analysis in this section, the mean log deviation is the measure of inequality. Unlike the Gini, it is additively decomposable, a mathematical property that is desirable in this context.

14. Region typically refers to the administrative region (for example, province) in which the household resides. Education denotes the highest level of education of the household head (none, incomplete primary, completed primary, completed lower secondary, university, other). Employment refers to the main economic activity of the household head (employee, employer/self-employed in agriculture, employer/self-employed outside agriculture, other). Gender and age refer to the household head. The demographic categories are one or two adults without children, one or two adults and fewer than three children, one or two adults and three children or more, three adults or more without children, three adults or more and up to three children, three adults or more, and four children or more.

15. The results for urban/rural and education are less pronounced than those in Belhaj Hassine (2015), who studies 12 countries in the Middle East and North Africa. She finds that gaps between regions account for a larger share of inequality than gaps within regions. Some of the inequality

across geographic areas reflects differences in the cost of living. Between-group inequality for regions and for urban/rural areas is lower if a delated measure of consumption is used rather than a nominal measure. Across countries, it declines by about 15 percent on average for both regions and urban/rural.

16. If a deflated measure of consumption is used, these ratios fall to 1.3 (Ethiopia), 2.2 (Democratic Republic of Congo), and 3.9 (Nigeria).

17. The focus here is on inequality of opportunity from the perspective of economic outcomes in adulthood. A third domain is the human opportunity index, which captures the extent to which circumstances such as school attendance, immunizations, and household infrastructure, including access to sanitation and water, contribute to gaps in outcomes for children. Dabalen and others (2015) present detailed analysis of the human opportunity index for Africa across many countries and years. They find that greater coverage for all was more important than changes in equity for improvements in human opportunities.

18. This approach is described as the ex ante approach to measuring inequality of opportunity, as opposed to the ex post approach (Checchi and Peragine 2010; Fleurbaey and Peragine 2013). In the ex post approach, there is no inequality of opportunity if people who exert the same effort end up with the same outcome. Inequality of opportunity in this approach is measured as inequality within responsibility classes (that is, within the set of individuals at the same effort level).

19. Exceptions are Cogneau and Mesplé-Somps (2008) for Côte d'Ivoire (1985–88), Ghana (1988 and 1998), Guinea (1994), Madagascar (1993), and Uganda (1992); Piraino (2015) for South Africa; and Brunori, Palmisano, and Peragine (2015a) for Uganda. Broader international comparisons of inequality of economic opportunity are presented in Ferreira and Gignoux (2011) for Latin America and in Brunori, Ferreira, and Peragine (2013) for 41 countries.

20. This subsection draws on Brunori, Palmisano, and Peragine (2015b).

21. Another circumstance that is particularly relevant for countries in the region hard hit by HIV/AIDS is orphan status. The empirical evidence on the consequences of being orphaned focuses on health indicators and education, with some studies showing a causal impact of orphanhood on schooling outcomes. Because orphanhood is not a random event (it is correlated with other household measures, such as urban status and household education and wealth), the correlation does not imply that education levels are generally worse among orphans. Indeed, the most recent Demographic and Health surveys show that in half of the countries surveyed, orphans are no less likely than nonorphans to be enrolled in school. In Nigeria and Chad, orphans are more likely than other children to be in school.

22. There are different methodological approaches to measuring inequality of opportunity, including the choice of inequality measure (Gini or MLD), the estimation approach (parametric or nonparametric), and the choice of circumstances to use if the set of circumstances differs across surveys. All circumstances available for each country are used. This choice is the best in analyzing a single country, but it poses some difficulties in terms of comparability across countries. There is a trade-off between the robustness and usefulness of the analysis in each country and the demands of comparability across countries. As the number of circumstances increases, the estimate of inequality of opportunity will also increase. The estimates reported here are based on a nonparametric estimation approach (Ferreira and Gignoux 2011). The MLD is commonly used as the measure of inequality in this literature, although some researchers propose using the Gini from a theoretical point of view (van de Gaer and Ramos 2015) and an empirical perspective (Brunori, Palmisano, and Peragine 2015b).

23. If data on these unobserved circumstances were available, the share of inequality attributed to circumstances would go up, as would the level and share of inequality of economic opportunity (though the extent of underestimation also depends on the degree of correlation between unobserved and observed circumstances).

24. This subsection draws on Azomahou and Yitbarek (2015).

25. Related studies include the following: Bossuroy and Cogneau (2013) cover

occupational mobility in Côte d'Ivoire in 1985–88 (four waves), Ghana in 1988–2006 (five waves), Guinea in 1995, Madagascar in 1994, and Uganda in 1993; Hertz and others (2007) examine educational mobility in Ethiopia in 1994, Ghana in 1998, and South Africa in 1998; and Lambert, Ravallion, and van de Walle (2014) analyze occupational mobility in Senegal.

26. These two measures of mobility—the intergenerational gradient and the correlation coefficient—can produce different findings in the same setting. The intergenerational gradient may decline over time (implying more mobility), but the correlation between the educational attainment of a child and parent can remain constant (implying no change in mobility) (Hertz and others 2007). This divergence may result from a reduction in the inequality of schooling in the child's generation (for example, achieving universal primary education) relative to the parents' generation and a drop in the persistence effect—that is, education in the recent birth cohort has become less dependent on parental schooling than parental education was on the educational attainment of the grandparents.

27. All billionaires included in this analysis are both citizens and residents of the region. Nathan Kirsh, a citizen of Swaziland who resides in London, is thus excluded. Forbes also excludes family fortunes, such as the Chandaria family in Kenya and the Madhvanis in Uganda, if the wealth is believed to have been dispersed among family members.

28. The Oxfam estimates also draw on the data from Credit Suisse (2014). Because information on assets and debts from household survey data is rarely available in African countries, estimates for the region are based largely on imputations from other low-income countries. In general, it is difficult to compare assets because the appropriate data are not available. For example, important assets held by the poor, such as landholdings, could be undervalued and assets held by the rich may be hidden.

References

Africa Progress Panel. 2013. *Africa Progress Report 2013: Equity in Extractives;* *Stewarding Africa's Natural Resources for All.* Geneva: Africa Progress Panel.

Alvaredo, Facundo, and Thomas Piketty. 2015. "Measuring Top Incomes and Inequality in the Middle East." Paris School of Economics.

Anand, Sudhir, and Paul Segal. 2015. "The Global Distribution of Income." In *Handbook of Income Distribution,* vol. 2, part A, edited by Anthony B. Atkinson and François Bourguignon, 937–79. Amsterdam: North-Holland.

Asian Development Bank. 2014. *Inequality in Asia and the Pacific: Trends, Drivers, and Policy Implications,* edited by Ravi Kanbur, Changyong Rhee, and Juzhong Zhuang.

Atkinson, Anthony B., and Andrea Brandolini. 2010. "On Analyzing the World Distribution of Income." *World Bank Economic Review* 24 (1): 1–37.

Atkinson, Anthony B., Thomas Piketty, and Emmanuel Saez. 2011. "Top Incomes in the Long Run of History." *Journal of Economic Literature* 49 (1): 3–71.

Azomahou, Théophile, and Eleni A. Yitbarek. 2015. "Intergenerational Mobility in Africa: Has Progress Been Inclusive?" Working paper, Maastricht University, Maastricht, the Netherlands.

Bagchi, Sutirtha, and Jan Svejnar. 2015. "Does Wealth Inequality Matter for Growth? The Effect of Billionaire Wealth, Income Distribution, and Poverty." *Journal of Comparative Economics* 43 (3): 505–30.

Banerjee, Abhijit, and Thomas Piketty. 2005. "Top Indian Incomes, 1922–2000." *World Bank Economic Review* 19 (1): 1–20.

Belhaj Hassine, Nadia, 2015. "Economic Inequality in the Arab Region." *World Development* 66: 532–56.

Berg, Andrew, Jonathan D. Ostry, and Jeromin Zettelmeyer. 2012. "What Makes Growth Sustained?" *Journal of Development Economics* 98 (2): 149–66.

Bhalotra, Sonia, Kenneth Harttgen, and Stephan Klasen. 2015. "The Impact of School Fees on Schooling Outcomes and the Intergenerational Transmission of Education." University of Bristol, United Kingdom.

Bhorat, Haroon, Karmen Naidoo, and Kavisha Pillay. 2015. "Growth, Poverty and Inequality Interactions in Africa: An Overview of Key Issues." University of Cape Town, South Africa.

Black, Sandra E., and Paul J. Devereux. 2011. "Recent Developments in Intergenerational

Mobility." In *Handbook of Labor Economics*, vol. 4, part B, edited by Orley Ashenfelter and David Card, 1487–541. San Diego: North-Holland.

Blau, Judith R., and Peter M. Blau. 1982. "The Cost of Inequality: Metropolitan Structure and Violent Crime." *American Sociological Review* 47 (1): 114–29.

Blundell, Richard, Luigi Pistaferri, and Ian Preston. 2008. "Consumption Inequality and Partial Insurance." *American Economic Review* 98 (5): 1887–921.

Bossuroy, Thomas, and Denis Cogneau. 2013. "Social Mobility in Five African Countries." *Review of Income and Wealth* 59 (S1): S84–S110.

Bourguignon, François. 2004. "The Poverty-Growth-Inequality Triangle." ICRIER Working Paper 125, Indian Council for Research on International Economic Relations, New Delhi.

Bruno, Michael, Martin Ravallion, and Lyn Squire. 1998. "Equity and Growth in Developing Countries: Old and New Perspectives on the Policy Issues." In *Income Distribution and High-Quality Growth*, edited by Vito Tanzi and Ke-Young Chu, 117–46. Cambridge, MA: MIT Press.

Brunori, Paolo, Francisco H. G. Ferreira, and Vito Peragine. 2013. "Inequality of Opportunity, Income Inequality and Mobility: Some International Comparisons." In *Getting Development Right: Structural Transformation, Inclusion and Sustainability in the Post-Crisis Era*, edited by Eva Paus, 85–116. Basingstoke, United Kingdom: Palgrave Macmillan.

Brunori, Paolo, Flaviana Palmisano, and Vito Peragine. 2015a. "Inequality of Opportunity during the Great Recession in Uganda." WIDER Working Paper 2015/039, United Nations University–World Institute for Development Economics Research, Helsinki.

———. 2015b. "Inequality of Opportunity in Sub-Saharan Africa." University of Bari, Italy.

Burgis, Tom. 2015. *The Looting Machine. Warlords, Oligarchs, Corporations, Smugglers, and the Theft of Africa's Wealth*. New York: Public Affairs.

Checchi, Daniele, and Vito Peragine. 2010. "Inequality of Opportunity in Italy." *Journal of Economic Inequality* 8 (4): 429–50.

Clementi, Fabio, Andrew Dabalen, Vasco Molini, and Francesco Schettino. Forthcoming. "When the Centre Cannot Hold: Patterns of Polarization in Nigeria." *Review of Income and Wealth*.

Cobham, Alex, and Andy Sumner. 2013. "Is It All About the Tails? The Palma Measure of Income Inequality." Center for Global Development Working Paper 343, Washington, DC.

Cogneau, Denis, and Sandrine Mesplé-Somps. 2008. "Inequality of Opportunity for Income in Five Countries of Africa." *Research on Economic Inequality* 16: 99–128.

Cornia, Giovanni Andrea. 2014. "Income Inequality Levels, Trends and Determinants in Sub-Saharan Africa: An Overview of the Main Changes." Università degli Studi di Firenze, Florence.

Cowell, Frank A. 2000. "Measurement of Inequality." In *Handbook of Income Distribution*, vol. 1, edited by Anthony B. Atkinson and François Bourguignon, 87–166. Amsterdam: North-Holland.

Cramer, Christopher. 2005. "Inequality and Conflict: A Review of an Age-Old Concern." United Nations Identities, Conflict and Cohesion Programme Paper 11, United Nations Research Institute for Social Development, Geneva.

Credit Suisse. 2014. *Global Wealth Databook 2014*. Zürich: Research Institute, Credit Suisse.

Dabalen, Andrew, Ambar Narayan, Jaime Saavedra-Chanduvi, and Alejandro Hoyos Suarez, with Ana Abras and Sailesh Tiwari. 2015. *Do African Children Have an Equal Chance? A Human Opportunity Report for Sub-Saharan Africa*. Directions in Development Series. Washington, DC: World Bank.

Davies, James B., Susanna Sandström, Anthony Shorrocks, and Edward N. Wolff. 2011. "The Level and Distribution of Global Household Wealth." *The Economic Journal* 121 (551): 223–54.

de la Fuente, Alejandro, Andreas Murr, and Ericka Rascón. 2015. *Mapping Subnational Poverty in Zambia*. World Bank Group and Republic of Zambia Central Statistical Office.

de Magalhães, Leandro, and Raül Santaeulàlia-Llopis. 2015. "The Consumption, Income, and Wealth of the Poorest: Cross-Sectional Facts of Rural and Urban Sub-Saharan Africa for Macroeconomists." Policy Research Working Paper 7337, World Bank, Washington, DC.

Deaton, Angus S. 2005. "Measuring Poverty in a Growing World (or Measuring Growth in a Poor World)." *Review of Economics and Statistics* 87 (1): 1–19.

Deaton, Angus S., and Salman Zaidi. 2002. "Guidelines for Constructing Consumption

Aggregates for Welfare Analysis." Living Standards Measurement Study Working Paper 135, World Bank, Washington, DC.

Deininger, Klaus, and Lyn Squire. 1996. "A New Data Set Measuring Income Inequality." *World Bank Economic Review* 10 (3): 565–91.

De Vreyer, Philippe, and Sylvie Lambert. 2014. "Intra-household Inequalities and Poverty in Senegal." Unpublished working paper, Paris School of Economics.

De Vreyer, Philippe, Sylvie Lambert, Abla Safir, and Momar B. Sylla. 2008. "Pauvreté et structure familiale: Pourquoi une nouvelle enquête?" *Statéco* 102.

Díaz-Giménez, Javier, Andy Glover, and José-Víctor Ríos-Rull. 2011. "Facts on the Distributions of Earnings, Income, and Wealth in the United States: 2007 Update." *Federal Reserve Bank of Minneapolis Quarterly Review* 34 (1): 2–31.

Easterly, William, and Ross Levine. 1997. "Africa's Growth Tragedy: Policies and Ethnic Divisions." *Quarterly Journal of Economics* 112 (4): 1203–50.

Elbers, Chris, Peter Lanjouw, Johan A. Mistiaen, and Berk Özler. 2008. "Reinterpreting Between-Group Inequality." *Journal of Economic Inequality* 6 (3): 231–45.

Ferreira, Francisco H. G., and Jérémie Gignoux. 2011. "The Measurement of Inequality of Opportunity: Theory and an Application to Latin America." *Review of Income and Wealth* 57 (4): 622–57.

Ferreira, Francisco H. G., Christoph Lakner, Maria Ana Lugo, and Berk Özler. 2014. "Inequality of Opportunity and Economic Growth: A Cross-Country Analysis." Policy Research Working Paper 6915, World Bank, Washington, DC.

Ferreira, Francisco, H. G., Julian Messina, Jamele Rigolini, Luis-Felipe López-Calva, Maria Ana Lugo, and Renos Vakis. 2013. *Economic Mobility and the Rise of the Latin American Middle Class*. Washington, DC: World Bank.

Ferreira, Francisco H. G., and Vito Peragine. 2015. "Equality of Opportunity: Theory and Evidence." In *Handbook of Well Being and Public Policy*, edited by Matthew D. Adler and Marc Fleurbaey. New York: Oxford University Press.

Fields, Gary. 2000. "The Dynamics of Poverty, Inequality and Economic Well-being: African Economic Growth in Comparative Perspective." *Journal of African Economies* 9 (Supplement): 45–78.

Fitz, Nicholas. 2015. "Economic Inequality: It's Far Worse than You Think." *Scientific American* March 31.

Fleurbaey, Marc. 2008. *Fairness, Responsibility, and Welfare*. Oxford, UK: Oxford University Press.

Fleurbaey, Marc, and Vito Peragine. 2013. "Ex Ante versus Ex Post Equality of Opportunity." *Economica* 80: 118–30.

Forbes Media. "The World's Billionaires." Jersey City, NJ. http://www.forbes.com/billionaires /list/41/#version:static.

Fosu, Augustin Kwasi. 2014. "Growth, Inequality, and Poverty in Sub-Saharan Africa: Recent Progress in a Global Context." *Oxford Development Studies* 43 (1): 44–59.

Gallup World Poll. 2013. http://www.gallup.com /poll/174263/belief-work-ethic-strong-across -africa.aspx.

Gandhi, Aditi, and Michael Walton. 2012. "Where Do India's Billionaires Get Their Wealth?" *Economic & Political Weekly* 47 (40): 10–14.

Guénard, Charlotte, and Sandrine Mesplé-Somps. 2010. "Measuring Inequalities: Do Household Surveys Paint a Realistic Picture?" *Review of Income and Wealth* 56 (3): 519–38.

Hertz, Tom., Tamara Jayasundera, Patrizio Piraino, Sibel Selcuk, Nicole Smith, and Alina Verashchagina. 2007. "The Inheritance of Educational Inequality: International Comparisons and Fifty-Year Trends." *B.E. Journal of Economic Analysis & Policy* 7 (2): 1–46.

Hlasny, Vladimir, and Paolo Verme. 2013. "Top Incomes and the Measurement of Inequality in Egypt." Policy Research Working Paper 6557, World Bank, Washington, DC.

Hoff, Karla. 2012. "The Effect of Inequality on Aspirations." Background paper for *Addressing Inequality in South Asia*, edited by Martín Rama, Tara Béteille, Yue Li, Pradeep K. Mitra, and John Lincoln Newman. Washington, DC: World Bank.

Huber, John D., and Laura Mayoral. 2014. "Inequality, Ethnicity and Civil Conflict." Unpublished working paper, Columbia University, New York.

Jenkins, Stephen P. 2014. "World Income Inequality Databases: An Assessment of WIID and SWIID." IZA Discussion Paper 8501, Institute for the Study of Labor, Bonn.

Jirasavetakul, La-Bhus, and Christoph Lakner. 2015. "The African Distribution of Consumption Expenditure." Unpublished working paper, World Bank, Washington, DC.

Kanbur, Ravi, and Adam Wagstaff. 2014. "How Useful Is Inequality of Opportunity as a Policy Construct?" Policy Research Working Paper 6980, World Bank, Washington, DC.

Keefer, Philip, and Stephen Knack. 2002. "Polarization, Politics and Property Rights: Links between Inequality and Growth." *Public Choice* 111: 127–54.

Klasen, Stephan. 2004. "In Search of the Holy Grail: How to Achieve Pro-Poor Growth." In *Toward Pro-Poor Policies: Aid, Institutions, and Globalization*, edited by Bertil Tungodden, Nicholas Stern, and Ivar Kolstad, 63–93. Washington, DC: World Bank.

Knight, Frank. 2015. *The Wealth Report 2015: Global Perspectives on Prime Property and Wealth.* London.

Korinek, Anton, Johan A. Mistiaen, and Martin Ravallion. 2006. "Survey Nonresponse and the Distribution of Income." *Journal of Economic Inequality* 4 (1): 33–55.

Krueger, Dirk, Fabrizio Perri, Luigi Pistaferri, and Giovanni L. Violante. 2010. "Cross-Sectional Facts for Macroeconomists." *Review of Economic Dynamics* 13 (1): 1–14.

Kuznets, Simon. 1955. "Economic Growth and Income Inequality." *American Economic Review* 45 (1): 1–28.

Lakner, Christoph. 2015. "The Ten Richest Africans Own as Much as the Poorest Half of the Continent." March 11, World Bank, Washington, DC. http://blogs.worldbank.org /developmenttalk/ten-richest-africans-own -much-poorest-half-continent.

Lakner, Christoph, and Branko Milanovic. 2015. "Global Income Distribution: From the Fall of the Berlin Wall to the Great Recession." *World Bank Economic Review.* Advance Access published September 26, 2015.

Lambert, Sylvie, Martin Ravallion, and Dominique van de Walle. 2014. "Intergenerational Mobility and Interpersonal Inequality in an African Economy." *Journal of Development Economics* 110: 327–44.

Langer, Arnim, and Frances Stewart. 2015. *Regional Imbalances, Horizontal Inequalities, and Violent Conflicts: Insights from Four West African Countries.* Fragility, Conflict, and Violence Group, World Bank, Washington, DC.

Lichbach, Mark Irving. 1989. "An Evaluation of 'Does Economic Inequality Breed Political Conflict?' Studies." *World Politics* 41 (4): 431–70.

Linton, Ralph. 1936. *The Study of Man.* New York: Appleton-Century.

Mansuri, Ghazala, and Vijayendra Rao. 2013. *Localizing Development: Does Participation Work?* Policy Research Report. Washington, DC: World Bank.

Marrero, Gustavo A., and Juan G. Rodríguez. 2013. "Inequality of Opportunity and Growth." *Journal of Development Economics* 104: 107–22.

Miguel, Edward, and Mary Kay Gugerty. 2005. "Ethnic Diversity, Social Sanctions, and Public Goods in Kenya." *Journal of Public Economics* 89: 2325–68.

Milanovic, Branko. 2005. *Worlds Apart: Measuring International and Global Inequality.* Princeton, NJ: Princeton University Press.

———. 2011. *The Haves and the Have-Nots: A Brief and Idiosyncratic History of Global Inequality.* New York: Basic Books.

Morival, Elodie. 2011. "Top Incomes and Racial Inequality in South Africa: Evidence from Tax Statistics and Household Surveys, 1993–2008." Master's thesis, Paris School of Economics.

New World Wealth. 2014. *Wealth in Kenya: The Future of Kenyan HNWIs.* Johannesburg.

OECD (Organisation for Economic Co-operation and Development). 2015. *In It Together: Why Less Inequality Benefits All.* Paris.

Olinto, Pedro, Gabriel Lara Ibarra, and Jaime Saavedra-Chanduvi. 2014. "Accelerating Poverty Reduction in a Less Poor World: The Roles of Growth and Inequality." Policy Research Working Paper 6855, World Bank, Washington, DC.

Olson, Mancur, Jr. 1965. *The Logic of Collective Action: Public Goods and the Theory of Groups.* Cambridge, MA: Harvard University Press.

Oxfam International. 2015. "Wealth: Having It All and Wanting More." Oxfam Issue Briefing (January), Oxford.

Palma, José Gabriel. 2006. "Globalizing Inequality: 'Centrifugal' and 'Centripetal' Forces at Work." *Revue Tiers-Monde* 186: (2): 249–80.

———. 2011. "Homogeneous Middles vs. Heterogeneous Tails, and the End of the 'Inverted U': It's All about the Share of the Rich." *Development and Change* 42 (1): 87–153.

Paris School of Economics. World Top Incomes Database. http://topincomes.parisschoolof economics.eu/#Database.

Pew Research Center. 2013. *Despite Challenges, Africans Are Optimistic about the Future*, Washington, DC. http://www.pewglobal.org/2013/11/08/despite-challenges-africans-are-optimistic-about-the-future/.

Piketty, Thomas 2014. *Capital in the Twenty-First Century*. Cambridge, MA: Belknap Press of Harvard University Press.

Pinkovskiy, Maxim, and Xavier Sala-i-Martín. 2014. "Africa Is on Time." *Journal of Economic Growth* 19 (3): 311–38.

Piraino, Patrizio. 2015. "Intergenerational Earnings Mobility and Equality of Opportunity in South Africa." *World Development* 67: 396–405.

Rama, Martín, Tara Béteille, Yue Li, Pradeep K. Mitra, and John Lincoln Newman. 2015. *Addressing Inequality in South Asia*. South Asia Development Matters Series. Washington, DC: World Bank.

Ravallion, Martin. 2001. "Growth, Inequality and Poverty: Looking Beyond Averages." *World Development* 29 (11): 1803–15.

Roemer, John. 2000. *Equality of Opportunity*. Cambridge, MA: Harvard University Press.

Roemer, John, and Alain Trannoy. 2015. "Equality of Opportunity" In *Handbook of Income Distribution*, vol. 2, edited by Anthony B. Atkinson and François Bourguignon, 217–300. Amsterdam: North-Holland.

Santaeulàlia-Llopis, Raül, and Yu Zheng 2015. "The Price of Growth: Consumption Insurance in China 1989-2009." Unpublished working paper, Washington University, St. Louis.

Shepherd, Andrew, Lucy Scott, Chiara Mariotti, Flora Kessy, Raghav Gaiha, Lucia da Corta, Katharina Hanifnia, and others. 2014. *Chronic Poverty Report 2014–2015: The Road to Zero Extreme Poverty*. London: Chronic Poverty Advisory Network, Overseas Development Institute.

Solt, Frederick. Forthcoming a. "The Standardized World Income Inequality Database." *Social Science Quarterly*.

———. Forthcoming b. "On the Assessment and Use of Cross-National Income Inequality Datasets." *Journal of Economic Inequality*.

Stewart, Frances, ed. 2008. *Horizontal Inequalities and Conflict: Understanding Group Violence in Multiethnic Societies*. Basingstoke, UK: Palgrave Macmillan.

Stiglitz, Joseph E. 2012. *The Price of Inequality: How Today's Divided Society Endangers Our Future*. New York: W. W. Norton.

Strauss, John, Germano Mwabu, and Kathleen Beegle. 2000. "Intra-household Allocations: A Review of Theories and Empirical Evidence." *Journal of African Economies* 9 (Supplement 1): 83–143.

Székely, Miguel, and Marianne Hilgert. 2007. "What's behind the Inequality We Measure? An Investigation Using Latin American Data." *Oxford Development Studies* 35 (2): 197–217.

UNDP (United Nations Development Programme). 2014. *Humanity Divided: Confronting Inequality in Developing Countries*. Bureau for Development Policy. New York: UNDP.

Van de Gaer, Dirk, and Xavier Ramos. 2015. "Measurement of Inequality of Opportunity Based on Counterfactuals." Paper presented at the Sixth Meeting of the Society for the Study of Economic Inequality (ECINEQ), Luxembourg, July 13–15.

World Bank. 2005. *World Development Report 2006: Equity and Development*. Washington, DC: World Bank.

———. 2011. *World Development Report 2012: Gender Equality and Development*. Washington, DC: World Bank.

———. 2014a. *Africa's Pulse*, vol. 10 (October), Washington, DC: World Bank.

———. 2014b. *Taking Stock: An Update on Vietnam's Recent Economic Developments*. Washington, DC: World Bank.